MW00448154

"I thought I'd seen every angle on the ██████████ John Tramazzo makes a compelling case ~~for the role of soldiers, the mil~~itary, and veterans in the story of America's favorite spirit—and he wraps it up in a pretty good yarn."
—Clay Risen, author of *American Whiskey, Bourbon, and Rye: A Guide to the Nation's Favorite Spirit*

"This book is more than just war stories about famous distillers, though there are plenty of those as well. It's about the spirit of America as told through the lens of distilled spirits as far back as the Revolutionary War, when whiskey was a standard part of rations. It's about dreams of better days ahead and honoring those who came before. Whiskey has always been a part of American culture, and this book is a perfect example of how that presence has changed over time."
—Maggie Kimberl, *Alcohol Professor*

"Whether one imbibes whiskey or not, the uniquely American character of the men to whose service the book is dedicated to rises to the top and resonates with the reader. So if you're a bourbon aficionado, pour yourself a finger or two of Maker's Mark, Blanton's, or whatever—or a Diet Coke if you don't drink alcohol—and maybe fire up a good cigar. Then settle back for a little history from a different and unique perspective."
—Col. Steve Patarcity, Association of the United States Army

"If you are a bourbon lover, if you have an interest in the history of this country, sit down and read this book—a fascinating portrait of some of America's military heroes and their connection to many brands of bourbon on the shelf today."
—Sally Van Winkle Campbell, author of *But Always Fine Bourbon: Pappy Van Winkle and the Story of Old Fitzgerald*

"The bourbon industry has long been filled with military veterans, but never have their valuable contributions been so finely documented until now. Captain Tramazzo's investigative book not only weaves together these veterans' military contributions but also provides an enlightening look at the impact they made on the spirits industry today."
—Mark Brown, president and chief executive officer, Sazerac Company

BOURBON AND BULLETS

BOURBON
&
BULLETS

TRUE STORIES OF WHISKEY,
WAR, AND MILITARY SERVICE

John C. Tramazzo

Foreword by Fred Minnick

POTOMAC BOOKS | *An imprint of the University of Nebraska Press*

Library of Congress Cataloging-in-Publication Data

Names: Tramazzo, John C., author. | Minnick, Fred,
1978–, writer of supplementary textual content.
Title: Bourbon and bullets: true stories of
whiskey, war, and military service / John C.
Tramazzo; foreword by Fred Minnick.
Other titles: True stories of whiskey,
war, and military service
Description: Lincoln, NE: Potomac Books, an
imprint of the University of Nebraska Press,
[2018] | "Highlights the relationship between
bourbon and military service to show the
rich and dramatic connection in American
history."—Provided by publisher. | Includes
bibliographical references and index.
Identifiers: LCCN 2018027388
ISBN 9781640121034 (cloth: alk. paper)
ISBN 9781640124288 (paperback)
ISBN 9781640121447 (epub)
ISBN 9781640121454 (mobi)
ISBN 9781640121461 (pdf)
Subjects: LCSH: United States—History, Military.
| Bourbon whiskey—Anecdotes. | Soldiers—
Alcohol use—United States. | Soldiers—United
States—Biography. | Bourbon whiskey—United
States—History. | United States—Armed
Forces—Military life—Anecdotes.
Classification: LCC E181 .T825 2018 | DDC
355.00973—dc23 LC record available at
https://lccn.loc.gov/2018027388

Set in New Baskerville ITC by E. Cuddy.
Designed by N. Putens.

Dedicated to all veterans of the American armed forces

Liquor was heat, after long exposure on the trail, promoting sleep in wet clothes when there was no sizzling steam radiator to welcome the traveler, and no hot coffee or chocolate at the corner drug store to take its place. It was part of the ration of both the British and American armies; a way of combating malarial chills when there were no nets against the storms of mosquitoes; a tonic for debility; preventive medicine for all manner of ailments which have been brought under control since Pasteur's genius flashed light into the darkness.

Frederick Palmer, *Clark of the Ohio*

CONTENTS

FOREWORD

Fred Minnick

When fighting in war, you anticipate mail more than a child does their birthday presents. I'll never forget the large tan box awaiting me with bolded letters—Staff Sgt. Fred Minnick. I picked it up, shook it, and heard a sloshing sound. Was it? Could it be what I asked for? Did they sneak it through customs?

Alone, on my bunk, and with my M16 by my side, I ripped the tape off more quickly than I thought possible, chunks of cardboard stuck to the tape. My hand reached in and pulled out a bottle of Listerine. Yes, Listerine. There was a note. "Fred, enclosed you'll find the Jack Daniel's you requested." My friend dumped the Listerine and filled it with Jack Daniel's. See, it was against our general orders to drink while in Iraq, and the fun-killing MPs searched packages to people like me. The Listerine trick was tried and true.

And that's the only military drinking story that I can share in public.

Most stories about whiskey and the military are fairly depicted as soldier-laden bar brawls. While sensationalized, that stuff happens, and I may or may not have participated in a few such shenanigans. That's the side of whiskey the public connects to the military.

The hidden side, the truer version, is what you're about to read in John C. Tramazzo's *Bourbon and Bullets*. For the first time in whiskey history, an author has tracked major brands and told their veteran stories, both war and whiskey.

This book has successfully shown how important whiskey has been to our country's history, from the Revolutionary War and the Civil War to Vietnam and today.

I think Tramazzo also answered a question I've long asked myself: Why was I drawn to bourbon? I mean, when I returned home from Iraq, I found a way to work in bourbon. Why? Was it the umpteen veteran charities run by bourbon companies? Was it the fact I just, um, really loved the stuff? No, to both. Tramazzo reinforced something I've always seen in bourbon but never could put my finger on it. There's a sense of selflessness in this community. Despite being competitors, bourbon companies help each other, even developing recipes and marketing strategies. This beautiful spirit is on perfect display, as Tramazzo shows how intertwined servicemen are with the whiskey industry. There are those who have written whiskey's history, like the great Sam Cecil and me, and we've made history through distiller toil, such as that of West Point graduate Dave Pickerell, whose hands have touched dozens of brands as a consultant or master distiller.

In this great book, we learn that heralded whiskey names—which to many are just faceless brands—belonged to those who fought in wars on behalf of the United States. George T. Stagg, a name that makes whiskey aficionados drool, was a fearless officer who led many battles in the Civil War. In whiskey circles, Stagg is known for its annual Buffalo Trace Antique Collection along with William Larue Weller and Thomas Handy. The real Weller served in the Mexican-American War and Handy—well, he was an elite Confederate soldier who sent many federals to the grave. These three men shared so many things in common: Stagg became one of the greatest all-time whiskey businessmen, Weller became a successful rectifier, and Handy planted the seeds that grew into Sazerac. Little did they know, their names and likenesses would be used centuries later and lead to long lines at liquor stores—the whiskey is that good!

Therein lies the beauty of *Bourbon and Bullets.* Tramazzo flawlessly weaves military and whiskey history together through time and adds a new must-read to the bourbon library.

Many bourbon books keep the narrow focus on this beautiful spirit and tell its history through distilleries. There's nothing wrong with that, but I believe Tramazzo tapped into the next wave of bourbon research. He provides broader context, giving tidbits of how things like the barrel entered into the picture, and seamlessly introduces veterans into the storyline, such as a World War I veteran congressman assisting bourbon becoming America's spirit. And furthermore, the book is structured around war, showing how whiskey and war coincided, making it far more appealing to your everyday history buff.

World War II is an especially illuminating time for both our country's history and whiskey. The distilling industry greatly sacrificed during this horrible war, allowing their equipment to be used for the greater good and losing many men to battle. But for the first time, we learn of the heroism from bourbon men on the battlefield. It's in these stories I find myself applauding Tramazzo most.

We're often so caught up in the history of bourbon—the mashbills, the distilling, aging, and branding—that we lose sight of the workers behind them. Oh, sure, we celebrate the master distillers, but what about the people behind the brands? It's in *Bourbon and Bullets* we learn the pain of losing a child, the guilt of being the survivor, and the rush of combat.

In other words, this isn't just a book on war and whiskey. It's about people. And through it all, Tramazzo never wavers in his quest to combine his two passions—bourbon and country. I'd expect nothing less from an army officer who doubles as a whiskey blogger.

Thank you, Tramazzo, for connecting so many dots of American whiskey history. You've done a great service to our country, sir.

INTRODUCTION

On August 22, 1848, twenty-six-year-old Lt. Hiram Ulysses Grant, a West Point graduate and Mexican-American War veteran from Ohio, married his sweetheart, Julia Dent, at her family's home in downtown St. Louis.[1] Following a short honeymoon cruise on the Mississippi River, Lieutenant and Mrs. Grant reported to the isolated garrison at Sackets Harbor, New York, the site of two engagements during the War of 1812.[2] Grant, who spent the first several years of his military career leading cavalry charges, quickly learned that garrison duty was a far cry from his prior adventures at Resaca de la Palma and Monterrey.[3] While at snowy Sackets Harbor, he coped with boredom by racing his "Cicotte Mare" to Watertown, playing checkers, and overindulging in whiskey, a habit he continued throughout his career.[4]

I can relate. I was a new lieutenant in the army when I married my college sweetheart in the North Carolina mountains on a perfectly crisp September evening. Not long after our honeymoon to Hawaii, I was ordered to report to the Tenth Mountain Division at Fort Drum, New York. The original Tenth trained at Camp Hale, Colorado, in the glorious Vail Valley, but it was deactivated in the 1950s after furiously fighting and defeating German forces in Italy's Apennine Mountains. In 1985, the division was reactivated at Fort Drum, just a few barren miles away from Sackets Harbor on the shores of Lake Ontario. Like Lieutenant and Mrs. Grant, my bride and I endured three frigid winters in the North Country, often making our way from Watertown to Sackets Harbor establishments to imbibe and dream of warmer weather.

Since leaving those simpler days in northern New York behind, war has dominated my army experience. Like most other soldiers serving since September 11, 2001, I have deployed to multiple conflict zones and seen unspeakable violence. I independently confirmed what Gen. William Tecumseh Sherman, who often carried a flask of bourbon on the battlefield, famously remarked: "[War's] glory is all moonshine" and "war is hell."[5]

However, I also verified the universal truth that challenging endeavors teach us valuable lessons. My proudest professional achievements, most of my close friendships, and countless comical moments are attributable to my wartime service. Whiskey has been a companion throughout, from the rare twenty-four-year-old Scotch I found in an African hotel bar, to the barrel proof Kentucky straight bourbon whiskey I discovered in a Middle Eastern market, to the Prohibition-era ryes and Stitzel-Weller Distillery bourbons available only at the Jack Rose Dining Saloon in my hometown of Washington DC.

As my army career and fascination with America's native spirit advance, I repeatedly discover military veterans' fingerprints upon the storied and complex history of our nation's whiskey industry. Even serious bourbon enthusiasts are surprised to learn that many popular brands on the shelf today were developed by or named in honor of distinguished combat veterans. Further, the modern whiskey industry is full of former soldiers, sailors, airmen, and marines. All of the major Kentucky distilleries employ veterans. Several dozen popular craft distilleries are veteran-owned or -operated. The nation's top still-maker, Vendome Copper & Brass Works in Louisville, is veteran-owned and operated. America's leading cooperage, Independent Stave Company, employs several veterans in positions of significant authority.

Through personal interviews, careful research, and the lens of my own military service, I am able to share their stories. In writing this book, I traveled to Kentucky to meet (and drink) with legends, explored historic distilleries, dug through wartime whiskey industry records, interviewed several of my whiskey idols, and discovered little-known accounts of valor.

I sat with members of the Van Winkle family and examined seventy-year-old newspaper clippings and a Japanese map captured by Julian Van Winkle Jr. in the Philippines. Sally Van Winkle Campbell, Kitty Van Winkle Terry, Julian Van Winkle III, and his wonderful wife, Sissy, graciously transcribed war letters written by Van Winkle Jr. to his father, Julian "Pappy" Van Winkle. I toured the grounds of the Buffalo Trace Distillery on a misty spring morning with Freddie Johnson, son of the late World War II veteran and distillery warehouse supervisor Jimmy Johnson Jr. Freddie, an icon himself, shared stories and insights about his father and Elmer Tandy Lee that I would have not discovered in any library. I enjoyed essential conversations with Four Roses brand ambassador Al Young, master distiller Dave Pickerell, members of the Weller, Willett, Handy, Lee, and Newman families, and others who care deeply about the lives and careers of the veterans discussed herein. I was fortunate to meet with or interview the diverse group of veterans discussed in the final chapter who are driving the American whiskey industry into the future.

Finally, while whiskey has comforted and intrigued me and played an important role in the American military community, one cannot ignore that it has been, and always will be, destructive when abused. No group understands that reality more than veterans of war do. I was proud to discover that a veteran who took his first sip of liquor as a new lieutenant in the U.S. Army founded Alcoholics Anonymous in 1935.

BOURBON AND BULLETS

1

Bourbon and Bullets

America was built, and occasionally damaged, by firepower and whiskey. Conflict, military service, and grain alcohol are foundations of our national story. American service members carried whiskey into battle, from Valley Forge to Gettysburg, Manila, and Da Nang, and it bolstered their courage, calmed their nerves, and treated their maladies. Many writers have discussed whiskey's place in history as it relates to military service. Chapters have been written about its utility as battlefield medicine and its presence in the canteens of Continental and Civil War fighters.

Until now, however, no writer has fully explored the depth of military service among the most notable American whiskey distillers and executives. Weller, Van Winkle, Stagg, and Bulleit all experienced combat before they became household names for American whiskey enthusiasts. Equally compelling are the successful craft whiskey distilleries currently owned and operated by veterans. In small towns and big cities across America, veterans of combat missions in Vietnam, Panama, Somalia, Iraq, Afghanistan, and elsewhere cook mash, operate stills, and push the booming industry to new heights.

To fully understand the significance of American whiskey, one must first explore its unbreakable connection to our pursuit of happiness and the occasional call to arms. The earliest American distilleries were constructed in New England to produce molasses-based rum. Colonial distilleries were "a link in a chain that dispatched ships freighted with rum to Africa to trade for slaves who were transported to the West Indies to grow sugar to make molasses to ship to New England to make rum . . . and so forth."[1] To the dismay of early American distillers and their patrons, the 1764 Sugar Act minimized profit margins on rum and slowed production of the spirit.[2] In an effort to obtain tax-free molasses, distillers engaged partners in the Spanish, Dutch, and French West Indies, but a Royal Naval blockade quickly cut that stream.[3] Instead of paying the tax on British molasses or risking their lives to smuggle it from other sources, frustrated colonists turned to local grains like rye and Indian corn.[4] English and Scots-Irish immigrants applied Old World methods to these New World resources to produce grain whiskey similar to what modern consumers might call moonshine. Whiskey was *the* American spirit by the time frustration with the king's taxes turned violent in the spring of 1775.

As Susan Cheever noted in her book *Drinking in America*, "American soldiers drink . . . and whiskey was the usual tipple."[5] Throughout the Revolutionary War, Continental soldiers, many of whom were farmer distillers, enjoyed a daily gill (about four ounces of liquor) as encouragement in the struggle for independence.[6] Gen. George Washington personally lobbied the Continental Congress for liquor rations and ensured through a series of general orders that sergeants in his command distributed brandy, rum, and heaps of whiskey to motivate and reward his battle-hardened soldiers.[7] The fledgling U.S. Navy followed suit by granting each sailor a half-pint of rum each day, which was quickly supplanted by American-made whiskey.[8] Evidently, it worked, as the Continental military's efforts gave birth to a new and powerful nation.

Following the American Revolution, the government paid off its war debt by heavily taxing whiskey production, a process that repeated itself with every conflict until Prohibition.[9] The original whiskey tax was necessary to replenish the national coffers, but it was expensive to enforce and caused more conflict. In 1794, a band of over five hundred frontier distillers in western Pennsylvania, many of them veterans of the revolution, attacked the fortified home of tax collector Gen. John Neville.

The retired general, a prominent war veteran and large-scale whiskey distiller himself, was a poorly selected target.[10] Neville grew up in Virginia near George Washington and served in Washington's regiment during the bloody French and Indian War. During the revolution they fought together at the battles of Trenton, Princeton, Germantown, and Monmouth and Washington brevetted Neville to brigadier general in 1783.[11] When Washington learned of the attack by the "Whiskey Boys" on his friend's estate, he rode with a massive contingent of federal troops to Bedford, Pennsylvania, to confront the insurrection, making him the only commander-in-chief to personally lead an army in the field.[12] The response to the so-called Whiskey Rebellion solidified the authority of the new federal government, and it pushed many frontier distillers further west toward the corn-rich commonwealth of Kentucky, where bourbon whiskey, a category of American whiskey described at length in chapter 2, was conceived.

In an ironic twist, when Washington retired from public service in 1797, he directed his Scottish farm manager to construct a distillery beside Mount Vernon's gristmill. Washington and James Anderson rapidly developed one of America's most productive and successful whiskey distilleries. In 1799, the year of Washington's death, Mount Vernon distilled rye, corn, barley, and wheat into nearly eleven thousand gallons of clear whiskey for nearby Alexandria taverns.[13] Washington's distillery burned to the ground during the War of 1812, but it was finally resurrected in 2007.[14] Today, former Maker's Mark master distiller and U.S. Army veteran David Pickerell oversees the production of several spirits at Mount Vernon based on Washington's actual recipes and documented preferences.[15] Before launching his remarkable career in distilling, Mr. Pickerell was a decorated cavalry officer and a professor of chemistry at his alma mater, the United States Military Academy at West Point.

The farmer distillers that settled the Kentucky territory following the Revolutionary War and Whiskey Rebellion significantly impacted military operations as America expanded its western border. During the War of 1812, hundreds if not thousands of early Kentucky distillers enlisted to fight hostile Indians in western territories. An estimated twenty-five thousand Kentuckians served in that war under the command of Revolutionary War hero and whiskey distiller Isaac Shelby.[16] As Richard G. Stone Jr. wrote in *Kentucky Fighting Men*, during the War of 1812, "each man carried a gun, a pack of cards, and a bottle of whiskey."[17] Even from their homesteads, distillers advanced the military effort. Between 1793 and 1827, Kentucky distillers provided the U.S. Army's commissary general of subsistence with more than half of the rationed whiskey needed to sustain men serving on the harsh frontier.[18]

During the Civil War, Gen. Ulysses S. Grant rode to victory under the influence of Dr. James C. Crow's Old Crow bourbon whiskey.[19] Following the Battle of Shiloh, Grant's critics complained about his excessive drinking to President Lincoln, a militia veteran, former tavern owner, and son of a distillery worker on Knob Creek in Kentucky.[20] Lincoln quipped, "I wish I knew what brand of whiskey he drinks. I would send a barrel to all my other generals."[21] Like Lincoln and Grant, many commanders acquiesced to whiskey in the field despite the fact that the U.S. Army formally abolished the liquor ration in the early 1830s.[22] Considering the brutal conditions and constant threat of death, the use of alcohol during the American Civil War was "small compensation for the freedom lost in other departments."[23]

Whiskey was not merely a witness to the Civil War. It was an active participant, from Fort Sumter to the obscure final surrender in Kentucky. Days before the first cannon shots were fired in Charleston harbor, Confederate brigadier general Pierre Gustave Toutant (P.G.T.) Beauregard sent his former West Point professor Maj. Robert Anderson, who commanded Fort Sumter, several cases of fine whiskey and a box of cigars, hoping to avoid "the horrors of a fratricidal war."[24] Anderson returned the liquor and cigars to his former pupil, and on April 12, 1861, Confederate batteries at Forts Johnson and Moultrie began their thirty-four-hour bombardment. Three years later, while the blue and gray were still at war, distiller James "Jim" Beauregard Beam was born and given his middle name in the Confederate general's honor.

The Civil War nearly ruined the American whiskey industry, as many distillers were wounded or killed in action, capital was invested in war bonds, and farms and stills were destroyed. In one instance, an old Kentucky distiller and his family fought off a blue-coated sergeant when he attempted to smash their treasured yeast jug.[25] Supplies of drinkable whiskey ran extremely low as both governments were forced to conserve grain for food rations and melt copper still components into war materiel. While Civil War surgeons employed quality whiskey as an anesthetic, a disinfectant, and very often as a preserving agent for amputated limbs, fighting men rarely enjoyed a decent tipple in the field. To cope, they stole whiskey or concocted dangerous bootleg liquor, nicknamed "rotgut," for the toll it exacted on their stomachs.[26]

During the final days of the Civil War, Gen. William Tecumseh Sherman rode to Columbia, South Carolina, where he laid siege to the city that sparked secession. Sherman, a regular bourbon drinker and acquaintance of the modern bourbon industry's founding father, Col. Edmund Haynes Taylor Jr., lost control of his men, who became utterly intoxicated on the city's barrels of whiskey. Along with newly freed African Americans, the troops overindulged and burned more than half of the Palmetto State's capital, an event that still rouses emotions 150 years later.[27] Among Sherman's foes on that February 1865 day was P.G.T. Beauregard, who chose not to destroy Columbia's abundant whiskey stocks before the federal siege.

Two months after the burning of Columbia, Gen. Robert E. Lee surrendered to Grant at Appomattox Courthouse, Virginia. In nearby Richmond, President Lincoln permitted federal officers occupying the "White House of the Confederacy" to consume Jefferson Davis's abandoned whiskey stock.[28] Several weeks later, a lesser-known but much greater surrender occurred when Confederate general Joseph E. Johnston relinquished eighty-nine thousand rebels to General Sherman near Durham, North Carolina.[29] While drafting the terms of the war's largest surrender, General Sherman retrieved his bourbon flask and shared it with Generals Johnston and John Breckinridge of Kentucky.

Before signing the documents, however, General Sherman absented himself, poured another drink, and returned the bottle to his saddle-bag without offering a second dram to either Confederate officer. "Did you see him take that drink by himself?" lamented Breckinridge. "No Kentucky gentleman would have acted that way."[30]

While almost every Confederate unit laid down its arms after Generals Lee and Johnston surrendered, one band of irregulars commonly referred to as "bushwhackers" refused. William Clarke Quantrill and his guerrillas, notorious for a raid on federal forces in Kansas, continued to resist until July 26, 1865.[31] When Quantrill was shot and killed in Nelson County, Kentucky, his fighters were chased to the town of Samuels Depot. They took refuge at a small commercial distillery run by Taylor William (T. W.) Samuels, who was also the town sheriff.[32] Samuels convinced the men (including Jesse James's brother, Frank) to lay down their rifles, which they finally did on the steps of his general store, becoming the very last Confederates to surrender. T. W. Samuels's kin continues to produce some of Kentucky's most well-known bourbon whiskey today, Maker's Mark.[33]

In the decades that followed the Civil War, many Americans, especially soldiers and veterans, consumed alcohol at an alarming rate. Increased public intoxication, drunk driving incidents, and alcohol-related deaths gave rise to the temperance movement, which was fueled by anti-German sentiments and World War I. Several states, and ultimately the federal government, outlawed the manufacturing, transportation, and sale of alcohol while millions of men were fighting in France.

However, the return of World War I veterans quickly injected life into the repeal movement. Rapidly growing organizations like the American Legion and Veterans of Foreign Wars helped build political will for repeal, which led to the passage of the Twenty-First Amendment in December 1933. Many Americans continued to abuse whiskey after Prohibition, but U.S. Army veteran Bill Wilson founded Alcoholics Anonymous in 1935 to help himself and others battle alcoholism.[34]

Following repeal, countless veterans went back to work in the whiskey industry, which was transformed by the necessities of World War II.

Between 1941 and 1945, American distilleries ran full blast seven days a week to supply U.S. military forces with high-proof industrial alcohol for torpedo fuel, smokeless gunpowder, penicillin, and other military purposes.[35] Tens of thousands of distillery workers and many whiskey company executives left to fight overseas. Other distillery employees and still manufacturers were exempted from conscription to maintain constant production for the War Department. Following victory over Germany, Gen. Brehon B. Somervell, the commanding general of the Army Service Forces, personally wrote to Schenley Distillers Corporation chairman Lewis Rosenstiel to express his appreciation and admiration for the company's role in defeating the Nazis.[36]

President Harry S. Truman, who spent thirty-seven years in the U.S. Army, began each day with a power walk and a shot of bourbon, usually Old Grand-Dad or Wild Turkey.[37] The Missouri native often worked up his nerves with the help of what he called "a little H2O flavored with bourbon."[38] Truman made no exception to his routine the day he authorized the nuclear attacks on Japan, a nation that now imports over $100 million worth of American-made spirits each year.[39]

Following World War II, the whiskey industry experienced a remarkable boom as production soared and veterans celebrated victory over the Axis. However, during the Vietnam War, a rebellious drinking crowd cast brown spirits aside for clear liquor like vodka, gin, and tequila. As U.S. Air Force veteran Reid Mitenbuler noted in his book *Bourbon Empire*, "bourbon became a symbol of the patriarchy and the Establishment. . . . As Vietnam fell apart, boomers protested the war that was being led by all those colonels with bottles of Jim Beam on their desks. Young people rejected everything their parents' generation stood for, from their bourgeois values to their straight, American whiskey."[40] While vodka-drinking war protesters raged during the 1960s, whiskey sales held on, particularly in foreign markets. Jim Beam and Stitzel-Weller whiskeys performed well, thanks in part to marketing efforts focused on military personnel serving overseas.

Throughout the Cold War, American whiskey companies competed with gin and vodka by lowering proofs from 86 to 80. Major distilleries even pushed "light whiskey" instead of their fully matured products to appeal to the changing market. In 1976, vodka sales surpassed those of bourbon, cementing the reality of whiskey's decline.[41]

Bourbon remained a has-been spirit until the mid-1980s when World War II veteran Elmer T. Lee introduced the single-barrel concept to the market. With the help of fellow veterans Bob Baranaskas and Jimmy Johnson Jr. Lee changed the industry by bottling bourbon from the best barrels, swapping consistency for superior, albeit varied, flavor profiles. When other distilleries followed Elmer T. Lee's lead with other unique and premium offerings, American whiskey climbed back to glory. Today, American whiskey, and bourbon in particular, is enjoying historic popularity. Over six hundred whiskey-focused distilleries have opened across the nation in the last ten years, dozens of them owned or operated by veterans of the recent campaigns in Iraq and Afghanistan.[42]

Consistent with their histories, the largest American whiskey companies proudly employ military veterans. The largest new bourbon distillery in America, the Bardstown Bourbon Company, recently hired John Hargrove, a decorated Special Forces veteran and former Sazerac master distiller, to lead its operations. The Brown-Forman Corporation encourages its veteran employees to join Brown-Forman Rallying All Veterans for Excellence, or BRAVE, an employee resource group dedicated to improving other veterans' lives. One BRAVE project resulted in the opening of the Woodford Reserve Bar and Room on the Fort Knox military installation.

Several other major distilleries donate profits to veterans' charities or otherwise celebrate the relationship between whiskey and the armed forces. Heaven Hill recently launched its Evan Williams American Hero Edition bottle campaign to salute American veterans.[43] Jim Beam produces one bourbon product to benefit Operation Homefront and has donated several million dollars to that charity, which assists military families and veterans in need. Wild Turkey's Boot Campaign has raised millions for veteran causes. Jack Daniels's Operation Ride Home relies on whiskey revenue to get troops home for the holidays. Diageo's Salute the Troops program supports several military charities including one that assists veterans who abuse alcohol.

Military veterans are prominent leaders within the ancillary industries that support distilleries. Thomas Sherman, the president of Vendome Copper & Brass Works in Louisville, Kentucky, served in the Kentucky National Guard from 1961 to 1968. Before taking control of the nation's top still-making company, Sherman was an army welder at Fort Knox, where he put his skills to use on armored vehicles bound for Vietnam. Tommy's brother Richard Sherman, Vendome's executive vice president, served on active duty during the same time frame. Richard spent eight years in the army, including a stint in Stuttgart, Germany, where he and fellow soldiers drank their fair share of exported Jim Beam bourbon, whiskey that began its life in a Louisville, Kentucky–made Vendome column still. Today, the Shermans employ veterans in every aspect of their business, from purchasing agent Gina Lesshafft, a former marine who recently attended her son's boot camp graduation at Parris Island; to project manager Erick Anderson, a former C-130 combat-tested loadmaster; to several young welders and mechanics who learned their craft on Humvees and helicopters.[44]

Independent Stave Company, the American whiskey industry's leading provider of new, charred oak barrels, employs several veterans in crucial positions. Two of the shift managers at the company's new Morehead Wood Products mill served on active duty during the Global War on Terror. Corey Barnes, who supervises the night shift, was a marine artillery officer who deployed three times to Helmand Province in southern Afghanistan. Two of the men on Barnes's shift are Kentucky National Guardsmen, as is the third-shift supervisor. Together, the men cut enough staves and heading to produce between thirteen hundred and fourteen hundred bourbon barrels a day, which barely meets current industry demand.[45]

The politicians who most significantly impacted bourbon whiskey were military veterans. President William Howard Taft, who developed the legal standards of whiskey recognized today, enlisted during World War I *after* his time in executive office. U.S. congressman Aime Forand, who introduced the legislation that extended the bonding period from eight to twenty years, allowing distilleries to create some of the most noteworthy brands available today, served as a noncommissioned officer in French trenches during World War I. U.S. senator Thruston Ballard Morton, who introduced the congressional resolution to declare bourbon a "distinctive product of the United States," was a naval officer during World War II. U.S. senator Wendell H. Ford, a tireless advocate for the bourbon industry during its darkest days, served on active duty during World War II and later commanded a tank company in the Kentucky National Guard. Senator Ford passed away in 2015, just before he was inducted into the Kentucky Bourbon Hall of Fame.

Military veterans have written several of the best-selling books about bourbon whiskey available. In 1999, U.S. Army veteran and longtime distiller Sam K. Cecil wrote *Bourbon: The Evolution of the Bourbon Whiskey Industry in Kentucky*, one of the most informative books about the beverage. Cecil began making whiskey at the T. W. Samuels distillery in Nelson County, Kentucky, in 1937 but left for five years of active military service during World War II.[46] After the war, Cecil remained in the Kentucky National Guard while pursuing a distilling career at Heaven Hill, J. W. Dant, and Maker's Mark, where he retired as plant manager. The aforementioned Reid Mitenbuler, who developed his palate for bourbon as a captain at the Bolling Air Force Base Officer's Club, wrote the popular *Bourbon Empire* in 2015. The prolific U.S. Army veteran Fred Minnick, who detailed his violent deployment to northern Iraq in *Camera Boy*, is the author of *Whiskey Women, Bourbon Curious*, and *Bourbon*, among others.

Thanks in part to the efforts of military veterans, the American whiskey industry is booming. Forgotten variations of American whiskey like Maryland-style rye are experiencing fervent comebacks. New creations, like bourbon/rye blends, hopped whiskey, and bourbon finished in beer and wine casks, have captured the drinking public's attention. Consumers enter lotteries and wait in long lines for opportunities to purchase limited-edition or cask-strength expressions from distilleries like Four Roses, Willett, and Buffalo Trace, which were all on the brink of demise thirty years ago. American whiskey makers sold more than $26 billion worth of product in 2017, helped by strong sales among the military community. Jack Daniel's master distiller recently boasted that the military purchases more of the brand's premium single-barrel

Tennessee whiskey than does any other group. Base exchanges, individual units, and other on-base entities like Officers' Clubs "have been some of the best friends of Jack Daniel's over the years."[47]

A review of what may be in the local liquor store reveals an enduring relationship between American military service and American whiskey, from the bottom shelf to the most elite heights. Barton 1792 Distillery produces Military Special, a four-year-old, 80 proof bourbon, sold in U.S. military post exchanges for nine dollars. Maker's Mark, as part of its collector's bottle series, recently released a series of camouflaged bottles, adorned with dog tags, to celebrate each branch of the U.S. military.

Woodford Reserve bourbon bears the name of Gen. William Woodford, the Revolutionary War hero who died as a British prisoner of war in 1780. Old Forester bourbon was named for Louisville physician Dr. William Forrester, a Civil War surgeon who relied heavily on whiskey to treat his wounded patients. The brand was created around 1870 by George Garvin Brown and his half brother John Thompson Street (J.T.S.) Brown Jr., whose father, J.T.S. Brown Sr., fought in the Confederate army as a major at the ripe old age of sixty-nine. For many years, consumers were led to believe that Old Forester was named for Confederate general Nathaniel Bedford Forrest, a myth the Brown-Forman Corporation now disclaims.[48]

The A. Smith Bowman Distillery, part of the veteran-established Sazerac profile, names its annual limited-edition bourbon for Col. Abraham Bowman, a regimental commander in the Continental Army. The Bower Hill whiskey line commemorates the 1794 confrontation between the "Whiskey Boys" of the Mingo Creek Militia and Gen. John Neville, the tax collector whose farm produced whiskey for troops at nearby Fort Pitt. Hood River Distillers recently produced a limited edition of their Pendleton whisky to "honor the integrity and patriotism of those who serve, and have served, our country with pride."

Prohibition Spirits' Hooker's House whiskeys pay homage to Gen. Joseph Hooker, infamous for his whiskey consumption during the Civil War. Novelist Robert Hicks produces Battlefield Bourbon, sales of which go to preserve the Civil War battlefield in Franklin, Tennessee.

Eastside Distilling in Portland, Oregon, produces a bourbon named for Gen. Ambrose Burnside, the Union general who liberated East Tennessee from Confederate control in 1863.

Fremont Mischief Distillery in Seattle produces Soldier Whiskey to honor those killed in action and donates profits to the nonprofit organization Growing Veterans. Patriarch Distillers in Nebraska sells bourbon in a WWII-era glass canteen replica as part of its mission to honor U.S. veterans. Boundary Oak Distillery produces Armored Diesel bourbon, a whiskey made in honor of Gen. George S. Patton Jr. and his unique wartime cocktail recipe. Heritage Distilling Company teamed up with Green Berets from the First Special Forces Group at Fort Lewis, Washington, to develop small-batch bourbon for their unit association. The 10th Mountain Whiskey & Spirits Company in Gypsum and Vail, Colorado, pays homage to the army division that trained for mountain warfare in Europe at nearby Camp Hale.

Ruthless demand for super-premium whiskeys like Buffalo Trace Distillery's William Larue Weller bourbon, Thomas H. Handy rye, George T. Stagg bourbon, Elmer T. Lee bourbon, and the Old Rip Van Winkle line has driven secondary market prices into the thousands. While many enthusiasts are knowledgeable about these special whiskeys, their mash bills, their alcohol content, and their flavor profiles, very few consumers are aware of their nexuses to military service.

William Larue Weller was once a private in the Louisville Legion, an elite outfit that fought with Gen. Zachary Taylor for twelve months during the Mexican-American War. Following his return from northern Mexico, Weller opened a whiskey rectifying operation and eventually hired his brother and sons, all military veterans. Weller's company became one of the, if not the, first to produce bourbon with wheat instead of rye in the mash recipe. The wheated bourbon concept has been emulated by many popular distilleries, including Maker's Mark, Buffalo Trace, Heaven Hill, and Barton.

Thomas H. Handy was a daring Confederate lieutenant who was wounded and twice spent time as a federal prisoner of war. In February 1864, Handy was decorated when his "Crescent Light Artillery" battalion sunk the federal ironclad USS *Indianola.* Five years later, Handy purchased the Sazerac Coffee House in New Orleans, improved and marketed the Sazerac cocktail, and laid the groundwork for the development of the behemoth Sazerac Company.

George T. Stagg was an officer during the Civil War in the Twenty-First Kentucky Infantry Regiment and led violent engagements in Kentucky, Tennessee, and Georgia. After completing his service to the Union army, Stagg launched a successful career selling whiskey for the most famous Kentucky distiller at the time, Col. Edmund Haynes Taylor Jr. When Colonel Taylor's financial situation deteriorated, Stagg acquired the Colonel's Old Fire Copper distillery on the banks of the Kentucky River in Frankfort, which bore Stagg's name from 1890 to 1952.

Elmer T. Lee served as the master distiller at the George T. Stagg Distillery until his retirement in the 1980s. Prior to being hired at the distillery in 1949, Lee was a B-29 radarman and flew several vital bombing missions over Japan. When he returned home from Northwest Field on the island of Guam, he finished his chemical engineering degree at the University of Kentucky and was hired by Orville Schupp and Col. Albert Blanton to work as an engineer. Lee ultimately became Stagg's master distiller and created Blanton's: The Original Single-Barrel Bourbon in 1983. Blanton's is widely recognized as the bourbon that saved the industry from its darkest days. Lee exported countless cases of Blanton's to his former enemies, the Japanese, who happily paid top dollar.

Today, the Stagg Distillery, known as Buffalo Trace since 1999, produces Old Rip Van Winkle bourbon and rye whiskey, a brand developed by U.S. Army veteran Julian Van Winkle Jr. in the 1970s. In the winter of 1942, Van Winkle left his job as treasurer of Stitzel-Weller Distillery to command a tank company in the Pacific. He was badly injured in the Philippines and was awarded the Silver Star Medal for valor after fighting in the single most critical battle of the entire campaign against the Japanese. According to his son Julian Van Winkle III, his father was the "consummate army guy."[49] His daughter Sally Van Winkle Campbell recalled that "he thrived on responsibility and challenge. He relished the training and the duty. He loved being fit and hard, being loaded down with equipment[,] . . . but most of all, he adored his men—'the boys.'"[50] Indeed, after the war, distillery employees fondly remembered how Van Winkle operated Stitzel-Weller as though he were still a tank commander.

In addition to describing the impressive military careers of whiskey men like Weller, Handy, Stagg, Lee, and Van Winkle, this book also pays tribute to all military veterans whose ideas and actions have impacted the industry. It honors veterans who work quietly in American cornfields, mills, fiery cooperages, distilleries large and small, whiskey warehouses, distribution centers, marketing departments, and visitor centers. It is ultimately a book for anyone who loves America and her native spirit.

2

Red Likker

Whiskey is an alcoholic distillate from a fermented mash of grain.[1] The first distillations of modern whiskey occurred almost a thousand years ago. In 1172, English soldiers invaded Ireland and found its people drinking the beverage *uisge-beatha*, a Gaelic term meaning "water of life."[2] The word *whiskey* is the anglicization of *uisge*, the Gaelic word for water. War influenced the spelling of its English name, as it is *whisky* in the loyal former British colonies, and *whiskey* in the rebellious ones, for the most part.[3] Bourbon whiskey is one distinctly American category of whiskey, noted by name as early as 1821, and is regulated by the U.S. Alcohol and Tobacco Tax and Trade Bureau (TTB).[4] The TTB was created in the wake of the September 11, 2001, attacks with the passage of the Homeland Security Act of 2002. TTB agents are tasked to ensure compliance with Title 27 of the Code of Federal Regulations. Part 5 of Title 27 mandates that

- Bourbon must be produced from a fermented mash of not less than 51 percent corn. Many bourbon mash bills include upwards of 70 percent corn; some contain 100 percent corn.

- It is not bourbon unless it is made in America (it can be made outside of Kentucky), although according to the Kentucky Distillers' Association, 95 percent of bourbon is made in Kentucky.
- Bourbon must be stored in charred new oak containers.
- Bourbon may not be produced in excess of 160 proof.
- Bourbon must be stored at 125 proof or less.
- Bourbon must be bottled at 80 proof or more.

Put simply, bourbon is a corn-based American whiskey that must age in new charred oak barrels and be bottled at 80 proof or stronger. To qualify as "straight," whiskey must be stored in oak for at least two years.[5]

The detailed regulatory requirements trace their roots to December of 1909, when President William Howard Taft rendered an executive decision on the disputed definition of whiskey. After a several-year struggle between Kentucky-based makers of "straight" whiskey and less scrupulous whiskey rectifiers (infamous for adding flavoring and coloring agents like prune, cherry, and tobacco juice to their products) in Indiana and Illinois, President Taft established the first whiskey labeling requirements in a nine-page pamphlet discussing the 1906 Pure Food and Drug Act.

The Pure Food and Drug Act was the brainchild of Civil War veteran Harvey Washington Wiley, who interrupted his studies at Hanover College to enlist in the Union army at the age of sixteen.[6] Wiley served in Company I of the 137th Indiana Infantry Regiment alongside his father and rose to the rank of corporal, but he fell ill while guarding railroads in Alabama and was sent home.[7] Following the completion of his education and a long career as a professor of chemistry at Purdue University, Wiley was appointed to serve as the nation's first commissioner of the U.S. Food and Drug Administration.

In developing his whiskey decision, President Taft closely consulted Wiley's findings on the use of artificial additives in consumer products, including alcoholic beverages. Wiley's studies reflected the strong preference for unblended, unadulterated whiskey codified in the U.S. Code of Federal Regulations. Had President Taft not defined whiskey at a time when rectifiers threatened its integrity, straight bourbon whiskey would not enjoy the sterling reputation it does today. In 2009, Taft was inducted into the Kentucky Bourbon Hall of Fame, the only president to receive that honor.[8]

President Taft is also the only president to serve in the military *after* leaving executive office. Taft was intimately involved in military affairs throughout his life and political career. His father, Alphonso Taft, served as President Ulysses S. Grant's secretary of war. [9] He followed in his father's footsteps, serving as President Theodore Roosevelt's secretary of war from 1904 to 1908 before defeating William Jennings Bryan for the presidency in 1908. Despite the fact that he lost his reelection bid to Woodrow Wilson in 1912, Taft continued to serve the nation. While employed as the dean of Yale Law School, Taft proposed the establishment of, and was selected to lead, the League to Enforce Peace, a hawkish organization that advocated for the use of military force to deter other nations' aggression.[10]

When the United States formally entered World War I in April of 1917, the portly ex-president enlisted in the Connecticut Home Guard, a body of armed troops dedicated to the defense of their state and its industries.[11] He also agreed to cochair President Woodrow Wilson's National War Labor Board (NWLB), a mediator of wartime industrial disputes between workers and employers. Taft's NWLB guaranteed workers' rights to organize and bargain collectively, and it mediated a threatened strike of Kentucky distillers, a dispute complicated by the Wartime Prohibition Act, which banned the sale of distilled spirits. Taft was later appointed to serve as the chief justice of the Supreme Court of the United States, a lifelong dream for the Ohioan. He died during Prohibition, but his whiskey decision lives on.

51 PERCENT CORN

Bourbon whiskey must be produced from a fermented mash containing at least 51 percent corn.[12] The regulatory emphasis on corn is a nod to early farmer distillers who settled Kentucky during and after the Revolutionary War. Several major Kentucky distilleries trace their roots to a family member who departed the East Coast for Kentucky's abundant land and corn: for example, William Brown (Brown-Forman); Jacob Boehm and Basil Hayden (Jim Beam); Robert Samuels (Maker's Mark); Henry Hudson Wathen (Medley and Wathen's); Daniel Weller (Buffalo Trace); William Willett Jr. (Willett); and Rev. Elijah Craig (Heaven Hill). Early American farmer distillers took advantage of Virginia governor Thomas Jefferson's 1776 "corn patch and cabin rights" law, which granted settlers four hundred acres if they would grow corn and build a cabin on the Virginia frontier in the region that became the Commonwealth of Kentucky in 1792.

Militia captain Jack Jouett, for example, left Albemarle County, near Charlottesville, in 1782 for what is now Woodford County, Kentucky.[13] The summer before he left, Captain Jouett saved Gov. Thomas Jefferson from being captured by members of the British Legion, including the infamous Banastre "Bloody Ban" Tarleton. Jouett spotted the enemy while drinking in a Louisa, Virginia, tavern and immediately rode over forty miles through the night to warn Jefferson, Patrick Henry, and three other signers of the Declaration of Independence of Tarleton's presence. Jefferson (who incidentally began producing corn whiskey at Monticello in 1813) rewarded Jouett with a bottle of fine Madeira wine before escaping with other key legislators into the Shenandoah Mountains.[14] The next year, "Paul Revere of the South" left his home for abundant, fertile land in the Kentucky territory, where he established a mill and whiskey distillery.[15] He operated the distillery until 1804, when he traded it to Charles and Peter Buck for a thousand gallons of their corn whiskey.[16]

American maize thrived in the rich soil of the frontier and it provided settlers with husk beds to sleep on, cobs for fires, and innumerable gallons of strong whiskey. Soldiers serving on the frontier had access to those farmer distillers' corn-based whiskey, as evidenced by early military records. In the spring of 1781, a new fort was established at the frontier village that later became Lexington, Kentucky. The expense account submitted by Fayette County militia commander Col. John Todd lists twenty-one quarts of liquor purchased for his men, including Lt. Col. Daniel Boone.[17] In a letter to the governor of Virginia, the colonel wrote that "rewards in liquor to the men proved powerful incentives to industry."[18] Three months later, Colonel Todd was killed at Blue Licks, one of the last battles of the Revolutionary War.

While countless Virginians moved to take advantage of Jefferson's corn patch law, many veterans moved to claim Revolutionary War service bounty land grants, given by the federal government to reward their military service. The number of Kentuckians nearly tripled between 1790 and 1800, from 61,133 residents to 179,873.[19] Thousands of veterans moved to Kentucky with their small pot stills and relied heavily on Kentucky corn to survive and to make whiskey. By 1797, Lexington was large enough to boast a Main Street, which included a tavern operated by Revolutionary War veteran Capt. John Postlethwait, whose customers included notable leaders of the day such as Andrew Jackson, James Monroe, Aaron Burr, Henry Clay, and Marquis de Lafayette.[20]

Many of the veterans who sailed the Ohio River or traversed the Appalachians sought to avoid the federal government's postwar tax on whiskey production, a sentiment that sparked violent rebellion in 1794.[21] In 1791, under the prodding of war hero Alexander Hamilton, the president approved an excise tax on liquor to pay back Revolutionary War debt, most of which was owed to European banks.[22]

Washington and Hamilton had a fraught relationship, forged in the fire of the revolution. Hamilton distinguished himself as a combat artillery officer during the Trenton-Princeton Campaign of 1776 and was selected to serve as General Washington's wartime aide-de-camp. After more than four years of serving the general, Hamilton resigned from the position when Washington reprimanded him for an act of tardiness. "You must change your watch, or I must change my aid," he wrote before accepting Hamilton's request for reassignment.[23] Later in the war, Hamilton was promoted to lieutenant colonel and led three battalions in a bayonet charge on Yorktown's Redoubt 10 alongside the Marquis de Lafayette.

After the revolution, Hamilton emerged as one of Washington's closest advisors and was appointed to lead the treasury, a position he used to torment whiskey distillers and implement his federalist views. In a letter to Congress, Hamilton justified the whiskey tax by arguing, "The consumption of ardent spirits . . . no doubt very much on account of their cheapness, is carried to an extreme, which is truly to be regretted, as well in regard to the health and the morals, as to the economy of the community. Should the increase of duties tend to a decrease of the consumption of those articles, the effect would be, in every respect, desirable."[24]

As a result of widespread animosity toward Hamilton's excise tax, Scots-Irish distillers in Maryland and Pennsylvania, still angry about a prohibitive tax on Highland stills in Scotland, refused to register their stills or pay. Over a period of nearly three years, gangs of distillers, most of them disillusioned war veterans, brutally attacked tax collectors, many of them also veterans, on the western frontier. Farmer distillers resisted the tax as part of a larger fight for economic equality. They did so by blackening their faces, donning deerskin breeches, sticking feathers in their hair, and terrorizing the government men invading their valleys.[25]

One such Revolutionary War veteran, Capt. James McFarlane, emerged as the popular leader of the rebellious Mingo Creek Militia. McFarlane, a forty-three-year-old whiskey distiller born in Northern Ireland, had commanded a company of militiamen from West Penns-borough Township, Pennsylvania, during the Revolutionary War. Like other rye whiskey distillers of the Monongahela River Valley, McFarlane refused to register his small still or submit to the federal tax collectors who demanded payment in cash.[26]

Tensions erupted in July 1794 when McFarlane and a contingent of angry country distillers threatened to scalp Capt. William Faulkner, who previously rented his property to tax collector, Gen. John Neville, a prominent Revolutionary War veteran and whiskey distiller himself. "They drew a knife on him, threatened to . . . tar and feather him and finally to reduce his house and property to ashes if he did not solemnly promise them to prevent the office of inspection from being there."[27] The next day, Revolutionary War veteran and whiskey distiller William Miller was served with a fine and notice of a court appearance for failing to register his still.[28] In response, McFarlane and the Mingo Creek men rode on horseback to General Neville's Bower Hill farm, intent on killing him.

Soldiers from nearby Fort Pitt responded to the attack, escalating the engagement on Bower Hill. Hundreds of distillers, including many expert riflemen, lay siege to Neville's residence, firing at his home for over an hour. In defense, Neville shot and killed William Miller's nephew Oliver. At one point, the rebels saw what they believed was the white flag of surrender rise from within from Neville's home. McFarlane stepped from behind a tree and directed his men to cease firing. Almost immediately, a shot rang out and struck him near the groin, killing him quickly. The outraged rebels stormed the house and forced the surrender of Maj. Abraham Kirkpatrick and his soldiers. Upon discovering that General Neville escaped in women's clothing, the rebels destroyed his house, crops, and animals, and they drank his whiskey.[29]

Thousands of frontier distillers attended James McFarlane's funeral, which became a recruiting rally for the rebel farmer cause. Within weeks, a force of some five thousand to seven thousand had gathered near Pittsburgh and began to train.[30] For President Washington and Alexander Hamilton, the prospect of Pittsburgh being overrun by defiant country whiskey distillers was unacceptable. On August 7, 1794, Washington issued a proclamation and requisitioned thirteen thousand grenadiers, dragoons, soldiers of foot, and pioneers, and he personally rode with them to Bedford, Pennsylvania.[31] Washington appointed several renowned Revolutionary War veterans to lead the column. Generals Light Horse Harry Lee and Daniel Morgan, infamous for the violent successes they enjoyed against redcoats like Bloody Ban Tarleton, rapidly advanced on the rebel distillers.

The deployment of their force and a terrible rainstorm brought a quick end to the uprising. Faced with a tremendous amount of firepower, the Whiskey Boys dispersed "like rye mash when the heat [is] applied."[32] Twenty men were arrested and tried in Philadelphia; only two were convicted and sentenced to death, but Washington pardoned their sentences having made his, and the federal government's, point.[33]

If fiercely independent farmer distillers needed a reason to continue their westward expansion, the whiskey tax was a good one. Unlike what they faced in western Maryland and Pennsylvania, enforcement of the excise tax in the newly chartered Commonwealth of Kentucky proved nearly impossible for the federal government. Prosecutors in Kentucky rarely found the courage to charge a distiller for violating the excise law, and when they did, Kentucky juries refused to convict.[34] Because many jurors were themselves defendants in tax evasion cases, the government banned whiskey distillers from serving on grand juries. Even so, judges and tax collectors were far more sympathetic to farmer distillers in Kentucky than in Maryland and Pennsylvania.[35]

As a result, droves of farmer distillers, including tens of thousands of Revolutionary War veterans, moved south and west. Distillers replaced East Coast rye with Kentucky corn, the most abundant crop, in their whiskey mash recipes. Over time, popular commercial distillers perfected their methods and used corn as the majority grain in their Kentucky whiskey recipes. Corn-based whiskey rapidly became the traditional beverage for spirited drinkers across the expanding nation.

CHARRED NEW OAK

In addition to the corn requirement, bourbon whiskey must be stored in charred new oak containers.[36] Most whiskey, regardless of national origin, must age in wooden containers to be labeled whiskey. The use of wooden barrels can be traced to the Celtic tribes of northern Europe. Before Romans incorporated wooden barrels into daily life, they encountered them on the battlefield. In the summer of 51 BC, when Julius Caesar's troops attacked a hilltop village in modern-day France, desperate Gallic defenders packed small wooden barrels with "pitch, tallow, and firewood."[37] They lit the primitive incendiary bombs and rolled them down toward the invading Romans. As Caesar's legionnaires worked to extinguish brush fires, the Gauls attacked with rocks, spears, and arrows. The Romans eventually overcame Gaul, and over time, Rome engaged in "cultural pillage" by adopting the Celtic methods for wood and metalworking.[38]

Roman historians called Celtic wooden barrels "cupae," from which the word "cooper" is derived. One early account describes the Roman military's use of wooden barrels to construct a pontoon bridge in AD 238. Throughout the Middle Ages, Celtic and Roman traders relied on coopers' barrels to transport provisions and liquids, especially by boat. Similarly, early Kentucky distillers relied heavily on coopers' work to store and transport grain and grain whiskey. During the nineteenth century, the use of barrels became customary in the American whiskey business, particularly upon the discovery that charred oak imparts a pleasant color, aroma, and flavor to corn whiskey during a flatboat journey to New Orleans.[39]

The requirement that bourbon age in *new* charred barrels dates to 1938 and is unique to the American spirit.[40] Such a requirement would be impossible for Scottish and Irish whiskey-makers, as naval conflicts nearly depleted oak forests in the United Kingdom.[41] Throughout the nineteenth century, most British oak trees were felled to build Royal Navy warships, forcing master distillers in Europe to turn to the French and Americans for proper containers. Americans are blessed with massive white oak forests, like those in the Missouri Ozarks, which produce cooperage ideal for mellowing whiskey and infusing distinct flavors. Present-day Scottish and Irish distillers are still left to rely on the Americans and French for used bourbon whiskey and wine barrels, although trees in some French regions like Argonne and Ardennes are too full of World War II shrapnel to be safely sawn.[42]

World War II also altered the physical makeup of the standard whiskey barrel. Today, a typical barrel can store fifty-three gallons or two hundred liters, a precise number necessitated by the demands of war. Prior to the 1940s, standard whiskey barrels could hold forty-eight gallons of liquid. Warehouses were originally constructed to accommodate forty-eight-gallon barrels. But as the Second World War continued on without an end in sight, resources like Missouri white oak became more precious. American coopers and distillery engineers figured out a way to continue to age whiskey while cutting back on the amount of wood used. By increasing the barrel size from forty-eight to fifty-three gallons, distilleries could store more whiskey per barrel and conserve wood for the war effort. Fifty-three-gallon barrels were the largest containers the original racks could safely hold, and they allowed American and European whiskey-makers to avoid massive upgrades to warehouse facilities.[43]

> 80 PROOF

Bourbon may not be produced in excess of 160 proof; it must be stored at less than 125 proof and bottled at more than 80 proof. Members of the Royal Navy developed the original "proof" test in the seventeenth century.[44] After England captured Jamaica and its rich sugar plantations in 1655, sailors became accustomed to generous rum rations. In the decades that followed, navy officials learned to soak pellets of gunpowder in their rum rations to determine their strength. If the rum-soaked pellets ignited, it served as proof that the liquor had not been overly diluted.

American and European distillers and chemists refined the proof test throughout the seventeenth and eighteenth centuries by mixing spirits with gunpowder and igniting it in more controlled environments. They found that the mixture burned with a steady flame at 50 percent alcohol by weight, which was referred to as "100 percent proved." While the invention of the hydrometer eliminated such tests, proof is still declared on many liquor labels, calculated as twice the percentage of a spirit's alcohol by volume in the United States. Liquor rations continued to flow in the U.S. Navy until World War I and in the British Navy until "Black Tot Day" in 1970.[45]

Under Title 27 of the Code of Federal Regulations, all whiskey must be bottled at 80 proof or higher, a requirement borne out of World War I. During the "Great War," British chancellor of exchequer David Lloyd George, with strong support from the king, established the Central Control Board, which developed regulations requiring whiskey to age for at least two years and to be produced at no more than 40 percent alcohol.[46] The goal was to conserve grain and promote efficiency in the whiskey industry. Eventually, American regulators adopted versions of both requirements, although 40 percent alcohol now represents the *least* potent a whiskey can be.

DISTINCTLY AMERICAN

Finally, bourbon whiskey must be made in America. On May 4, 1964, the 88th Congress of the United States declared bourbon whiskey to be "a distinctive product of the United States." Congress directed the appropriate agencies to prohibit the importation of any foreign "whisky designated as bourbon whiskey."[47]

Among the strongest supporters of the 1964 congressional resolution were the nine men in Congress from the Commonwealth of Kentucky.[48] Seven of the nine served in either the army or the navy, and all seven of them saw action on World War I or World War II battlefields. U.S. senator John Sherman Cooper, the son of a coal miner in Harlan County named for Gen. William Tecumseh Sherman, joined the army in 1942 as a lawyer and dashed across Europe with Gen. George Patton's Third Army. He was awarded the Bronze Star for reorganizing the German justice system in Bavaria and facilitating repatriation efforts in General Patton's occupation zone.[49]

His close friend and colleague in the Senate was Thruston Ballard Morton, who grew up milling corn into flour on a farm near Louisville.[50] Morton served as a naval officer in the Pacific during World War II and remained in the navy reserve as he became increasingly involved in politics.[51] Morton was elected to the U.S. Senate in 1956 and personally introduced the now famous bourbon whiskey resolution on September 12, 1963. Morton's proposed declaration was intended to elevate bourbon to the same level as Scotch, Canadian whisky, and cognac and to end the importation of foreign-made "bourbon." At the time, a New York heiress named Mary Dowling was importing "bourbon whiskey" from her family's Mexican distillery, Waterfill & Frazier, which moved from Kentucky to Juarez during Prohibition.

However, Morton's resolution was primarily driven by the overproduction of bourbon during the Korean War.[52] When the bourbon-drinking veteran President Truman committed U.S. forces to the conflict in Korea, Schenley Distillers Corporation executive Lewis Rosenstiel gambled that the Korean War would cause a whiskey shortage like the one America suffered during World War II. In preparation, Schenley's many distilleries went into overdrive, pushing total stocks of American whiskey past 637 million gallons.[53] When the conflict in Korea ended without the shortages Rosenstiel anticipated, he was left with an enormous surplus of aging straight whiskey.

Federal law at the time required distilleries to pay taxes on whiskey after aging eight years, at which point it had to be sold or destroyed (i.e., to be "forced out of bond").[54] Concerned that he might have to sell bourbon at a loss or destroy millions of gallons in order to avoid heavy taxation, Rosenstiel formed the Bourbon Institute, which lobbied for a law that would make whiskey taxes due at twenty years instead of eight.

Rosenstiel looked to Congressman Aime Forand, a World War I veteran from Rhode Island.[55] Congressman Forand, a member of the House Ways and Means Committee, was a zealous advocate for war veterans. Forand had been a sergeant first class in the army and experienced combat in France as a member of the American Expeditionary Force's Motor Transport Corps.[56] As a civil servant in the mid-1930s, he served as the commandant of the Rhode Island Soldiers' Home, an experience that later inspired him to cosponsor the legislation that created Medicare.[57]

Persuaded by Rosenstiel's dilemma, the influential congressman agreed to introduce a measure to extend the bonded period from eight to twenty years. In September 1958, the "Forand Bill" became law, relieving pressure on companies like Schenley.[58] Distilleries took advantage of the expanded bonded period to create brands of bourbon whiskey like Very Old Fitzgerald and much older expressions of Old Charter, Ancient Age, and I. W. Harper.

With the 1958 Forand Act in place, Rosenstiel looked for other ways to capitalize on his massive, aging bourbon stock. To protect it from foreign competition, the Bourbon Institute began its work on the congressional resolution that declared bourbon a "distinctive product of the United States." In May 1964, Senator Morton's resolution passed, and Rosenstiel sent a case of bourbon to every U.S. embassy in the world.[59] Today, Senator Morton's resolution has been broadly interpreted by marketing agencies and legislators alike, who have stretched its language to designate bourbon whiskey "America's Native Spirit."[60]

ETYMOLOGY

Despite bourbon's familial relationship with the bald eagle, baseball, and apple pie, its name is French. But even its moniker is deeply rooted in military history. During the Revolutionary War, King Louis XVI of France was the main source of foreign support for the colonists in the fight against George III. King Louis XVI was a member of the Royal House of Bourbon.[61] Members of the French Army fought alongside

Continental troops beginning in 1778 and participated in notable battles at Newport, Rhode Island, Savannah, Georgia, and Chesapeake, Virginia. Nearly nine thousand French regulars fought at the decisive siege of Yorktown that forced Cornwallis to surrender to Washington and Rochambeau on October 19, 1781.[62]

Following the war, the Virginia General Assembly made the Marquis de Lafayette, France's most ardent supporter of the patriot cause, an honorary citizen of the Commonwealth of Virginia. Lafayette bled with the Americans at Brandywine, and he remained with the Continentals through the bitter Valley Forge winter of 1777–78. Washington, Lafayette, and their men drank whiskey, rum, and applejack together to restore their cold and beaten bodies.[63] Beginning in 1785, members of Virginia's legislature, some of whom fought beside the French at the Battle of Yorktown, honored their brothers-in-arms by naming many towns and counties after French people and places.[64]

A drive through northern and central Kentucky today, formerly part of Virginia, brings one through Bourbon County, and the towns of Bellefonte, Bellemeade, Bellevue, Frenchburg, La Center, La Grange, LaFayette, Paris, Versailles, and of course the commonwealth's largest city, Louisville, named for the Bourbon King. By the time Kentucky became an independent commonwealth in 1792, thousands of frontier distillers were producing corn-based whiskey in and around Bourbon County. Soon their uniquely aged distillate would bear that name.

After the outbreak of the French Revolution and Reign of Terror, a man named Louis Tarascon fled the Cognac region of his native France for Philadelphia in 1789. His brother Jean followed in 1797.[65] The Tarascons quickly built a successful shipyard in Pennsylvania, but they continued to explore the Ohio Valley, eventually settling at the Falls of the Ohio River in present-day Louisville. The Tarascons founded a thriving French community known as Shippingport, where they established a mill and purchased a warehouse east of the falls. Shrewd businessmen, the brothers purchased whiskey from distillers in the area and aged it in charred barrels to make it taste more like French cognac or brandy.[66]

Following the United States' purchase of Louisiana in 1803, Americans flooded New Orleans, joining the French and Creole residents in and around the established Vieux Carre, or French Quarter.[67] As the population grew, the street life blossomed. Around 1807, the Tarascon brothers and their partner, Jacques Berthoud, began shipping their charred barrel–aged, corn-based whiskey on steamboats, where it was sold to other Frenchmen in New Orleans.[68] Many New Orleans residents had also fled the chaos of the French Revolution and were loyal to the French monarchy. Bourbon Street establishments called the aged whiskey from Kentucky "Bourbon Whiskey" to appeal to royalists in the city, but it was sometimes called "Bourbon County Whiskey" so as not to offend the revolutionists.[69]

The Tarascons may or may not have been the first Kentucky whiskey producers to age their product in charred barrels. Available records do not answer the question to a reasonable degree of certainty, but that has not stopped whiskey companies or scholars from offering opinions about who "invented" bourbon whiskey. In one of the most recent and well-researched efforts, author and U.S. Army veteran Fred Minnick surmised that Jacob Spears of Bourbon County was most likely the "father of bourbon."[70] Spears moved from Dutch Pennsylvania to Paris, Kentucky, in Bourbon County in the late 1780s and began making whiskey around 1790. Several sources strongly suggest he was the first to label his product as "bourbon whiskey."[71]

It is, however, impossible to conclude that Spears was the first Kentucky distiller to age his corn whiskey in charred cooperage or to call it bourbon. There is some evidence that Jacob Spears was *not* the first man to call his whiskey bourbon.[72] For example, Revolutionary War veteran Capt. John Hamilton moved to Kentucky following the 1791 Whiskey Rebellion and, according to several sources, produced "bourbon whiskey" before Spears.[73] What is not in dispute, however, is that before Jacob Spears began distilling whiskey in Kentucky, he served as a private soldier during the Revolutionary War.[74]

At the outbreak of war, Spears enlisted alongside other Pennsylvanians and fought as a member of Capt. John Hoagland's company. He participated in one of the war's final battles during Col. William Crawford's "Sandusky Campaign."[75] In 1782, both Captain Hoagland

and Colonel Crawford were captured, tortured, and killed in Ohio, which "caused profound sensation throughout the country."[76] Private Jacob Spears survived the campaign, reunited with family in Virginia's Kentucky territory, and began distilling whiskey shortly thereafter. In 1792, he was commissioned a captain in the Bourbon County, Kentucky, militia.

Confusing the history is the fact that Jacob Spears's first cousin (also named Jacob Spears) was another Revolutionary War soldier who settled in Lincoln County, Kentucky, to manage his family's farm.[77] *That* Jacob Spears, originally from Virginia, fought Indians with Maj. Joseph Bowman's company during Gen. George Rogers Clark's Illinois Campaign.[78] Jacob Spears was a sergeant when Major Bowman, the brother of the famed Col. Abraham Bowman, was killed by celebratory artillery fire at the conclusion of the Illinois Campaign in 1779.[79] In 1818, that Jacob Spears's sister, Catherine Spears Frye Carpenter, recorded the first known sour mash recipe (the method of sparking fermentation in one batch of whiskey by adding material from a spent batch) in their family's bible, lending credence to the belief that he too was an early Kentucky distiller.[80]

While the Spears families were developing distilling methods in Bourbon and Lincoln Counties, thousands of other Kentucky distillers began advertising and identifying their product on barrelheads as Old Bourbon Whiskey, no matter where it was actually made. Beneficiaries of shipments from places like Shippingport and Maysville considered the barrel-aged whiskey labeled "Old Bourbon" to be the best whiskey available. As early as 1821, advertisements for the corn whiskey being loaded onto flatboats in Kentucky identified it as Bourbon whiskey.[81]

The name did not become a permanent part of the American language, however, until the American Civil War. As author Henry Crowgey wrote in 1971, the Marquis de Lafayette returned to tour the United States in 1824–25, and he visited Ashland, the home of Kentucky statesman Henry Clay.[82] It is written that the guest of honor was offered a glass of *whiski*. "Had the finest in Kentucky hospitality been known as bourbon whiskey at the time, it would certainly been referred to as such."[83] In 1861, however, when Prince Napoleon came to America and inspected the military camps at Staten Island, New York, he sipped from a bottle of liquor carried by an army private. "What is it?" he asked. "Old Bourbon, sir," replied the soldier. "Old Bourbon indeed," was the prince's response. "I did not think I would like anything with that name so well."[84]

3

War and Whiskey Persist

It is somewhat surprising that a private would have openly carried a bottle of liquor in the presence of superior officers, let alone foreign dignitaries, in 1861. In the decades leading up to the Civil War, significant elements of society began to criticize binge drinking made common by the presence of cheap, untaxed liquor and harsh living conditions. As one author observed, "I am afraid my brave Tennesseans indulge too great a fondness for whiskey. When I was in Virginia it was too much whiskey. The Ohio story was the same: too, too much whiskey."[1] Military commanders and surgeons, observing the same levels of indulgence, took note of whiskey's impact on good order and discipline.

In 1832, liquor rations for the U.S. Army were eliminated when General-Officer-turned-President Andrew Jackson signed an executive order substituting coffee and sugar for the daily gill of liquor established by Gen. George Washington.[2] Congress followed the president by passing a law in 1838 that officially eliminated the daily gill.[3] Justification for ending the ration was documented by U.S. Army assistant surgeon L. A. Birdsall and other officers in a letter to Congress published in the

May 24, 1838, *Army and Navy Chronicle*. The letter was entitled "Temperance in the Army" and included a statement that

> the undersigned officers of the United States army beg leave respectfully to represent that, in their opinion, the substitution of sugar and coffee for the whiskey part of the ration allowed to soldiers, has been productive of great good to the service, and also the means of preserving the health, efficiency, and happiness, and frequently affecting the moral reformation of that part of our army.[4]

That President Jackson replaced the soldier's daily gill with coffee is ironic considering that Old Hickory was a large-scale Tennessee whiskey-maker himself. In 1799, the hero of the Battle of New Orleans obtained licenses to operate a 127-gallon still and a 70-gallon pot still at the Hermitage, his estate in Nashville. Jackson's distillery was destroyed by fire in 1800, which burdened his estate with a tax obligation on the burned stills, a dilemma he worked for years to resolve. The Hermitage distillery was rebuilt in 1802, the same year he was elected major general of the Tennessee Militia. The year after Jackson was appointed to command the Tennessee Militia, the general petitioned Congress for a refund on the whiskey taxes he paid in 1799 after the fire.[5]

Further, Jackson's troops during the War of 1812 and Seminole Wars were supplied with liquor, and his inauguration party in 1829 was a whiskey-soaked affair.[6] There is even an enduring rumor that Jack Daniels Old No. 7 Tennessee whiskey brand is a reference to the seventh president. Old Hickory and Hermitage were popular whiskey brands in the nineteenth century, and today one can enjoy Old Hickory whiskey, produced by Nashville-based R. S. Lipman Company, in his honor. Yet modern-day soldiers in basic training at Fort Jackson, South Carolina, have their post's namesake to thank for the Folgers coffee and generic sugar packets shrink-wrapped in their meals ready-to-eat (MREs).

Despite President Jackson's edict and the will of Congress, whiskey continued to flow in the army, whether made available at commanders' discretion or smuggled in by industrious and creative soldiers. When the army inspector general George Croghan toured the forts in "the new West" along the Mississippi River, he noted that where there is money, there is "no lack of whiskey."[7] Soldiers at Fort Crawford, Wisconsin, were observed smuggling whiskey into camp by soaking their blankets in whiskey and wringing them out. During an inspection at the fort, two senior officers observed "the strange antics of an approaching cat." The two men stepped over in its direction, and suddenly the animal stopped. "Major Garland reached down, picked it up, and discovered he held a cat's skin stuffed with a bladder full of whisky. He had stopped the cat's mysterious journey toward a thirsty soldier within the barracks."[8]

AMERICAN CIVIL WAR

American alcohol consumption continued to rapidly rise around the time Prince Napoleon visited the conflicted United States. Throughout the 1850s, the annual alcohol intake for an average American drinker increased from 3.9 gallons to 6.4 gallons.[9] By comparison, today's average drinker consumes 2.3 gallons of alcohol per year.[10] Huge percentages of men were rejected from military service because of drunkenness. Records of Union courts-martial during the Civil War show that those percentages should have been even higher.

Most troops were "young, hot-blooded, and an inch away from chaos."[11] Consequently, many were disciplined for getting drunk and wandering behind enemy lines, straggling behind formations, cursing at superior officers, fighting, stealing whiskey, and falling off of horses. Gen. Braxton Bragg believed that "more than half the labor of the courts-martial result from" whiskey.[12] One rebel private was convicted by court-martial and made to stand on the head of a barrel with a whiskey bottle hanging from his neck two hours each day for a month.[13] Some men were executed for drunken misconduct.

Within the whiskey industry, high demand for alcohol among Civil War soldiers gave rise to new brands and marketing strategies. The war and wartime sentiments inspired the creation of Rebel Yell, Jeff Davis, and Deep Spring, a Tennessee whiskey featuring Robert E. Lee on horseback and a Confederate nurse holding a glass of whiskey to the lips of a wounded rebel soldier. General Lee was, however, one of the rare Civil War leaders who avoided whiskey, which he called the universal balm. In a letter to his son, Lee wrote, "I am sorry to say that there is great proclivity for spirit in the field."[14] Not even Gen. Thomas "Stonewall" Jackson, Lee's trusted lieutenant, could stifle the rebels' thirst for liquor.

In August 1862, just days before the Battle of Second Manassas, Jackson's men plundered a massive Union depot near Manassas Junction, Virginia. The rebels gorged on enemy supplies, including several casks of whiskey. When General Jackson ordered the whiskey to be destroyed, many of the soldiers fell to their hands and knees to drink the liquor from the ground. Members of the Fifth Virginia Volunteer Infantry Regiment, a component of the Stonewall Brigade, once purchased three casks of rye whiskey near Winchester, Virginia, and "woke not sure where it was."[15] One of the intoxicated Virginians climbed a tall tree during their night of revelry and hung the regimental colors from the tallest branch.

While General Jackson mostly avoided alcohol, he supported medicinal whiskey for wounded men. When he was wounded by a friendly gunshot during the Battle of Chancellorsville in Virginia, doctors immediately administered whiskey as he lay wounded on the battlefield.[16] As John Bowers noted in his book *Stonewall Jackson*, as soon as the general was struck, a bottle of whiskey materialized. Jackson took a large mouthful. He was later transferred to a warmed tent in the wilderness, where he took more whiskey before dying several days later. "On the battlefield there was always whiskey."[17]

While Stonewall Jackson's death was a tragic loss for Robert E. Lee personally and foreshadowed the fate of the Confederacy, the Battle of Chancellorsville was a stunning tactical success for the South. Following the battle, President Lincoln's secretary of the navy, Gideon Welles, criticized Maj. Gen. Joseph Hooker for "indulging too freely in whiskey" during the battle.[18] Welles believed that whiskey made Hooker unsafe and unreliable. He also wrote that "if there had been no whiskey in the army after crossing the Rappahannock we should have had complete success."[19] Gen. George McClellan, who did not drink, also criticized General Hooker's division, writing that "no one evil agent so much obstructs this army . . . as the degrading vice of drunkenness."[20] Today, the California distillery Prohibition

Spirits' Hooker's House Bourbon Whiskey pays homage to the hard-drinking commander.

General Hooker was not the only senior leader to be criticized for indulging too freely on the battlefield. At Antietam, Irish Brigade commander Briga. Gen. Thomas Meagher was allegedly "too drunk to keep the saddle" and fell from his horse several times as his men were slaughtered at Antietam's "Bloody Lane."[21] During the second Battle of Murfreesboro in Tennessee, Confederate general Benjamin Franklin Cheatham drunkenly fell from his saddle as thousands of men around him were wounded or killed in action.[22] Cheatham had been introduced to whiskey during the war by Jack Daniel himself and praised the Lynchburg, Tennessee, distiller in a letter by telling Mr. Daniel his product was "beyond a doubt the finest whiskey I ever tasted. . . . Once one has sampled his first sip, it is impossible to refuse a second."[23]

General Grant, one of the best horsemen in U.S. military history, suffered a fall from his steed in New Orleans on September 2, 1863, attributed by many to the effect of whiskey.[24] While intoxication was only the rumored cause of the New Orleans debacle, Grant famously downed an entire "goblet" of Old Crow bourbon in the presence of an aide during the siege of Vicksburg.[25] The same month, Grant mounted his horse and went for a drunken gallop in the presence of *Chicago Times* reporter Sylvanus Cadwallader, who recorded the event in his manuscript "Three Years with Grant," which was not published until 1955.[26]

While the generals drank decent straight whiskey produced by reputable distillers in Kentucky and Pennsylvania, foot soldiers in both blue and gray mocked the infamous whiskey made available to them by the commissary, believing that it was made from bark juice, tar water, turpentine, brown sugar, lamp oil, and perhaps alcohol.[27] As a consequence, men dedicated huge amounts of time searching for quality whiskey in the towns they swept through. The First Special Battalion, Louisiana Volunteer Infantry, stole so much whiskey en route to the Battle of Gettysburg that Pennsylvania whiskey distillers buried their rye to prepare for their arrival.[28] The misbehaving "Louisiana Tigers" dug it all up. As one lieutenant noted, "the whole Brigade got drunk."[29] They later carried a pilfered barrel of whiskey to Gettysburg, where they charged the Union's Eleventh Corps at Cemetery Hill.[30] Union troops noted that following the battle, Tigers lay on the field with whiskey-filled canteens in their cold, dead hands.

Mississippi lieutenant John Brynam noted that "a soldier will get whiskey at any risk."[31] A company from his regiment smuggled a half-gallon of whiskey into a tent in the center of a hollowed-out watermelon, which the men buried beneath the tent floor and tapped into with a long straw.[32] Whenever one of the rebels wanted a drink, he would simply lie flat on the floor and suck through the straw. During an engagement in Middletown, Virginia, Confederate general Turner Ashby's men plundered Union supply trains containing barrels of whiskey, and became so intoxicated that Gen. Nathaniel Banks's Union forces escaped what would otherwise have very likely been a decisive Confederate victory.[33]

For federal troops, the U.S. government and distillers in the North had the means and resources to continue producing potable whiskey. One young Massachusetts fifer who abstained from alcohol when he joined up yielded to his commander's "better judgment" when he brought out a barrel.[34] Supplies dwindled over time, however, as did the quality of whiskey in the field. One Chicago solider wrote about an incident in New Orleans where the "Boys cleaned out a Bar."[35] For Christmas 1864, the colonel of the Ninety-Fifth Illinois Regiment did what he could for his men and "turned out fifteen gallons of Rotgut."[36]

For rebel soldiers, demand for whiskey was extremely strong, but the Confederate government badly needed to conserve grain and repurpose copper and brass. Several southern states imposed heavy fines on whiskey production unless it was for hospital use or chemical, mechanical, or industrial purposes.[37] Other states ordered outright prohibitions. When the Confederate War Department opened a medicinal whiskey distillery in Salisbury, North Carolina, Gov. Zebulon Vance threatened to arrest the distillers and reminded the secretary of war that his state "positively [forbade] the distillation of any kind of grain within its borders under heavy penalties."[38]

Many southern stills were confiscated and their components were melted into cannons and ammunition. While the Confederate navy distributed liquor rations throughout the war to attract foreign sailors to its fleet, most southern states prohibited liquor for fighting men in the field. Whiskey supply was so low in the South that rebels drank blends of whiskey and cleaning solvent. Some rebels drank mixtures of gunpowder and whiskey.

Following a battle in Helena, Arkansas, one Wisconsin soldier wrote that "the Rebels were fed on gunpowder and whiskey, and they were just crazy."[39] Adequate containers were so scarce that one soldier from Tennessee was seen drinking whiskey from the barrel of his rifle.[40] Even if Confederate leaders had the means to ration whiskey for their troops, men fighting in the Deep South were cut off from the cornfields and country stills of Kentucky by massive Union columns.

At the war's bitter end, veterans of both sides returned to their homes and contributed to the whiskey industry's revival. One example is William "Billy" Pearson, a veteran of the Second South Carolina Spartan Militia and the Battle of King's Mountain. After the war, Pearson moved to Big Flat Creek near modern-day Lynchburg, Tennessee. He apparently brought his grandmother's Pennsylvania whiskey recipe with him, which he eventually sold to a local distiller named Alfred Eaton. The recipe called for corn-mash whiskey to be filtered through charcoal made from hard sugar maple wood. In 1865, Eaton sold the recipe to distiller Jack Daniel, who perfected the method now known as the Lincoln County process.

Another is Wiley Searcy, the son of a Kentucky tavern owner, who served as a private in Company E of the Twenty-First Kentucky Infantry Regiment. Searcy fought at the Battle of Perryville in October 1862 and was rewarded with sergeant's stripes. Late in the war, Sergeant Searcy accepted a commission in Company L of the Ninth Kentucky Cavalry, commanded by his relative, Capt. William M. Searcy.[41]

In 1864, Wiley Searcy was promoted to captain and helped raise Company G of the Thirtieth Kentucky Mounted Infantry, which he later commanded.[42] He led his troops in a furious pursuit of the daring Confederate cavalryman John Hunt Morgan (whose likeness appeared on advertisements for Old Crow in the years that followed the Civil War) and Morgan's raiders. Searcy also fought in Virginia and East Tennessee and survived having two horses shot from under him in one afternoon. In October 1864, he was "severely wounded" at the First Battle of Saltville in Virginia.[43] After recovering, Searcy rejoined his unit and fought "bushwhackers" like the infamous William Quantrill until the last of them surrendered on the steps of a Nelson County distillery owned by T. W. Samuels. Following the war, Captain Searcy returned to his home in Kentucky, where he remained in the militia until his first wife bore a child.

In 1886, Searcy, who continued to use his rank on official documents, purchased the Anderson County distillery originally owned by "Old Joe" Peyton, considered to be the creator of the very first bourbon "brand." Searcy's small distillery featured two simple warehouses where he aged whiskey called "Old Joe" in honor of Peyton's original label. Captain Searcy advertised himself as an independent distiller and his product as "the best whisky that can be made."[44]

In 1909, the Wiley Searcy Distillery was completely destroyed by fire. The sixty-six-year-old combat-wounded veteran ultimately sold his property to Thomas Beebe Ripy and James Porter Ripy, who rebuilt the distillery and operated it until Prohibition.[45] Forty-five years before they sealed the deal, James Porter Ripy was a young rebel cavalryman in John Hunt Morgan's command on the opposite end of the battlefield from Capt. Wiley Searcy and his Kentucky mounted infantry.[46] After the sale, the Ripy family maintained control of the distillery and were involved in almost every other distillery in Anderson County, Kentucky, including those known today as Four Roses, Wild Turkey, and the Hoffman Distillery, last used as a warehouse facility and bottling plant for the Van Winkle family.[47]

In the decades that followed the Civil War, however, whiskey became a bane to American society and the military. "Liquor became the scourge of the army, particularly in the lonely outfits on the plains during the Indian Wars in the 1880s."[48] Soldiers spent months at a time patrolling rugged, dangerous lands, but upon returning to their frontier forts, they spent their time and money in local saloons drinking whiskey. Veterans across the nation attempted to heal their physical and psychological wounds of these conflicts with whiskey.

Overindulgence among Civil War and frontier veterans gave life to a powerful temperance movement. Calls for prohibition strengthened as prominent figures like Carrie Nation gained notoriety with anti-saloon "raids." Nation's anti-drink zeal was ignited by the severe alcoholism and death of her first husband, Charles Gloyd, a Civil War doctor. Whiskey's negative reputation in the late nineteenth century spiraled toward national prohibition after several scandals involving prominent veterans.

WHISKEY RING AND GEN. JOHN MCDONALD

The first major scandal erupted within the administration of the bourbon-reliant President Ulysses S. Grant when it was revealed that federal tax collectors were colluding with whiskey distillers seeking to avoid paying taxes. Following the Civil War, the whiskey tax increased sharply, to a high of two dollars per gallon, prompting distillers to bribe tax collectors to avoid paying exorbitant sums.[49] In 1875, government storekeepers maintained the keys to bonded warehouses, and when tax payments came due, the whiskey was dumped and sold. The only relief from the tax was fraud.

Gen. John McDonald, a senior army commander during the war, personal friend of President Grant, and the supervisor of internal revenue in St. Louis, led a massive conspiracy to accept bribes from undercapitalized distillers eager to remain profitable. During the war, McDonald rose to the rank of brigadier general and served under the immediate command of Gen. William T. Sherman. He raised and outfitted the Eighth Missouri Regiment, which saw action in many of the western campaigns, fighting in the Battles of Fort Henry, Fort Donelson, and Shiloh.[50] His postwar conspiracy involved distillers, many of whom were also veterans of the Civil War, in St. Louis, Chicago, Peoria, Milwaukee, Cincinnati, and New Orleans.

When whiskey salesman and Civil War veteran George Thomas Stagg complained about McDonald's scheme, the federal government launched an investigation. The inquiry revealed not only that distillers and tax collectors had been defrauding the government of taxes, but also that some of the stolen revenues were used to finance Republican Party campaigns. General McDonald was summoned to Washington, where he admitted to falsifying tax records and stealing tax revenues.

A special prosecutor named John Brooks Henderson, a brigadier general in the Missouri State Militia during the Civil War, ordered raids on other federal tax offices. Investigators seized records and arrested scores of distillers and government officials. Henderson discovered that over 350 whiskey distillers, storage managers, distributors, and others had been bribing tax collectors to ignore various irregularities in whiskey manufacturing since at least 1870.[51]

In Washington DC, another prominent veteran was implicated but denied wrongdoing. The flamboyant Gen. Orville Babcock, a heavy whiskey drinker, served as General Grant's chief of staff during the Civil War, fought at almost every major battle in which General Grant commanded forces, and personally escorted Robert E. Lee at Appomattox to surrender to his boss. After the war, Grant hired Babcock to be his personal secretary in the White House, a position he probably used for personal profit. When Babcock was indicted for his role in the whiskey tax ring in 1875, President Grant personally testified on his behalf, and he was exonerated.[52]

Despite General McDonald's admissions, Grant resisted prosecuting him. Grant even fired prosecutor John Henderson for challenging his interference in the case and appointed James Overton Broadhead to replace him. Broadhead, a lieutenant colonel in the Third Missouri Cavalry during the war, indicted and tried nearly two hundred people for tax fraud, including General McDonald, who was convicted, fined $5,000, and sentenced to three years in jail.[53] On January 26, 1877, at the peril of his political career, President Grant pardoned McDonald.[54] Between 1870 and 1876, between twelve and fifteen million gallons of whiskey went untaxed (i.e., nearly $20 million in lost tax revenue each year), an appalling number considering that 50 percent of federal revenue during Grant's administration came from the alcohol tax.[55]

PEORIA WHISKEY TRUST AND JOSEPH GREENHUT

Several years later, America experienced a second whiskey scandal involving a prominent veteran. Civil War hero Joseph Benedict Greenhut established a whiskey trust, which briefly monopolized the whiskey industry before being dissolved by state and federal government action.

Greenhut was born at the Austrian military post of Teinitz in 1843, but he moved with his mother to Chicago after his father died in 1847.[56] When the Civil War erupted in April 1861, Greenhut became the second man in the state of Illinois to join the Union army.[57]

He enlisted as a private in the Twelfth Illinois Infantry in Chicago and served with the regiment throughout General Grant's campaigns in Kentucky and Tennessee. Greenhut was promoted to sergeant after being badly wounded in the right arm at Fort Donelson. Upon his recovery, in August of 1862, he was appointed captain of Company K, Eighty-Second Illinois Infantry Regiment. He fought for Generals Burnside, Hooker, and Meade in the Virginia Campaign at the Battles of Fredericksburg and Chancellorsville and he commanded two companies at the Battle of Gettysburg. On the second day of the infamous battle, Greenhut led a "storming party" of one hundred men to kill Confederate sharpshooters on Cemetery Hill.[58] His regiment later repelled a charge of seventeen hundred Louisiana Tigers, infamous for stealing whiskey and drinking it on the battlefield. Greenhut's Eighty-Second Illinois killed fourteen hundred of them. Later that year, the highly decorated Captain Greenhut was selected by Gen. Friedrich Hecker to serve as his staff adjutant, a position he held until February 24, 1864, when he resigned his commission.[59]

Following the Civil War, Greenhut returned to Illinois and went to work for the Great Western Distillery as a coppersmith.[60] At that time, production of distilled spirits in America was between three and four times consumption, which was economically acceptable until European distilleries recovered from a devastating drought, eliminating the export market. Demand for American whiskey dwindled, but distillers were under pressure to continue operating at high levels to meet the parallel demand from cattle lot owners, who needed spent mash to feed their livestock, a lucrative business they could not afford to lose.

In 1869, when Greenhut became the secretary and treasurer of the Keller Distilling Company, he instituted a plan to control production levels, stymie competition, and maximize profits for trust executives. Using John D. Rockefeller's Standard Oil Trust as a model, he created the Distillers & Cattle Feeders Trust and was elected its first president.

When the Peoria-based Whiskey Trust formed, sixty-five distilleries joined it, including twenty-four in Illinois and twelve in the city of Peoria alone.

In its early years, the Whiskey Trust was profitable, paid dividends, and openly tried to convince other distilleries to join. But as it expanded, the trust circumvented state securities laws by tempting independent distillers to join through share offers that yielded little profit. Occasionally, the Whiskey Trust used force if other methods failed to convince stubborn competitors to join. The Whiskey Trust dynamited H. H. Shufeldt distillery's facilities in Chicago when it refused to join.[61]

By the early 1890s, Greenhut's Trust was producing more than 80 percent of the nation's total alcohol spirits, over three hundred million gallons in a seven-year period. Greenhut and other trust executives amassed great wealth, built mansions in Peoria and elsewhere, and invested in other industries. In September 1891, when Greenhut delivered a rousing speech to a group of Eighty-Second Illinois veterans at the Gettysburg Battlefield, he was not only the president of the Distilling & Cattle Feeding Company, but he was also the president of the Central Railway Company, a principal owner of the Peoria Steel and Iron Company, and a director for the German American National Bank and National Bank of the Republic.[62]

In June of 1893, Greenhut's trust crumbled. First, the state of Illinois filed suit, alleging that the Whiskey Trust "exceeded powers granted by its charter, destroyed competition, and was repugnant to public policy."[63] Congressional hearings about the trust's activities revealed many of its nefarious actions, including the bombing of the Shufeldt distillery. In December 1893, the state succeeded in canceling the trust's certificate of incorporation.[64] Appellate litigation kept the trust operating for several more years, but in the court of public opinion, the entire whiskey industry was increasingly viewed as corrupt and harmful to society.

In 1890, concerned with the "morality, sobriety, and discipline" of the troops, Congress imposed a limited prohibition on the army by banning "ardent spirits" for enlisted men while they were on their military posts.[65] In 1901, Congress expanded the army prohibition with the Canteen Act, which prohibited "the sale of, or dealing in, beer, wine or any intoxicating liquors by any person in any post exchange or canteen or army transport or upon any premises used for military purposes by the United States."[66]

Political leaders in both the United States and Great Britain called on grateful citizens to "omit any alcoholic beverage of any kind in sending favors to the soldiers."[67] Sadly, despite the increased regulation of alcohol, many Americans, and a large proportion of Civil War veterans, continued to abuse and self-medicate with whiskey. Drunkenness and alcoholism became major societal problems. Even President Grant, who carried his Civil War experiences into the Oval Office, struggled with alcoholism up until his death. As one scholar noted, "the courageous soldier who defeated the Confederates lost his longer war with the disease of alcoholism."[68] Decades of American overindulgence gave rise to the ill-fated temperance movement, whose leaders exploited World War I fever to pass the Eighteenth Amendment.

WORLD WAR I AND PROHIBITION

The United States' experience during the First World War provoked its final march to Prohibition. From a practical perspective, the government restricted the production of beverage alcohol in response to the Allied military establishment's demand for more grain, metal, and men. From an emotional perspective, the temperance movement advanced as Americans came to see Germany, a proud drinking nation, as the aggressor in Europe. Temperance advocates adopted the declaration that "we are fighting Germany, Austria, and drink, and, as far as I can see, the greatest of these deadly foes is drink."[69] The powerful Anti-Saloon League went so far as to refer to the Milwaukee brewing industry (e.g., Pabst, Schlitz, Blatz, Miller) as "the worst of all our German enemies."[70]

World War I–era propaganda posters featured sober, upright, patriotic men preparing for battle against booze-soaked Huns. Germans were often depicted as intoxicated beasts and cartooned into whiskey or beer barrels by pro-temperance organizations. William Fraunce, the president of Brown University, told the graduating class of 1917 that "patriotism spells prohibition."[71] Even ex-president William Howard Taft, the man responsible for establishing national standards for the whiskey industry, directed his alma mater Yale University (where, as a student, he was known to drink an occasional beer) to prohibit liquor at class reunions.[72] Several other American universities followed suit, tying the temperance effort to patriotism and support for the military.

On June 28, 1914, a Yugoslav nationalist assassinated Archduke Franz Ferdinand of Austria, sparking the violent, near-global conflagration. Coincidentally, on July 1, 1914, the secretary of the U.S. Navy, the devout Methodist and teetotaler Josephus Daniels, published General Order No. 99, prohibiting "the use or introduction for drinking purposes of alcoholic liquors on board any naval vessel, or within any navy yard or station."[73] Sly sailors exploited liberal prescriptions of the navy's "official" medicinal whiskey, Old Overholt rye, but Daniels's General Order 99 reflected a broader national sentiment.[74]

Despite the federal government's official stance of neutrality, state governments instituted a series of measures to prepare for war, which included bans on the production of beverage alcohol. By 1917, thirteen states had enacted total prohibitions to conserve grain and war materiel for the armed forces.[75] Also that year, the federal government raised the whiskey tax from $1.10 to $3.20 per gallon and passed a conscription statute that prohibited the sale of liquor to soldiers, sailors, and marines in uniform and to anyone within five miles of a military base.[76] Finally, after Congress declared war on Germany, it enacted a nationwide temporary "wartime prohibition" on the production of beverage alcohol, banning the production of distilled spirits from any produce that could be used as food.[77]

Across the Atlantic, British citizens and politicians wrestled with similar issues relating to temperance and the production of alcohol. Prominent English leaders considered a total ban on the production of beverage alcohol but opted to significantly raise taxes on whisky instead, causing a major reduction in Scotch sales.[78] While distilleries were permitted to continue operating, alcohol advertising was banned in some areas of England.[79] The 1915 Immature Spirits Act and additional regulations mandated that whisky be aged for at least two years and diluted to contain no more than 40 percent alcohol. Licensing laws limited public house operating hours to two hours each afternoon and three hours each evening.[80] A "no treating" order required drinkers to pay for their beverages at the time they were supplied to discourage running tabs and rounds of drinks.[81]

The military communities also grappled with how to balance their soldiers' demand for alcohol with the burgeoning temperance movement. U.S. Army doughboys were expected to fight dry, and possession of alcohol could be punished by a court-martial with the maximum sentence being death. The Royal Army, however, continued to ration rum to fighting men in the murderous trenches, and Englishmen, Frenchmen, and Canadians provided American allies with access to brandy, wine, and rum. One war correspondent wrote that while "some people at home feel very uncomfortable about the small rum ration that the troops receive, almost every man I have met who has served during the winter is in favour of it."[82]

Life in the trenches was a combination of sweltering heat, freezing cold, and exposure to constant shelling and rotting corpses. Private Ernest Spillett of the Canadian Army's Forty-Sixth Battalion wrote in a 1917 letter about having to remove corpses from the battlefield, saying, "They don't have to prime me with rum before I can handle a man; altho' I have and do certainly drink it . . . to take the taste of dead men out of my mouth."[83] Private G. Boyd of the Canadian Eighth Battalion remembered that "if we had not had the rum we would have died."[84] Capt. Alexander Stewart wrote that "the finest thing that ever happened in the trenches was the rum ration."[85] Smuggled whisky also served as a strong combat motivator and to soothe the mental wounds of war. Author Robert Graves noted that some men, including pilots, drank two bottles of whisky each day to cope with the brutality and constant threat of violent death. Graves himself, an abstainer before the war, began drinking a bottle of whisky a day.[86] Hospital trains and Royal Navy ships maintained whisky and rum stocks to serve to the wounded.

The British government, in dire need of U.S. capital, continued to export Scotch whisky to the United States. However, German U-boats patrolling in the Atlantic destroyed an untold number of westbound shipments. Still, Chancellor of Exchequer David Lloyd George, founder of the "Central Control Board," publicly declared that "drink is doing more damage in the war than all the German submarines put together."[87]

Thus, a host of prominent Scotch whisky executives and distillers directed their companies to focus on the production of industrial alcohol for Lloyd George's Ministry of Munitions. Ultimately, it was the German policy of unrestricted submarine warfare and the sinking of a British ocean liner carrying 128 American passengers that gave President Woodrow Wilson no choice but to seek a congressional declaration of war against Germany in April 1916.

Following America's entry into the "war to end all wars," just five distilleries were contracted to produce industrial alcohol for the U.S. War Department: Peerless Distilling Co., Midway Distillery, George T. Stagg Distillery, James E. Pepper, and the Glenmore Distilling Company in Daviess County, Kentucky.[88] Glenmore owner James Thompson's son, Frank Barton Thompson, a new graduate of the University of Michigan's College of Engineering, quickly enlisted in the U.S. Army. Thompson, who was born on the Fourth of July in 1895, answered the call to arms by reporting to Fort Benjamin Harrison, Indiana, in the summer of 1917. After just three months of basic and officer's training, Thompson commissioned as a second lieutenant and immediately shipped to France.[89] Thompson fought in every major campaign involving the American Expeditionary Force, but there are few specific details available about his service. According to those who knew him, Frank Thompson rarely discussed his time in the French trenches. In fact, his family knew nothing of his combat experiences until his mother discovered the Croix de Guerre, awarded by the French government for gallantry, in "some Army clothing."[90]

As historian Michael Veach noted, "Prohibition became a foregone conclusion" when the United States entered the Great War.[91] When the federal government passed the Selective Service Act in May 1917, more than three million American men, including thousands of distillery workers, were mobilized and deployed to fight. Military-aged American men were, therefore, mostly absent for the final rounds of the political debate that resulted in the passage of the Eighteenth Amendment. As U.S. Army veteran and master distiller Sam K. Cecil noted in his book *Bourbon: The Evolution of Kentucky Whiskey*, World War I soldiers felt that Prohibition "was steamrolled in their absence.

Had they been at home, so the thinking went, they would not have permitted it to happen."[92]

In January 1919, the requisite number of American states ratified a new amendment to the U.S. Constitution, which completely prohibited the manufacture, sale, and transportation of beverage alcohol. In October 1919, Congress passed the National Prohibition Act to implement the amendment, formally introduced by Minnesota congressman Andrew Volstead (who never served in the military and did not drink). President Woodrow Wilson, a casual Scotch whisky drinker whose 1912 campaign featured a slogan stolen from the Baltimore based Hunter-Wilson whiskey company ("Wilson, That's All!"), vetoed the so-called Volstead Act, but Congress quickly overrode it.[93]

The federal government immediately halted grain and sugar shipments to breweries and distilleries. In Newport, Kentucky, Col. Henry Denhardt's Thirty-Eighth Tank Company captured and destroyed "moonshine" stills.[94] Tens of thousands of men lost their jobs. Small-scale distillers fled Kentucky for places like Mexico and Montana, where an obscure local law permitted limited whiskey distilling. Joseph "Elmo" Beam, who served as a combat engineer during World War I, spent Prohibition making liquor in the mining town of Butte, Montana.[95] Only six whiskey distilleries were granted licenses to continue operating for medicinal purposes: Schenley Distillers Corporation, the American Medicinal Distillers Spirits Company, the Brown-Forman Distillery Company, Frankfort Distilleries Inc., the A. Ph. Stitzel Distillery, and Glenmore.[96]

After the brutal war's end in November 1918, Frank Barton Thompson quietly returned to civilian life in Kentucky, where his father had secured one of the coveted medicinal whiskey licenses. When their father passed away, Frank and his brother James T. Thompson assumed responsibility for operating the distillery during Prohibition. The Thompson brothers rapidly transformed Glenmore into a multimillion-dollar enterprise by serving as a medicinal whiskey production and distribution center. In 1923, Frank Thompson facilitated an armed guard's movement of six thousand mature barrels of Henry Kraver's Peerless whiskey in Henderson, Kentucky, to the Glenmore warehouse in Owensboro.[97] Glenmore later received permits to produce sixty-five hundred more barrels to replace a depleted medicinal whiskey stock.[98] While serving as the president of Glenmore in the 1930s, Frank Thompson also continued to serve in the Kentucky National Guard. Despite his financial success, associates recalled that it took "some rather urgent persuasion by his wife" to get the distillery president to abandon his army-type shoes for formal occasions.[99]

Once all of America's World War I veterans returned from European battlefields, many of them mobilized to fight for repeal. Nearly 90 percent of World War I's four million veterans strongly opposed Prohibition.[100] The American Legion and the Veterans of Foreign Wars were two of the most vocal organizations of the repeal movement.[101] One 1919 California newspaper reflects the VFW's strong opposition to Prohibition: "It would throw one million people out of employment, confiscate property and condemn as illegal a business in which our Government has been a partner and from which it has received millions of dollars in revenue. That if prohibition is right, our Government has been a partner in crime and is in duty bound to return every dollar accepted in revenue from the manufacture, sale and use of alcoholic drinks. If a crime now, it has been a crime since 1776."[102]

The American Legion, formed just two months after the passage of the Eighteenth Amendment, remained an aggressive repeal advocacy group throughout the 1920s by sponsoring repeal rallies and demanding national referendums on the alcohol ban. In October 1933, the American Legion invited presidential candidate Franklin Delano Roosevelt, assistant secretary of the navy during World War I, to give the keynote address at its annual National Convention in Chicago after he wrote to Congress and urged repeal of the Eighteenth Amendment.[103]

One of the more prominent repeal advocates was Col. Ira Louis Reeves, a daring war veteran and teetotaler. Reeves first served in the U.S. Army from 1893 to 1902 but was wounded during the Philippine-American War and retired. He was later selected to lead Norwich University, the military college of Vermont, but resigned from Norwich in August 1917 to serve again during World War I. On November 11, 1918, Armistice Day, Reeves was wounded in action for a second time.

He remained in France and commanded the American Expeditionary Forces University in Beaune until 1919.

After the war, Reeves moved to Newark and became a prominent businessman. In the fall of 1926, he was appointed to enforce Prohibition in New Jersey, one of the three states that did not ratify the Eighteenth Amendment, where cases of whiskey were being sold in open-air markets at pre-Prohibition prices. In his eight months as the deputy Prohibition administrator for the Fourth Enforcement District (New Jersey), Reeves directed or personally led over four hundred raids on stills, speakeasies, and safe houses. However, he quickly became disillusioned and concluded that all he had done was "raise the price and lower the quality of alcohol in the state."[104] After resigning his post, Reeves became a vocal advocate for repeal, joining the leadership of the Crusaders, an anti-Prohibition organization based in Chicago. In 1931, he even published a book, *Ol' Rum River*, about his futile experience, arguing that Prohibition was "out of harmony with the American ideals of liberty as fought for by our forefathers."[105]

When the Twenty-First Amendment was ratified in December of 1933 and Prohibition ended, the alcohol industry rehired Veterans of Foreign Wars, Legionnaires, and an untold number of others.[106] Whiskey production immediately went into overdrive. Elmo Beam, whose estranged wife turned him in to Montana authorities for illegal "moonshining," returned to Kentucky and became the first master distiller at Star Hill, known today as Maker's Mark.[107] Over the next ten years, American distilleries produced tens of millions of gallons of bourbon alone.

World War I veterans overindulged to a dangerous degree despite Roosevelt's charge for men to resist the "curse of excessive use of intoxicating liquors, to the detriment of health, morals and social integrity."[108] As a result, government regulation and temperance lingered throughout the 1930s. The ban of alcohol sales on military posts remained, and in early 1934, the whiskey industry agreed to refrain from using "pictures of men in the uniform of our armed services or to illustrate military or naval equipment" in liquor advertisements.[109] The temperance narrative was proven to be erroneous, however, as Prohibition caused more drunkenness in America, not less. Public intoxication, drunk driving, and alcohol-related deaths all increased during Prohibition. One positive development came in 1935 when U.S. Army veteran William Griffith Wilson, who took his first drink while encamped as a second lieutenant in the Sixty-Sixth Coastal Artillery Battalion, founded Alcoholics Anonymous after struggling with alcoholism for years.[110]

WORLD WAR II

Only nine years after the repeal of Prohibition, America was attacked at Pearl Harbor in December 1941. President Roosevelt, the notorious martini man who repealed Prohibition in the first week of his presidency, immediately vowed to strike back. Within one year, several million men and women flocked to join the service or were conscripted. The government again ceased production of beverage whiskey, diverting industry resources for military purposes. As it had been during the Great War, the whiskey industry was called upon to support the armed forces in a variety of ways.

Men like Schenley Distillers sales associate Curtis G. Culin III enlisted to fight Nazis. "Bud" Culin left his job creating promotional items for Schenley's home office to join the New Jersey National Guard's Essex Troop, 102nd Cavalry Reconnaissance Squadron. Culin, an enlisted engineer, earned his first Purple Heart on June 6, 1944, when his unit stormed the beaches of Normandy, but he fought on with his tank crew. As the American tankers cleared Normandy, thick bushes and trees rendered tanks immobile. While in the vicinity of St. Lo, France, Sergeant Culin quickly invented a tusk-like, hedgerow-breaching device from recovered German steel, which he welded onto the front of his crew's tank.[111] Gen. Omar Bradley was notified and watched in awe as other tanks outfitted with Culin's invention tore through Norman hedgerows. Bradley ordered "Culin Cutters" to be mounted on the front of as many tanks as possible and later awarded the twenty-nine-year-old distillery sales associate the Legion of Merit.[112]

Several months later, Culin stepped on a land mine in the Hurtgen Forest and was thrust into a second explosive. He completely lost his left foot from the first blast and a portion of his right leg to the second, but he was evacuated to Belgium and then to England, where he recovered. Once back in New Jersey, Culin's fame persisted, as he was recognized to be a "very American kind of national hero."[113] While back at work for Schenley, General Bradley praised Culin in his autobiography, and Dwight Eisenhower recognized "the little sergeant's" ingenuity in one of his final addresses as president.[114] In 1989, the U.S. Army renamed its Fort Knox Armor School maintenance facility for Culin, who died in his hometown of Cranford, New Jersey, in 1963.[115]

Harvey L. Treace, an employee at the James E. Pepper Distillery in Lexington, Kentucky, enlisted as a B-24 gunner in the Ninety-Eighth Bombardment Group. Treace and his crew flew dozens of bombing missions from their temporary bases in North Africa and Italy. Twice he had to make parachute landings because his B-24 was hit by anti-aircraft fire. Once he landed in the Mediterranean near the Isle of Malta and swam to shore. Nine enemy planes and a German submarine "bit the dust due to Treace's Kentucky marksmanship." During a secret raid on German-controlled oil fields in Romania, enemy fighter planes engaged Treace's crew in the air. His gun jammed, but he pulled a can of oil from his pocket to lubricate and keep it firing. Treace was decorated with the Distinguished Flying Cross, Silver Star Medal, and an incredible fifteen Air Medals during the war.[116]

While blue-collar distillery workers like Bud Culin and Harvey Treace joined the fight, well-known whiskey company executives fought right alongside them. Bourbon enthusiasts may be familiar with the story of how Austin Nichols executive Thomas McCarthy coined the name Wild Turkey for the bourbon made at the Ripy Brothers Distillery in Anderson County, Kentucky. In 1940, while on a turkey hunting trip in South Carolina, McCarthy pulled out a bottle of undiluted bourbon to share with the hunting party. McCarthy's buddies enjoyed it, and when they insisted he bring "that wild turkey bourbon" to the next year's hunt, the name stuck.[117] What does not appear in Wild Turkey promotional material is the fact that Thomas McCarthy left his position at Austin Nichols the next year to join the U.S. Marine Corps. In 1942, McCarthy fought on the island of Guadalcanal in the U.S. military's first major offensive in the Pacific Theatre, Operation Watchtower.[118]

During the offensive, Admiral Chester Nimitz, the commander of U.S. Pacific Fleet, sent cases of Old Crow bourbon whiskey to marines to boost their morale.[119] The Allied victory on the island was the first in a long string of battles that led to the eventual Japanese surrender. McCarthy later fought during the invasion of Iwo Jima and during the U.S. occupation of Japan. When he rejoined Austin Nichols after the war, he purchased the Ripy Brothers Distillery and proudly renamed it Wild Turkey in 1971.[120]

Ernest W. Ripy Jr., the distiller of "that wild turkey bourbon," left his position at the Ripy Brothers Distillery to take a commission as a second lieutenant in the Forty-Fifth Field Artillery Battalion.[121] Ripy and his soldiers trained in arduous conditions at Fort Sill, Oklahoma, Fort Leonard Wood, Missouri, and Yuma, Arizona, before boarding the SS *Shawnee* for a trip to Northern Ireland in late 1943. Ripy quickly rose through the ranks to become a major during training exercises in the cold, dark, wet Irish winter and peat bogs. In July 1944, Major Ripy led his artillerymen across the English Channel to Utah Beach in Normandy, France, to fight a series of intense engagements with well-trained German artillery units. After breaking through enemy lines in Normandy, Ripy traversed northern France in support of the Twenty-Eighth Infantry Division's efforts. His battery fired hundreds of thousands of artillery rounds at Brest, Crozon, and Bastogne, and in the Hurtgen Forest, suffering a number of casualties along the way.

In February 1945, when the commanding officer of the Forty-Fifth Artillery was medically evacuated, Major Ripy assumed command in the field. He led the battalion across all of Germany, leapfrogging with other artillery battalions in a drive toward the town of Schwerin. On April 9, 1945, Major Ripy and his reconnaissance party were caught in an incoming enemy artillery barrage, and a round landed within five yards of his position, killing four men. Ripy remained calm and led the men out of the kill zone and completed the reconnaissance mission. For his bravery under fire, Major Ripy was awarded the Silver Star Medal.[122] After the war, he returned to the distillery and trained a young man named Jimmy Russell how to make Wild Turkey bourbon. Over sixty years later, Russell is still making whiskey in Anderson County.

Ripy retired from Austin Nichols as a vice president and from the army reserve as a full colonel in 1973.[123]

At the Glenmore Distillery in Owensboro, Kentucky, World War I veteran Frank Barton Thompson was again mobilized and offered a desk job in Washington. The forty-five-year-old lieutenant colonel was much more interested in leading men in the field, however, and volunteered for service with Kentucky's historic 149th Infantry Regiment. "I know Army life and Army discipline, and I like it," he declared.[124] During the war, Colonel Thompson led the regiment's Third Battalion in campaigns against the Japanese in New Guinea, the Bismarck Archipelago, and the Philippines. His unit reconnoitered beach landing sites in preparation for larger amphibious assault forces like the one Capt. Julian Van Winkle Jr. led on the Filipino island of Leyte.[125] Van Winkle had left his job as the treasurer of the Stitzel-Weller Distillery to command a company of men from the Forty-Fourth Tank Battalion in combat and was wounded during the invasion. For his bravery and dedication to the mission, Van Winkle was awarded the Silver Star Medal, the nation's third-highest decoration for valor.

Richard B. Wathen, a descendant of one of Kentucky's original distillers and the son of a principal at National Distillers Products Corporation, graduated from Princeton University two years after Julian Van Winkle Jr. did and joined the navy. He commissioned as an ensign in 1942 and served aboard the aircraft carrier *Guadalcanal* (CVE-60). On June 4, 1944, Wathen was part of a navy "hunter-killer" task force that attacked, boarded, and captured the German submarine *U-505* off the coast of French West Africa. Wathen and the other sailors involved in the operation were awarded a Presidential Unit Citation for heroism.

The Second World War exacted a heavy price from the Willett Distilling Company in Bardstown, Kentucky, as all four of founder Thompson Willett's brothers joined the service. Paul A. Willett and Joseph W. Willett served overseas as army air corps pilots before they came home to help manage distillery and testing lab operations.[126] Robert E. Willett was a P-51 Mustang fighter pilot in the army air corps before returning home to practice law in Washington DC. He eventually left the beltway for Bardstown and became the president of the family's distillery in the 1970s.[127] Charles D. Willett was a student in the navy's V-12 College Training Program. He served as naval officer before returning to Bardstown to work as a distributor of Willett whiskey products.[128]

Louis Forman, the creator of Michter's Original Sour Mash Whiskey, also left his distillery to serve in World War II. Forman entered the whiskey business as a small-scale liquor broker in Philadelphia after the repeal of Prohibition and, in 1937, Forman purchased the small but historic Bomberger's Distillery in nearby Schaefferstown, Pennsylvania.[129] Named for Abraham Bomberger, a Mennonite farmer whose family owned the distillery from the Civil War until Prohibition, the site had been in use since 1753. It is believed that the original owner, John Shenk, provided his whiskey to George Washington and his troops encamped at Valley Forge in 1777. On July 17, 1941, Lou Forman incorporated the Philadelphia Brokerage Company and purchased Bomberger's as quickly as he could gather the funds.

In August 1942, Forman was drafted into the U.S. Army and, uncertain whether he would survive World War II, sold the distillery to the Logansport Distilling Company, which in turn became a subsidiary of the Schenley Distillers Corporation. During the war, Schenley modified and directed Bomberger's to make industrial alcohol for the War Department. After the war, Forman was discharged from the army and regained control of the old Bomberger's Distillery from Schenley. He appointed master distiller Charles Everett Beam to cultivate a premium niche market by making old-fashioned pot-still mash whiskey, which he called "Michter's" in honor of his sons, Michael and Peter. Though Forman's Michter's went out of business in 1990, his brand was revived several years later by Chatham Imports and combat-wounded Korean War veteran Richard Newman. Today, Michter's produces several of the most sought-after whiskeys on the market.

As whiskey men like McCarthy, Ripy, Thompson, Van Winkle, Wathen, the Willetts, and Forman left to fight overseas, their distilleries were retrofitted to make 190 proof industrial alcohol for antifreeze, insecticide, torpedo fuel, smokeless gunpowder, synthetic rubber, rayon for parachutes, and penicillin. The U.S. War Production Board oversaw the production of industrial alcohol for the war effort and coordinated the movement of massive grain shipments to distilleries all over the country.

Between 1941 and 1945, distilleries produced 1.7 billion gallons of alcohol to support military operations. The beverage alcohol industry produced nearly half of the 1.2 billion gallons used to produce synthetic rubber, 200 million gallons for ammunition, 126 million gallons for antifreeze, 66 million gallons for tetraethyl lead, 75 million gallons for plastics in the aviation industry, 115 million gallons for the production of lacquer and insecticide, and 30 million gallons for medical supplies.[130] One gallon of alcohol could be used to produce sixty-four hand grenades or two 155mm Howitzer shells.[131]

Stills ran twenty-four hours a day, seven days a week. Employees at Vendome Copper & Brass Works in Louisville were exempt from conscription to make more stills. Cooperages, like the one owned by Brown-Forman, built airplane wings for the Allies.[132] Across the Atlantic, Scotch distilleries also served as war materiel production sites, sources of fighting men, and even ammunition hubs. Laphroaig Distillery manager "Bessie" Williamson became an important "war operative" by subtly facilitating soldiers and huge amounts of Allied ordnance through the Sound of Islay to the battlefield. Had Hitler known that the pastoral island distillery was shipping small arms rounds, high explosive shells, and bomb carrier cases to his enemies, it would have not survived the war.[133] Indeed, in 1941 alone, Nazi bombers destroyed the Auchentoshan distillery near Glasgow, the Banff distillery in Inverboyndie, and the Bushmills distillery's office in Dublin.

Thanks to steady government demand, companies like Schenley fared well financially, but they produced very little alcohol for consumption. Wartime rationing essentially eliminated available stocks of quality whiskey for the drinking public and servicemen in the field. Sailors operating submarines in the Pacific were left with no choice but to drink Schenley's Black Velvet Blended Canadian whisky, which they held in very low regard and called "Schenley's Black Death."[134] Marines improvised by filtering hair tonic through bread and mixing it with grape juice, a concoction they called "jungle juice."[135]

Other units incorporated whiskey into their official planning efforts.

Just days before his infantrymen steamed across the Atlantic, Col. Robert Sink, commander of the 506th Parachute Infantry Regiment, ordered Lt. Richard "Dick" Winters on a mission from Fort Bragg, North Carolina, to his home state of Pennsylvania to stock up on bourbon whiskey. Lieutenant Winters was later directed by the regimental executive officer to personally meet with a Schenley distributor in New York City and secure whiskey for his paratroopers. Despite the fact that he was a lifelong teetotaler, Winters noted that "right then and there, that man did his part in helping to win World War II."[136]

As author Steven Ambrose wrote in *Band of Brothers*, Winters's Easy Company carried whiskey throughout their epic deployment, from the initial D-Day airborne operation to its many firefights in France, the Netherlands, Belgium, and Germany. Winters's best friend, Lewis Nixon, an alcoholic, considered his stock of Vat 69 Scotch blended whisky to be essential gear. When Easy Company cleared Hitler's Eagle's Nest in the Bavarian mountain town of Berchtesgaden in May 1945, the men captured a vaulted cellar holding ten thousand bottles of Nazi liquor, wine, and champagne. Capt. Lewis Nixon spent V-E Day drinking the best of Hitler's private stock.[137]

As Easy Company celebrated with good European whiskey, army interrogators at Camp Pine Grove in Pennsylvania discovered that German prisoners of war enjoyed good American whiskey. One German naval officer "dug in his heels," so the Americans left two bottles of Jack Daniel's in his cell. The Tennessee whiskey loosened his tongue, and the ceiling Dictaphone recorded everything he and his cellmate discussed. Several days later, the Americans bombed a Nazi submarine pen, once a closely held Third Reich secret.[138]

While the demands of war brought production of beverage alcohol to a halt, Americans at home continued to consume whiskey at a steady pace. The enormous stock of bourbon produced between the repeal of the Eighteenth Amendment and the beginning of World War II was almost eliminated. As a result, American distilleries resorted to blending straight whiskey with grain neutral spirits or water to stretch supplies. American importers turned to European spirits like Scottish single-malt whisky, which narrowly survived a wartime prohibition of its own. Recognizing its importance as an export, Winston Churchill demanded that "on no account reduce the barley for whisky. [Whisky] takes years to mature, and is an invaluable export and dollar producer."[139] Unfortunately, for American consumers and British merchant marines, history repeated itself as dozens of cross-Atlantic shipments of Scotch whisky were sunk by German U-boat attacks.

The Axis's alcohol industries faced a supply crisis as well. Hitler's *weinführers* used force to seize spirits and wine for the Wehrmacht and for sale to fund Nazi activities. At the same time, Hitler severely punished Nazi soldiers who "allowed themselves to be tempted to engage in criminal acts as a result of alcohol abuse."[140] In Italy, severe grain shortages eliminated amaro production, and most of the Luxardo family (famous for its Maraschino cherry liqueur) was killed. In Japan, the massive rice shortage that led to widespread starvation also eliminated sake production. Dozens of breweries, vineyards, distilleries, and the people who worked there were damaged or destroyed by Allied ordnance, particularly late in the war.[141]

On April 12, 1945, with the end of the war in sight, President Roosevelt suffered a cerebral hemorrhage at his "Little White House" in Warm Springs, Georgia. When word of his death was passed to Washington, the bourbon-drinking veteran Harry S. Truman was immediately sworn in to the office of the presidency. Both sides of Harry Truman's family were from Kentucky, and he was very fond of Kentucky whiskey, especially Old Grand-Dad. In 1946, the *New York Times* ran a story by Luther Huston called "Bourbon on the Potomac." Huston wrote, "President Truman does not settle momentous controversies on the basis of teetotaler vs. tippler, but anyone who knows him is aware that there is quite likely to be a stronger bond between him and a Southern gentleman who likes a hooker of red likker than between him and an arid Iowan."[142] Shortly after Truman was sworn in as America's thirty-third president, the German High Command surrendered to General Eisenhower at Reims in northwestern France.

Truman immediately turned his attention to the Pacific, where 5.5 million men were still fighting for the Japanese Imperial Army. After briefly considering an invasion of mainland Japan, Truman instead ordered a firebombing campaign to destroy Japanese industrial centers. B-29 crews like Lt. Elmer Tandy Lee's directed ordnance onto Japanese targets from their bases in Guam and Tinian.

On July 26, 1945, while visiting occupied Germany, Truman signed the Potsdam Declaration, in which he threatened "prompt and utter destruction" unless the Japanese surrendered on Allied terms.[143] Before returning to the United States, the president scheduled a meeting with King George VI on the British ship *Renown* to discuss the atomic bomb. After their lunch of soup, fish, and lamb chops, Truman invited the king to tour the USS *Augusta*, the ship that carried Gen. Omar Bradley and his staff on D-Day, anchored in Plymouth. While aboard the cruiser, the British king happily inspected the American sailors and took "a snort of Haig & Haig" whisky,[144] prompting Truman to note that the king was a "good man."[145]

Two weeks later, after the Japanese ignored his demand for surrender, Truman dispatched B-29 pilot Col. Paul Tibbetts from the 509th Composite Group in the Mariana Islands and waited for the news that "Little Boy" had detonated in Hiroshima. Sixty-six thousand were killed and another 69,000 were injured to varying degrees. One surviving Japanese doctor recalled that all of his medical supplies were burned. He used whiskey to help revive the unconscious in his neighborhood.[146] Three days later, a second bomb was dropped in Nagasaki. Over 250,000 people were killed in the devastating attacks and their aftermath.[147] The Second World War formally ended for the United States on September 2, 1945, when Japan's foreign affairs minister, Mamoru Shigemitsu, signed an instrument of surrender on board the USS *Missouri*. Shigemitsu returned to devastated Tokyo and drank Suntory Whisky with his aides in defeat.[148]

Following "V-J Day," millions of veterans flocked home and exchanged green suits for blue or white collars. For the first time in generations, distilleries enjoyed sustained, unrestricted whiskey production. A strong economy put disposable income in veterans' pockets and bourbon whiskey made its way into decanters in every home, bar, and workplace. Bourbon whiskey sales skyrocketed in postwar America, and production boomed throughout the Korean War and early Cold War to keep up with unprecedented demand. The whiskey industry maintained its bullish production schedule as the United States expended new resources to counter the spread of communism. By 1967, there were 8 million barrels (approximately 424 million gallons) resting in Kentucky warehouses.[149] Sales figures rose each year in the 1960s, but changing social norms would soon degrade bourbon's place as America's leading spirit as hundreds of thousands of men and women were sent to fight in the jungles of Southeast Asia.

VIETNAM

The nation's mood changed dramatically during the Vietnam War. A generation of young drinkers rejected everything their parents stood for, to include their alcoholic beverage of choice. Young people turned to clear, exotic spirits like vodka, gin, and tequila. Bourbon nearly disappeared from the American drinking scene, forcing large distilleries to dramatically cut production. However, overseas sales helped keep bourbon afloat, thanks in particular to sales on military bases. The dispersion of American soldiers around the world during the Cold War sparked an extraordinary international interest in American whiskey that continues today.

As Michael Veach noted in his book *Kentucky Bourbon Whiskey,* "just as Scotch whisky went global by following the armed forces of Britain to every corner of its empire, so too bourbon whiskey followed the U.S. military to its bases in South Korea, Japan, Germany, and Italy. Initially available only through base exchanges, bourbon whiskey was soon among the standard offerings at local bars catering to servicemen, giving the locals a chance to develop a taste for it as well. American distilleries began marketing their products internationally." [150] Veach also pointed out that "Jim Beam . . . is the singular success story when it comes to international marketing. It had an initial advantage in that Jim Beam was one of the whiskeys made available by the U.S. Army in its base exchanges, and American soldiers became its unpaid salesmen."[151] In the 1960s, Jim Beam even opened bottling plants in Germany to better supply American soldiers and fulfill growing demand abroad.[152]

Just as Revolutionary War minutemen relied on their daily gill and

Civil War soldiers on medicinal whiskey they culled from generous medics, veterans of jungle warfare in Vietnam relied on whiskey to cope with fear, loss, and boredom. Timothy Dunn, who served with Second Platoon, H Company, Second Battalion, First Marines remembered how his platoon commander, Lt. Brian O'Connor, passed around a bottle of Jim Beam on Christmas Eve 1966: "He had an aggressive fighting spirit and at the same time a deep concern for his men. Christmas Eve of 1966 was rainy, cold, and generally miserable. Our platoon stood perimeter watch (three men to a fighting hole) with no other comfort than a shared blanket. At midnight, Lt. O'Connor visited each fighting hole with a bottle of Jim Beam to let each one of us have a taste. No other officer did the same that night and it left a lasting impression on all of us."[153]

Four weeks later, on January 29, 1967, 2nd Lt. Brian Richard O'Connor was killed in action during an intense ambush. O'Connor exposed himself to withering fire in order to maneuver and communicate with his men, allowing several marines to locate and destroy an enemy bunker. According to his posthumous Silver Star citation, O'Connor's actions permitted other men to withdraw from the field of fire and "undoubtedly saved the lives of many of the Marines in the other platoon."[154] According to Timothy Dunn, "his loss was particularly hard to take because he disregarded his wounds to insure the care for other wounded and lapsed into unconsciousness attempting to get off the medical evacuation helicopter to be with his men. It was an honor to serve with him."[155]

Army veteran Ed St. Clair "found out that war is hell, big time" and described an encounter with one of those colonels with Jim Beam on his desk:

> The light colonel asked me why I was looking for Bill, and I told him. . . . Bill and I had been Platoon Leaders in B Co, 317th Engineer Battalion in Frankfurt Hochest in 1959. Bill later became our company commander. Under his command, with four first lieutenants, some damn good NCOs and troops, we became the best company in the battalion. The colonel invited me to sit down, and he closed

the door. He pulled a bottle of Jim Beam out of his desk, poured drinks, and told me, 'Bill was killed a month ago.' I guess I must have stared at him, with tears in my eyes, choking on the booze. I felt as bad as the day JFK was shot, only this was more personal. Of all the soldiers I knew, Bill was the one who was supposed to come through Vietnam without a scratch.[156]

Reporter Joe Galloway, coauthor of *We Were Soldiers Once . . . And Young* and the only civilian ever awarded the Bronze Star Medal for Valor in Vietnam, recalled being on Plei Me Special Forces Camp in October 1965. It was under siege by North Vietnamese regulars, and he was attempting to go there and take photographs. After "stomping up and down the flight line" he found Ray Burns, who agreed to give him a ride in his Huey helicopter.

Galloway said, "I still have a picture I shot out the open door of Ray's Huey. We are doing a kind of corkscrew descent and the triangular berms and wire of the camp below fill that doorway . . . along with the puffs of smoke from the impacting mortar rounds inside the camp. Hell . . . I can scare myself bad, just looking at that photo." When the Huey landed, a sergeant major ran up to Galloway along with an angry field grade officer. He continued, "The dialogue goes something like this: Who the hell are you? A reporter. Son, I need everything in the goddamn world from food and ammo to water . . . to medevac . . . to reinforcements . . . and I wouldn't mind a bottle of Jim Beam. But what I do not need is a goddamn reporter!"[157]

Veteran Austin Wilcox recalled serving in a logistics cell just northwest of Tam Ky "on some hill." After a harrowing encounter with incoming fire one evening, the men built a table out of ammunition crates, covered it with a white cloth taken from the medics, and "had a Jim Beam party right there in the open" to calm their nerves.[158] Veteran John O'Meara, who served just outside of Saigon, "knew an alcoholic sergeant who worked in shipping and receiving. When there was an opportunity for a case of steaks or chicken, we would get out our ration cards and someone would be chosen to go to the army liquor store and buy two bottles of Jim Beam. The downside was that when we got one of these cases, that was all we ate for two weeks because the freezer section of our refrigerator could only hold so much."[159] Richard Boyd, a marine serving on Da Nang Airbase, liked to trade unarmed airmen "grenades, AK's, NVA flags and clothing, even M-16's and .45's, etc., for bottles of Jim Beam."[160] Army veteran James Mulvaney, who served in a United Nations operation in the Chorwon Valley, remembered trading a Thai army officer a bottle of Jim Beam for a bottle of Thai whiskey: "He conned me into trading my Jim Beam for Thai whiskey and the Thai whiskey is like Log Cabin Syrup. What a mistake."[161]

Despite bourbon's steady popularity with fighting men in Vietnam and foreign drinkers, bourbon sales hit an all-time low in the United States during the 1970s. In 1969, bourbon whiskey was holding on as America's best-selling spirit. In 1970, the Bourbon Institute reported that a remarkable 84.2 million gallons of bourbon were sold in the United States and abroad.[162] Bourbon was exported to 102 countries that year, with the most being sold in West Germany where the U.S. Army's First, Third, Eighth, and Twenty-Fourth Infantry Divisions and First, Third, and Fourth Armored Divisions maintained their head-quarters. In Australia, bourbon sales rose 54 percent between 1969 and 1970, as hundreds of thousands of American service members on twelve-month tours in Vietnam traveled there for rest and recuperation leave.[163] However, 1970 was the last year that bourbon sales increased in the United States. Domestic bourbon sales decreased every year from 1970 to 1985, when World War II veteran Elmer T. Lee's single-barrel bourbon sparked renewed interest in the distinctly American whiskey.[164]

The lack of interest in America's native spirit forced a number of mergers and the closure of historic operations like Kentucky's Stitzel-Weller, Pennsylvania's Michter's, and Maryland's Majestic and Pikesville distilleries. As the industry stumbled into the 1980s, executives at the George T. Stagg Distillery in Frankfort, Kentucky, pinned their hopes on Elmer T. Lee to develop something new. Lee's beloved Stagg Distillery, like many other historic Kentucky operations, was in dire financial straits. While it employed 250 people in 1949, only 50 worked there in the mid-1980s.[165] Lee was in the final year of his career when distillery executives Ferdie Falk and Bob Baranaskas, an army veteran, came to him and anxiously requested that he develop a special brand for the relatively stable Japanese whiskey market. What followed was the tipping point that brought bourbon from near demise to the golden era of today.

Lee considered his options and chose to fill bottles with bourbon dumped from the highest-quality single barrels in Warehouse H. Col. Albert Blanton built the metal warehouse after Prohibition in order to age whiskey faster, as it gets warmer during the summer days than traditional wooden warehouses, and it is steam-heated during the winter. Blanton relied on Warehouse H to throw infamous parties and pull samples for special guests to the Stagg Distillery.

As Lee and his army buddy warehouse manager Jimmy Johnson sampled barrels from Warehouse H, they developed a plan to refrain from blending the barrels from Warehouse H, and to offer a "single-barrel" product, the first bourbon of its kind on the market. They bottled their highest-quality whiskey straight from the barrels in unique, barrel-shaped bottles featuring horse-and-jockey stoppers. Lee's decision not to blend barrels piqued interest, particularly among drinkers of single-malt Scotch whisky and in Japan, where bourbon interest was high. Thus, the single-barrel genre was born, giving rise to other single-barrel, super-premium, and limited-edition bourbons.[166]

Initially, the American market failed to take notice of Elmer Lee's single-barrel bourbon. But Blanton's was so uncommonly good for its time and unique from barrel to barrel. Intrigue became fascination, which translated into high demand. It sold for up to one hundred dollars overseas, compared with an average price of ten to fifteen dollars for most other bourbons. Lee's brand slowly built a devoted customer base. "We had to have cases and cases of it every Friday, or else," said Eric Gregory, who as a University of Kentucky student worked part-time in a liquor store in the mid-1980s and is now president of the Kentucky Distillers' Association. Mr. Gregory credited the premium market that Mr. Lee pioneered as a major factor in the bourbon industry's turn-around in the last decade: "Elmer T. Lee was first. He transformed our industry."[167]

When Blanton's was released in 1984, it would have been difficult to convince Elmer T. Lee that his beloved bourbon whiskey would become as popular as it has today. According to the Kentucky Distill-ers' Association, annual production of the spirit has increased nearly 300 percent, from under 500,000 barrels in 1999 to over 1.8 million barrels in 2016. It is nearly impossible to find a bottle of Blanton's on a shelf today, let alone a bottle of Elmer T. Lee Single-Barrel Bourbon, a Buffalo Trace Distillery product since 1990. For an industry on the brink of demise thirty years ago, it is miraculous that bourbon sales now generate $3 billion a year.

Seventeen thousand, five hundred Kentuckians are paid over $800 million each year to produce the beverage. Kentucky Bourbon and Tennessee whiskey account for $1 billion worth of exports. The tax appraisal on aging Kentucky bourbon whiskey is nearly $2 billion, nearly double the value assessed ten years ago. Each year, bourbon sales pump hundreds of millions of dollars in tax revenue back into Kentucky infrastructure, schools, and roads.[168] As Buffalo Trace tour guide Freddie Johnson likes to tell visitors, there are two million more barrels of bourbon aging in Kentucky (6.6 million) than there are people living in the commonwealth (4.4 million). Between now and 2021, the industry will spend more than $1.3 billion on new projects, including new distilleries, warehouses, bottling facilities, and tourism centers. Bourbon is booming.

4

George Washington

The benefits arising from the moderate use of liquor have been experienced in all armies, and are not to be disputed!

> George Washington to John Hancock (president of the Continental Congress), August 16, 1777

George Washington was born in Westmoreland, Virginia, in 1732. He served as the commander of the Continental army during the American Revolutionary War and as the United States' first commander in chief. Following his retirement from American politics, Washington and his Scottish farm manager, James Anderson, became the new nation's most productive and successful whiskey-makers. Washington sold nearly eleven thousand gallons of his rye whiskey in 1799, the year of his death.

In 1755, having expertly surveyed the Shenandoah Valley, twenty-three-year-old George Washington was commissioned the "Colonel of the Virginia Regiment and Commander in Chief of all forces now raised in the defense of His Majesty's Colony."[1] The Virginia Regiment was the first full-time American military unit in the colonies and was tasked with defending the Old Dominion from French and Indian troubles.

The young colonel of the regiment spent several years leading Virginians on the rugged frontier, and he armed his men with weapons and liquor in accordance with the Virginia legislature's will to provide "a gill of spirits" for each officer and soldier in the state.[2]

On August 7, 1756, Washington issued his daily orders, promising each man a daily ration of liquor "as an encouragement to them to behave well, and to attend diligently to their Duty."[3] Among the younger officers in Washington's regiment were William Woodford, for whom Woodford County, Kentucky, is named; Evan Shelby, father of Kentucky's governor Isaac Shelby; Gen. John Neville, the tax collector whose home was attacked during the short-lived Whiskey Rebellion; and Capt. Thomas Bullitt, who later surveyed and laid the plans for what is now Louisville, Kentucky.

Unfortunately for Colonel Washington and subordinate officers like Woodford, Shelby, Neville, and Bullitt, a daily gill of liquor was not enough for the brave Virginians. Soldiers took advantage of their proximity to the many "tippling houses" in Winchester and engaged in what Washington described as "villainous Behaviour."[4] When the Virginia Regiment was accused in the papers of drunkenness, Washington declared war on the taverns. He whipped his men when they became drunk, ordered them away from the public houses, and even closed one saloon by force. In a letter to the colonial governor, Washington lamented that his men were "incessantly drunk and unfit for service."[5]

Washington had good reason to punish his men for overindulgence. For one, he knew that his regiment was directly responsible for the security of Virginia's frontier population. In ten months, they fought twenty brutal battles with hostile Indians. At the battle of Fort Necessity, one-third of Washington's men were killed or wounded. He watched in horror, in a driving rainstorm, as the survivors broke into a supply building and began drinking rum, not knowing whether French soldiers and vengeful Natives would come back and overrun them all.[6] In addition to his commitment to keeping Virginians safe, Washington sought in vain to secure political office and a commission in the British army; a drunken defeat would be catastrophic for the young colonel's career.

In the summer of 1757, Washington campaigned for the Frederick County seat in the Virginia House of Burgesses. In colonial times, it was traditional for candidates to "treat" voters with alcoholic beverages on Election Day.[7] Perhaps soured by his frontier experience in Winchester, however, Washington chose not to ply voters with any of the rum, whiskey, beer, cider, brandy, or punch that his opponents did. As a result, he garnered just 40 votes, while Thomas Swearningen and Hugh West earned 270 and 271 votes respectively.[8]

The next summer, Colonel Washington ran for office again. It was a busy year for the young commander, as he prepared for an expedition to the French-held Fort Duquesne, and he became engaged to the recently widowed Martha Dandridge Custis. Still, Washington sought a seat in the House of Burgesses that July. Throughout his campaign, Washington capitalized on the lesson he learned the previous summer. He directed his friend and campaign manager James Wood to roll out the booze—fifty gallons of rum punch, forty-six gallons of beer, thirty-four gallons of wine, twenty-eight gallons of rum, and two gallons of hard cider, nearly enough for a half-gallon per voter. Wood spent a total of thirty-eight pounds and seven shillings for the campaign, of which over thirty-four pounds was on alcohol. Washington actually feared that Wood "spent with too sparing a hand."[9] It was apparently enough, as he won the election by a comfortable margin.

Shortly after his political victory, Washington departed for Fort Duquesne, a site where the Virginia Regiment had been defeated by the French and Indians in 1754 and 1755. As the men trudged across Pennsylvania, they used liquor to entice members of the Catawba and Cherokee tribes to join their effort despite General Braddock's orders that "no officer, soldier, or others give the Indian men, women or children any rum or other liquor."[10]

The 1758 attempt to capture Fort Duquesne was a violent one from the start. Morale among the Virginians plummeted after a disastrous assault by Maj. James Grant in late September. Three hundred British soldiers were killed or wounded, including six Virginia officers. Only the heroic actions of Capt. Thomas Bullitt prevented complete disaster.[11] Washington wrote in a letter that Captain Bullitt "acquired immortal honour in this engagement by his gallant behaviour and long continuance in the field of action."[12]

On November 12, 1758, a force of 30 French-Canadians and 140 Native Americans attacked British troops guarding horses. Gen. John Forbes sent George Washington's regiment and Col. Hugh Mercer's troops toward the gunfire. Mercer's men moved in an arc behind the French positions as Washington's men advanced. The events of that night are not entirely clear, but it is likely that Mercer's scouts opened fire on Washington's men after mistaking them for the enemy. Washington realized that the colonials were firing on each other, rode his horse down the line, furiously knocking muskets into the air with his sword to stop his men from firing. The incident left 35 soldiers and 2 officers dead, but could have turned out much worse without Washington's action.[13]

While the Virginians suffered another tactical defeat at Fort Duquesne, ultimately the French burned it to the ground and abandoned the site. The battle-hardened Washington returned home desiring peace and quiet. Upon his return to Virginia, he resigned his commission in December 1758, and did not return to military life until the outbreak of the American Revolution.[14]

Back at Mount Vernon, which he referred to as "my Vine and Fig tree," Washington avoided drunkenness, although he drank in moderation frequently.[15] His preferred beverage was Madeira, a fortified wine made in Portugal, and he kept hundreds of gallons of it on hand. Washington was also quite fond of peach brandy and fermented apple cider. In 1760, as a private tobacco farmer, he wrote to the Laird family of New Jersey and requested their secret "applejack" recipe in order to produce similar cider on his Virginia estate.[16]

In 1770, Washington switched from tobacco to rye and wheat and oversaw the construction of a state-of-the-art gristmill on Mount Vernon. Washington used the mill to produce several hundred thousand pounds of high-quality wheat flour each year, which he exported to lucrative markets in the West Indies and Europe. Around the same time, Washington ordered the construction of a small copper still and began distilling rum with imported molasses, the heavily taxed British commodity. But like his fellow planters, Washington felt exploited by British merchants and hampered by British taxes and regulations. As the quarrel with his mother country grew, he voiced resistance to the duties and restrictions.

When the Second Continental Congress assembled in Philadelphia in May 1775, Washington, one of the Virginia delegates, arrived in his old regimental uniform, indicating his willingness to fight.[17] Inspiring great confidence in the other delegates, he was elected commander in chief of the Continental army. On July 3, 1775, at Cambridge, Massachusetts, he took command of his ill-trained troops and embarked upon a war that lasted six grueling years.

Despite the abuses of liquor he dealt with on the rugged Virginia frontier, Washington lobbied the Continental Congress for liquor rations, arguing that "the benefits arising from the moderate use of liquor have been experienced in all armies, and are not to be disputed!"[18] Washington recommended the establishment of public distilleries for the purposes of supplying the army with beverage alcohol. He believed it was "necessary and essential" to supply his army with a "Sufficient Quantity of Spirits" regardless of whether his soldiers were "marching in hot or Cold weather, in Camp or Wet, on fatigue or in Working Parties."[19]

Actual liquor allowances ranged from a half-gallon a week for a colonel to a pint and a half for a subaltern, or junior officer. For the ordinary soldier, the liquor issue was limited to rainy weather and "fatigue duty," and never more than a gill per man.[20] With the traditional ration of rum so difficult to acquire, soldiers starting seeing more American grain whiskey, and they certainly enjoyed it.

Whiskey undoubtedly served as a motivator and sustainer for the patriot soldiers that endured through final victory at Yorktown. During Washington's retreat across New Jersey in 1776, one Continental patrol stumbled upon a barrel of whiskey and drank it all on the spot.[21] Some undisciplined patriot soldiers traded their uniforms, which were in great demand, for whiskey. During the winter of 1777–78 Continental quartermasters struggled to provide troops with adequate amounts of food, but they did provide over five hundred thousand whiskey rations, between a gill and a half-pint of whiskey per man each day.[22] After losing the Battle of Germantown, Pennsylvania, in 1777, Washington and his men were pleasantly surprised when the Continental Congress shipped them thirty casks of whiskey as encouragement to continue the fight.[23] After the revolution, Congress made it law that "every noncommissioned officer, private, and musician shall receive the following rations of provisions, to wit: one pound of beef or three-quarters of a pound of pork, one pound of bread or flour, half a gill of rum, brandy, or whiskey."[24]

On the eve of the Battle of Monmouth, New Jersey, Washington made a point to dine with Moses Laird of the applejack family to whom he had written in 1760. After the war, Moses Laird's nephew Robert Laird, who served in Washington's army during the Revolutionary War, founded the nation's first licensed distillery. To this day, Lairds produce aged applejack by fermenting Virginia apples and blending them with grain neutral spirits in New Jersey.[25]

Washington wrote about liquor throughout the war in both public and private correspondence. In his general orders from May 16, 1782, he criticized the "vile practice of swallowing the whole ration of liquor at a single draught" and ordered "the Serjeants to see it duly distributed daily and mixed with Water at stated times; in which case . . . it will become refreshing and salutary."[26] Toward the final days of the war in 1781, Washington briefly returned home to Mount Vernon, the only time he visited home during the six-year war. During his rapid ride from New York to Virginia en route to Yorktown, he sent a set of orders to Capt. William Colfax, then commanding his personal guard, to ensure his baggage, papers, and liquor supply would be protected, writing, "Sir[,] . . . the best security for your liquors and other stores which are liable to be pilfered or otherwise wasted, will be to place them in a situation in the hold where they cannot be got at easily."[27]

From Mount Vernon, Washington joined French forces in Williamsburg, where hopes were high for a final victory against Lord Cornwallis. American and French men frequented Williamsburg's taverns, placing bets over spirituous beverages on when Cornwallis would surrender. On September 28, 1781, the joint American and French army left Williamsburg invigorated and prepared to lay siege to British forces in Yorktown.

After a series of skirmishes along the way, General Washington's main siege began on October 9 when Rochembeau asked him to do the honor of firing the first cannon. Their bombardment lasted several days and destroyed British fortifications, ships, and lives. Hundreds of cannons on both sides erupted in chaos while men engaged in hand-to-hand combat. Despite the brisk return fire of artillery shells and musket fire, General Washington exposed himself, as he often did, without revealing fear of the enemy snipers' skill. Washington rode confidently around the battlefield, giving speeches to men tasked to perform bayonet charges against British redoubts. With cannons blasting away, the foot soldiers overran British positions and made way for American and French cannons to move closer to British ships just offshore. As a result of their efforts, the Americans and French were able to array their guns in a large semicircle and commence enfilade firing, hitting British positions and ships from several angles.

When a squall prevented Cornwallis from crossing the York River and escaping the brutal artillery fire, the British realized their situation was hopeless. Their professional force was made to surrender to an army of former blacksmiths, shopkeepers, farmers, and whiskey distillers. Humiliated, Cornwallis sent word to the Americans that he was ill, and he sent Irish general Charles O'Hara to surrender to Rochambeau. The Frenchman would not talk to the Irishman, however, and he pointed across the road to where General Washington awaited. When Washington laid eyes on O'Hara, a second in command, he refused to accept his sword. He made the disgraced Irishman surrender his sword to Gen. Benjamin Lincoln.

Observers believed that British soldiers and sailors had been drinking heavily on the day of O'Hara's surrender in Yorktown. British men were angry, embarrassed, tearful, and mostly drunk, having consumed their remaining supply of rum to keep the liquor from falling into the hands of the Americans. For General Washington, a military career that began in Virginia's mountains ended on Virginia's coast, and liquor was there for better or worse.

Sixteen years later, when Washington retired from public life, he returned to his gristmill at Mount Vernon. He wondered how he would make his retirement "more tranquil and freer from cares."[28] He hired a new farm manager, James Anderson, a Scottish immigrant and whiskey distiller. Knowing that the revolution had created a deep loyalty to the spirit, Anderson viewed Mount Vernon's fields of rye with an appraising eye. Despite Washington's concern that he was "entirely unacquainted" with whiskey-making, he permitted Anderson to convert a cooper's shop into a distillery.[29] He wrote, "I consent to you commencing a distillery and approve of you purchasing the mill and I shall not object to your converting part of the coopers shop at the mill for this operation."[30]

In late 1797, workers constructed the distillery beside the workhorse gristmill. The retired general and president apparently had a difficult time not micromanaging the work, a challenging task for the closest thing America ever had to a king. In the spring of 1798, the distillery began pumping out corn- and rye-based whiskey. Anderson and six African American slaves focused their efforts on milling, mashing, and distilling "Rye . . . and Indian Corn" and selling whiskey wholesale to taverns in nearby Alexandria.[31] At the end of the year, Washington fulfilled a $332 tax obligation on 616 gallons of whiskey produced on his farm.[32]

In 1799, Washington's distillery produced 10,500 gallons of clear rye whiskey, which netted the former president $7,500 (nearly $142,000 in modern dollars), making him the new nation's most productive and successful commercial distiller. Sadly, Washington enjoyed less than three years of retirement at Mount Vernon, as he died of a throat infection December 14, 1799. For months the nation mourned their loss. In 1814, his distillery was completely destroyed by fire. It would be forgotten for a very long time.

In 1992, two young archeologists by the name of Esther White and Dennis Pogue were playing croquet on land owned by the Commonwealth of Virginia behind the sprawling Fort Belvoir Army installation. White and Pogue, newly hired employees at George Washington's Mount Vernon estate, gazed up at the founding father's historic but abandoned gristmill and discussed their desire to explore what lay beneath it. They would soon get their chance.[33]

By that time, over a million visitors flocked each year to admire Washington's meticulously preserved mansion, gardens, and gravesite.

However, fewer than three thousand people ventured down the road to explore Washington's gristmill, the site of his forgotten whiskey-distilling operation. Commonwealth officials had offered the small parcel of land many times to Mount Vernon's board of trustees, but preservation of Washington's reputation was tantamount. Prohibition had been repealed just two years before the first offer in 1935, and the board couldn't see the value in reconstructing a long-abandoned whiskey distillery. Preserving Washington's image was much more important than rebuilding five copper pot stills, so the board politely declined. Years passed. Vegetation grew around the stone mill. A road was constructed near the small creek that fed Washington and Anderson's mill and mash tanks.

A break came in 1995 when the Mount Vernon Ladies Association developed a new educational program known as "George Washington: Pioneer Farmer." The program was intended to spark interest in the lesser-known aspects of Washington's career, particularly his farming accomplishments in the 1760s, 1770s, and 1780s. The ladies had come to regard the forgotten gristmill as a natural complement to the Pioneer Farmer exhibit and as a means to expand the public's interpretation of George Washington's agricultural enterprises. When the commonwealth made another offer to Mount Vernon in 1997, it was promptly accepted and the land was deeded to Mount Vernon. Within a year, excavation work began and Dennis Pogue took on a project to fully restore the gristmill.

The Distilled Spirits Council of the United States, a descendant of Lewis Rosenstiel's Bourbon Institute, paid for the project, which reflects a historically faithful reconstruction of the original buildings and equipment. Everything from the grain hopper, to the copper pot stills, to the water wheel is just as it was in 1797. In 2007, after a nearly two-hundred-year hiatus, the George Washington Distillery & Gristmill reopened and began producing the same rye whiskey, with some modern twists, like filtration, that George Washington preferred (65 percent rye, 30 percent corn, 5 percent malted barley). Mount Vernon hired West Point graduate and decorated cavalry officer David Pickerell, the former Maker's Mark master distiller, to oversee production.

5

Evan and Isaac Shelby

When we encounter the enemy, don't wait for a word of command. Let each of you be your own officer, and do the best you can.

Col. Isaac Shelby before the Battle of King's Mountain, North Carolina, October 1780

Evan Shelby was born in England around 1720 and sailed to the New World in 1735, eventually settling with his parents, Evan and Catherine, in the colony of Maryland. In 1750, he and his first wife, Letitia Cox Shelby, had a son named Isaac, born near present-day Hagerstown, Maryland. Evan Shelby served on several British expeditions against the French and their Native American allies. He was also an early distiller of rum and rye whiskey. During the Revolutionary War, Evan and Isaac Shelby fought alongside one another as officers in the Virginia militia. Later, both men engaged Native Americans on the frontier and produced whiskey for other settlers in present-day East Tennessee. In the 1780s, Isaac Shelby moved to Kentucky and established one of the territory's earliest and more prolific whiskey distilleries. He was later elected the first governor of Kentucky and commanded the Kentucky Militia in the War of 1812.

Western Maryland was a dangerous patch of earth in the 1750s for settlers of the New World. Men like the rugged Evan Shelby, who emigrated as a child from England to Frederick County in 1735, constantly worked to improve the security of their homesteads and protect their families from Indian attacks. The best defense was often offense, so Shelby joined the militia to counter French and Indian aggression on the frontier.

In 1755, thirty-five-year-old Evan Shelby, then a private soldier in the Maryland militia, participated in Gen. Edward Braddock's expedition to capture the French- and Indian-held Fort Duquesne at the confluence of the Ohio, Monongahela, and Allegheny Rivers. Accompanying Shelby and his men was General Braddock's twenty-three-year-old aide de camp, George Washington, from Virginia. Following a violent defeat described in the preceding chapter, Shelby returned to Maryland, where his wife, Letitia, cared for their three young sons, Isaac, James, and Evan.

In the summer and fall of 1758, colonial governor Horatio Sharpe, a commander in the British Army and friend to George Washington, promoted Evan Shelby to the rank of captain in the Maryland militia. Captain Shelby was personally selected to lead Gen. John Forbes's advance party in a second trek across Pennsylvania. Shelby and his rangers marked out the route of a road to Fort Cumberland and conducted a daring reconnaissance of Fort Duquesne. His efforts preceded a massive British assault of the fort, which was ultimately abandoned by the French in November 1758.

Two days after the enemy withdrawal, while serving in a detachment of Col. George Washington's Virginia regiment, Shelby killed an enemy fighter with a hatchet, impressing superiors with his courage and great physical strength: "he gave chase to an Indian spy, in view of many of the troops, overtaking and tomahawking him."[1] As a military officer, Shelby was blunt in speech, prompt to take initiative, and fearless in the presence of his men.

Throughout the 1760s, Evan Shelby worked as a surveyor along Maryland's border with Pennsylvania, but he sustained heavy financial losses in the Indian trade and was forced to sell much of his property to satisfy debts. He briefly moved his family to Pennsylvania and was offered a land grant in West Virginia in 1768, but "it failed confirmation by the Crown."[2]

In 1771, Shelby moved his family to a 1,900-acre tract of land in the Holston region of southwest Virginia, near present-day Bristol, Tennessee, where he planned to quietly farm and raise cattle. Between 1771 and 1773, the resourceful frontiersman and combat veteran opened a general store, tavern, and inn, and built a distillery with the assistance of his son Isaac who inherited his father's "iron constitution" and skill with a rifle.[3]

Records from his store show that Evan Shelby sold legendary pioneer Daniel Boone "2 Quarts of Rume" in 1773.[4] Later records show that Evan Shelby became proficient in the production of rye whiskey, a valuable commodity on the American frontier.[5] A contract between Shelby and another farmer distiller named Pierce Wall reflects an agreement to provide "Rye Meal Malt and Malt at his Distillery, Logs for Fuel and Candles . . . and to allow the said Pierce Wall the Fifth part of all the Whiskey He . . . makes Which is to be Divided Weekly." In exchange, Wall agreed to "Cut his Firewood, make malt and two Gallons of Whiskey of Every Bushel of Rye Distilled by Him or more if the Rye will produce it."[6] According to author Henry Crowgey, Evan Shelby was the source of much of the rye whiskey sold in taverns in eastern Tennessee.[7]

War continued to occasionally call Evan and Isaac Shelby away from their farm and still. The Shelby men battled a party of almost one thousand Indians in "Lord Dunmore's War" of 1774 while under the command of the hard-drinking general George Rogers Clark. Later that year, Col. William Preston appointed Isaac Shelby a lieutenant in the militia. "When Isaac thoughtlessly sat down instead of remaining at attention while his commission was being written out by Col. Preston, his father, with characteristically imperious manner, sternly admonished him: 'Get up, you young dog, and make your obedience to the Colonel!'"[8] As Archibald Henderson noted in his book *Revolutionary Patriot and Border Hero*, "in time to come, the graceless 'young dog' was to prove himself, as a soldier and statesman, the superior of his bull-dog father, the grizzled veteran and Indian fighter."[9]

The next year, Isaac Shelby, having distinguished himself with wilderness skills and leadership in combat, left his family's farm and distillery to survey wild lands in the Kentucky Territory. That July, as colonial tensions erupted in violence against the crown, Gen. William Thompson sent a letter to Evan Shelby, indicating the high reputation he held back home: "Had General Washington been sure you could have joined the army at Boston without first seeing your family, you would have been appointed Lieut. Colo. [of the] Rifle Battalion."[10] Instead, Gov. Patrick Henry appointed Evan Shelby a major in the Virginia militia.

Governor Henry also promoted Isaac to captain and appointed him the commissary of supplies for all frontier posts. From 1777 to 1779, Isaac Shelby was fully engaged in securing supplies, sometimes at his own expense, for the Continental army. In the spring of 1779, however, he was elected to political office in the Virginia Assembly and was quickly promoted from captain to major to colonel in the Sullivan County militia by Gov. Thomas Jefferson.

In May of 1780, Col. Isaac Shelby was surveying land to settle in Kentucky when he received news that the British had captured Charleston. When Gen. Charles McDowell requested his aid, he hurried east to recruit frontiersman to fight. Shelby immediately assembled militiamen from his Sullivan County and marched with three hundred of them to General McDowell's camp in northwestern South Carolina. During the next three weeks Shelby and his men tore through British and loyalist Tory forces in the Carolinas.

On October 7, 1780, Shelby and his "Overmountain Men" won a decisive battle in the woods of western South Carolina at a place called King's Mountain. In a battle that lasted just over an hour, Shelby's men killed almost 300 Loyalists and captured 668 more. According to Thomas Jefferson, Isaac Shelby's cunning and violent strike against Loyalists at King's Mountain was "that turn of the tide of success which terminated the Revolutionary War."[11]

The following April, Isaac Shelby returned to Boonsborough, Kentucky, and married Susanna Hart, the second daughter of Gen. Nathaniel

Hart. He established a plantation where he focused on building a family (Shelby and his wife had eleven children), the raising of livestock, cultivation of the soil, and distillation of corn whiskey. Shelby remained an active civil servant, and in 1783 he chaired a convention of military officers who met to debate separation from Virginia. He served in the convention that drafted the first Kentucky constitution in 1792 and was elected to serve as the commonwealth's first governor that May.

During his first term, he instituted a tax system and fundamental laws, formed military divisions, developed a court system, extended the Wilderness Road, and kept Indian fighters at bay. In 1796, Shelby declined a second gubernatorial term so that he could return to his farm and successful whiskey distillery. A 1797 document reveals the scale of his operation. Shelby promised a customer named Andrew O'Hare "seven hundred and three gallons of good whiskey in eleven casks at my house."[12] Like his father before him, Isaac Shelby also negotiated rental agreements involving his distillery so that smaller farmers could convert their grains into a more profitable and moveable commodity.

With the outbreak of the War of 1812, the people of Kentucky cried out for leadership. Shelby, intent on aggressively prosecuting the war against Indians in the Northwest Territories, emerged as the popular candidate to lead the commonwealth, and he was elected for a second time in August 1812.

As the second war for American independence expanded, Governor Shelby personally raised over four thousand Kentucky volunteers and led them in an invasion of Canada. Shelby and his rugged militiamen fought valiantly against the British and their Indian allies at the Battle of Thames, for which Shelby was awarded a Congressional Gold Medal. During the war, Shelby served under the command of Gen. William Henry Harrison, who established his own whiskey distillery in Ohio shortly after the campaign.[13]

In 1813, Shelby appointed Charles S. Todd, his aide-de-camp and future son-in-law, to be a colonel in the Kentucky militia. Following the War of 1812, Governor Shelby bestowed honorary colonels' commissions on all of the men who served in his command, beginning a rich tradition. Eventually, the colonels were reconstituted as the Honorable Order of

Kentucky Colonels, a charitable organization focused on philanthropy in the commonwealth. Today, there are more than 100,000 Kentucky Colonels who donate millions of dollars to promote health and education initiatives. Notable Kentucky Colonels include General of the Army Omar Bradley, Medal of Honor recipient Rear Admiral Richard Byrd, U.S. senator and army veteran John Sherman Cooper, Gen. Norman Schwarzkopf, Ronald Reagan, and George H. W. Bush. The Colonels' official toast celebrates that "in a trying world darkened by hate and misunderstanding, he is a symbol of those virtues in which men find gallant faith and of the good men might distill from life. Here he stands, then. In the finest sense . . . a patriot."[14]

After Governor Shelby retired for a second time, President James Monroe recruited him for service as the United States' secretary of war. By 1816, Shelby had grown weary, and at the age of sixty-six, he desired to return to his farm. Governor Shelby may have declined a position in the president's cabinet for the farm, but he continued to serve. He was elected the first president of the Kentucky Agricultural Society and chairman of the first board of trustees of Centre College in Danville, Kentucky. In 1818, he joined Gen. Andrew Jackson, another noted whiskey distiller, in negotiating the "Jackson Purchase" from the Chickasaw Indians.

In 1820, he suffered a stroke that paralyzed his right arm and leg. However, the six-foot-tall, iron veteran survived for another six and a half years. Gov. Isaac Shelby passed away on July 18, 1826. He was buried at a family graveyard on his estate, Traveler's Rest, in Lincoln County. The Commonwealth of Kentucky erected a monument over his grave in 1827. Counties and towns in nine states are named in his honor.

6

The Weller Family

From the Battle of New Orleans . . . where all Kentucky manned her warrior sires through Buena Vista and Monterey, and the reddest fields of Mexico, on to the Civil War, and through its bloody course, the men of Kentucky have ever been at the front when the cause of the country, or of duty, called.

Col. Ernest Macpherson, 1891

Johannes Weller and Catherine Ambrose emigrated separately from Germany to Maryland in the 1740s. After marrying in Frederick County, the Wellers produced twelve children, including a son named Daniel in 1762. After serving alongside his brothers in the Revolutionary War, Daniel moved to Kentucky, where he began distilling whiskey. Daniel's son Samuel Weller, born in 1787, fought in Isaac Shelby's regiment during the War of 1812 and inherited his father's stills and barrels when he returned from the war. Samuel's son William Larue (W. L.) Weller, born in Hardin County, Kentucky, in 1825, served as a private in Company D, First Regiment, Kentucky Infantry (Louisville Legion) during the Mexican-American War with Gen. Zachary Taylor. After the war, Weller founded the whiskey wholesale company W. L. Weller & Sons with his younger brother John and his two sons, all Civil War veterans. In 1893, Weller hired a young salesman named Julian "Pappy" Van Winkle, who led the company through Prohibition and into the twentieth century.

In 1743, Johannes Weller left Diedenshausen in Westphalia, Germany, crossed the Atlantic on the ship *Lydia*, and settled in Maryland's rolling Catoctin Mountains on a fifty-acre parcel he called "Beauty."[1] Wasting no time, Weller married his neighbor's daughter, Catherine Ambrose, who bore twelve children, including a son named Daniel in 1762. Throughout the 1760s, while Charles Mason and Jeremiah Dixon were surveying the nearby border with Pennsylvania, Weller laid claims to several additional tracts of land, and he helped to establish the town known today as Thurmont, near Emmitsburg, Maryland.[2]

Germans like Weller flocked to America as hostilities with England erupted in 1775. Many of the German immigrants living in Maryland and Pennsylvania generally supported the patriot cause. Barred by colonial law from voting, men like Johannes Weller felt alienated from civic life. Weller came to America to escape religious persecution, and efforts to tighten imperial control did not sit well with him or other Germans who prized religious and political freedoms. The Continental Congress, knowing that these frontier farmers were a potential source of firepower, authorized the raising of volunteer rifle companies and recruited men like Weller, his neighbor Mathias Ambrose, and their many hardy sons to fight the king's men.

Like most residents of the Catoctin Mountains, the Weller men chose to fight in the American Revolution. In 1776, Johannes traveled to Philadelphia to enlist as a private in the First German Battalion,[3] and he "rendered provisional aid to the Continental Army" throughout the conduct of the war.[4] In 1778, he and several members of his family signed Oaths of Fidelity, swearing allegiance to Frederick County, Maryland, and denying obedience to Great Britain.[5] His sons John and Philip later joined a unit called the Toms Creek Hundred. John was commissioned an ensign in Capt. Jacob Ambrose's company, and Philip Weller served as the company's fifer.[6] Elements of the Toms Creek Hundred joined the Continental Army in the north, fighting at White Plains and Long

Island, although the muster records for this period are lost. They were called again to active service during the 1781 Chesapeake Campaign that culminated in the Battle of Yorktown.[7] In recognition of its war efforts, the new federal government granted the Weller family a land bounty in western Virginia, in present-day Nelson County, Kentucky, although they did not immediately move to claim it.[8]

Following the revolution, Johannes Weller's sons returned to Frederick County, where they cultivated their father's land and distilled excess rye into whiskey. Most farmer distillers like the Wellers used whiskey as a substitute for currency, and they traded it for other goods, supplies, and land. In 1784, Daniel Weller married Anna Margaret Firor and they started a family on a parcel called "Arnold's Delight," not far from "Beauty." Daniel Weller followed in his father's footsteps and learned to distill whiskey, a skill carried across the Atlantic by so many European settlers and further refined in the New World.[9]

Life became more costly in 1791 when Alexander Hamilton's treasury department levied a tax on whiskey production in support of the indebted federal government. Despite the fact that most farmers rarely distilled more than two months a year, the government gauged still capacity, assumed full-time production, and assessed a tax on whiskey that, often, was never even made. Distillers resisted the tax in a variety of ways. Some turned violent, tarring and feathering tax collectors or attacking their properties. Others left their homes in Maryland and Pennsylvania to take advantage of opportunities in lands further west, where tax collectors and judges were less aggressive or more sympathetic.

In March 1792, as the seeds of the Whiskey Rebellion were being sown in Frederick County, Maryland, Johannes Weller died at the age of seventy-five, leaving his real and personal property, livestock, and currency to his beloved wife and children.[10] Daniel Weller and Anna Margaret made the most of their inheritance, continuing to work on the farm and make whiskey. But in 1796, Daniel Weller made a decision that would significantly alter his family's story. He left Maryland for the brand new commonwealth of Kentucky, where the Wellers' Revolutionary War land grant awaited.[11] His widowed mother, Catherine, joined his family to head west, leaving the only home she had known since she came to America as a seven-year-old girl.

Along with Daniel Weller on the trek from Maryland to Kentucky were his wife of twelve years, Anna Margaret, and their six children, including nine-year-old son Samuel. The grueling exodus took the Wellers to Pittsburgh, then up the Ohio River on a flatboat. Like thousands of other settlers, the Wellers ultimately landed at Beargrass Creek in Louisville, moved inland, and claimed their land in Nelson County, Kentucky, near Bardstown.

By 1800, records show that Daniel Weller was operating a ninety-gallon copper still in Bardstown, converting excess corn into clear Kentucky whiskey.[12] Each September, he licensed use of the still to his neighbor Jacob Hirsch, who operated it for two weeks and paid the taxes on the approximately one hundred gallons of whiskey he produced.

The Wellers became acquainted with the Boehm family, whose patriarch, Jacob Boehm, was also a German-born farmer distiller. Boehm moved his family from near Frederick, Maryland, to Kentucky in 1788 and later amended the German spelling of his surname to the more Americanized "Beam." Daniel Weller's daughter Anna Maria ("Mary") married Jacob Beam Jr., whose brother David grew the family distillery, eventually passing it off to his grandson, distiller James "Jim" Beauregard Beam.

While life was challenging for early settlers of Kentucky like the Beams and Wellers, it undoubtedly became much more difficult for Anna Margaret Weller, her children, and Catherine when Daniel Weller died in 1807 at the age of forty-five. When his estate was inventoried, his son Samuel paid about $200 for his father's stills, mash kettles, barrels, and other cooper's tools.[13] While Samuel intended to remain at home, make whiskey, and care for his family, military duty called.

By 1807, tens of thousands of Americans were moving to western states and territories like Kentucky, Ohio, Indiana, Illinois, and Michigan. By 1810, the population of the white settlements in those places amounted to 270,000. More white settlers meant less land and freedom for Native Americans, who numbered fewer than 70,000.[14] The U.S. Army was constantly engaged in skirmishes with Native Americans as territorial governors negotiated lopsided treaties and pushed Natives onto reservations. The young Shawnee warrior Tecumseh, whose people were forced out of the Kentucky territory and into Ohio during the Revolutionary War, retaliated by stealing horses, ransacking settlements, and attacking civilians and soldiers. Tecumseh and his brother, The Prophet, even stole the settlers' valuable whiskey and became "addicted to the fiery fluid," which became a priority Indian target during raids.[15]

In 1810, Tecumseh and a number of his warriors met with territorial governor and whiskey distiller William Henry Harrison to discuss the Treaty of Fort Wayne. Tecumseh was angry that Americans were settling the lands ceded in the treaty, as he had not been included in the negotiations. While Harrison offered to pay Tecumseh for the land, the Natives were not interested in money. Tecumseh made it clear at his meeting with Harrison that if the United States did not change its policies, there would be war. In the event of war, he warned, he would accept British arms and gunpowder.[16] Tecumseh "spoke for some time with great vehemence and anger," but Harrison remained calm.[17]

Meanwhile, British agents were courting the tribes' favor and quietly urging the Natives to take up their hatchets against Americans. The British hoped to reconstitute that region as a Native state and harmonize it with British fur-trading interests. In November 1811, Tecumseh launched an attack against an American encampment in Indiana. As William Henry Harrison fought back, a larger conflict burst open between the British and the Americans.

According to the U.S Army Center of Military History, American frontiersmen had "no doubt that their troubles with the Indians were the result of British intrigue."[18] Americans may have exacerbated the problem by "[circulating stories] after every Indian raid of British Army muskets and equipment being found on the field."[19] Early settlers were convinced that they could solve their problems with Indians by forcing the British out of America. Thus, the War of 1812 was a "second war of independence" for frontiersmen like Samuel Weller.

Good fighting men were in demand, especially those from the backwoods of Kentucky and Tennessee, whose reputation for bravery and ability with a rifle was unmatched. Samuel Weller was busy providing for his family when Congress declared war on the United Kingdom in June 1812. He was twenty-five years old when he joined the whiskey-making Gov. Isaac Shelby and the Kentucky Militia's Second Regiment to fight Redcoats and adversarial Native Americans in the Illinois Territory. Weller, a private, was assigned to Capt. Caleb Hardesty's Mounted Militia with other men from Nelson and Washington Counties.[20] He served under Revolutionary War veteran Col. (later Maj. Gen.) John Thomas. In 1814, his younger brother George was drafted into the Kentucky militia, inspiring their other brother David Weller to enlist.[21]

While specific details of Samuel Weller's service in the war are scant, both David and George Weller served in the Fifteenth Regiment of the Detached Kentucky Militia commanded by the aptly named Lt. Col. Gabriel Slaughter. David Weller served as Capt. John Farmer's first sergeant and George was a corporal. On December 19, 1814, while en route to New Orleans with Gen. Andrew Jackson, a noted Tennessee whiskey-maker, a young officer named John Figg drowned. The following day, David Weller was commissioned an ensign to replace Figg.

During the Battle of New Orleans, David and other Kentuckians like George Beam performed brilliantly and displayed expert marksmanship. "I don't suppose there ever were men who fought more bravely than the whole of the troops engaged," he wrote to Samuel. "There was only one man killed near us, he had his brains shot out on me, and I was bloody as a Butcher."[22] An unidentified Kentucky soldier corroborated what David Weller wrote when he noted that "during the action . . . a ball passed through [a Tennessee man's] head, and he fell against Ensign Weller."[23] When David Weller returned home to Kentucky in May 1815, he wore his bloodstained shirt, which terrified his mother.

Nearly twenty-five thousand Kentuckians, about one in six, engaged in some type of military service during the War of 1812.[24] Kentucky men like the Wellers and Beams were so deadly with their long rifles that men across the nation began referring to all American long rifles as "Kentucky Rifles," a name that endures today.[25] Sixty-four percent of the soldiers killed in action were sons of Kentucky, meaning that the Bluegrass State suffered more casualties than did all other states combined. Today, twenty-two Kentucky counties are named for men who fought during the War of 1812.

By mid-1815, all of the Wellers had returned safely to Kentucky. Samuel followed in his late father's footsteps by putting his two pot stills to use, producing corn-based whiskey for consumption, sale, and trade. Over the next decade, Samuel tended to his farm and family, and in 1825, his son William Larue ("W. L.") was born. W. L. Weller would ultimately leave an indelible mark on the whiskey business, but not until he had experienced war for himself, in northern Mexico.

In the lead-up to the Mexican-American War, the United States maintained two armies. In 1789, Congress authorized a standing army, commonly referred to as the U.S. Army. That force was composed of regular commissioned officers and private men who enlisted for a period of five years. In 1792, Congress authorized a second army intended to be an auxiliary to the regulars called "the militia." In 1846, Kentucky governor William Owsley issued a call for men to join the Kentucky militia and fight in Mexico where the chaotic Mexican government stood in the way of American expansion, particularly along the border with Texas.[26]

Twenty-one-year-old William Larue Weller promptly enlisted in the newly created First Regiment, Kentucky Infantry, referred to as the "Louisville Legion."[27] Competition to be accepted into the Legion was fierce, and, once in, few left. The Weller family was well known in and around Louisville, and W. L. impressed senior militiamen with his military bearing and discipline. Members of the Legion were renowned for their high standards, and companies prided themselves on drill and discipline. While other Kentucky militia units used their muster and drill dates as social occasions, the Legion trained and drilled faithfully.[28]

The Legion was the first unit in the commonwealth to respond to Governor Owsley and the first to be mustered into service by the federal government. In the summer of 1846, the Legion was mobilized for combat in northern Mexico. Volunteers supplied their own uniforms, horses, and equipment, while the U.S. government provided the arms. The Kentucky volunteers wore full beards, three cornered hats, and hip boots lined with red morocco.

Before embarking for Mexico by steamboat, W. L. Weller and the Legion were treated to a patriotic send-off by the citizens of Louisville. Sally Ward, the most beautiful woman in the city, presented the Legion with its regimental colors, which would later be riddled by enemy bullets at Buena Vista.[29] The Legion traveled down the Ohio and Mississippi Rivers to New Orleans before taking ships to Monterrey. There, they joined the forces of Gen. Zachary Taylor.

In September 1846, the Louisville Legion saw its first major action in the Battle of Monterrey. During the three-day-long conflict, W. L. Weller and his company guarded a mortar battery while Tennessee volunteers and Texas rangers raided the homes of Mexican soldiers. The raids inflicted staggering casualties upon Mexican forces and convinced Mexican general Pedro de Ampudia to begin negotiating a truce with General Taylor. One of the regular officers present at the Battle of Monterrey was West Point graduate Jefferson Davis, a native Kentuckian and son of a whiskey distiller. Davis later resigned his commission to lead the Confederate States of America as its president. Several other notable future leaders fought at Monterrey. Ulysses Grant and George Meade were regular army lieutenants on the battlefield. Braxton Bragg, a strong opponent of whiskey rations, was a regular army artillery captain at Monterrey and nearly lost his life when American militiamen tried to kill him out of disdain for his authoritarian style.[30]

Following the battle, General Taylor was heavily criticized for negotiating a two-month armistice with the Mexicans. Even President Polk publicly lambasted General Taylor, insisting that "the army had no authority to negotiate truces, only to kill the enemy."[31] However, Monterrey was the beginning of the end for the Mexican Army, as it led to desertion and disenchantment within the Mexican ranks. While the Mexicans achieved one more victory at Buena Vista, the battle in which Henry Clay Jr. was killed in action, the greater conflict ended in the winter of 1848 with the creation of the modern-day U.S.-Mexican border.

On January 9, 1849, W. L. Weller, though "much impaired in health," celebrated his return from Mexico by forming a liquor distribution company in Louisville with his friend George Gonterman and brother Charles D. Weller.[32] The men began purchasing and rectifying whiskey on downtown Louisville's Eighth Street, at times adding various ingredients for color and flavor. Weller later built a small alcohol distillery in downtown Louisville, which burned to the ground within a year. Weller continued to purchase whiskey from other distillers, including "Old Joe" Peyton, the maker of the first branded bourbon, and his father, Samuel, and selling it in his company's name.[33]

According to many, "W. L. Weller's whiskeys were so popular that he had to put his thumbprint in green ink on all invoices and barrels of whiskey sold to insure his customers that they were getting the real item."[34] Weller produced "honest whiskey at an honest price" like Old W. L. Weller, Mammoth Cave, Cabin Still, Harlem Club, Hollis Rye, Silas B. Johnson, and Stone Root Gin.[35] (After Weller's death, in 1915, the government seized and destroyed one hundred cases of Stone Root and Gin, a punishment for wrongfully labeling the product as "excellent preparation for Kidney, Bladder, and all Urinary troubles . . . and excellent relief for Nervous Debility and Dyspepsia" in violation of the Food and Drug Act.[36] Perhaps the whiskey in that era was not always so "honest.")

In 1850, W. L. Weller married Sarah B. Pence of Shelby County. Sarah gave birth to George Pence Weller in 1852, the same year W. L. Weller bought out his partner, Gonterman. While Weller enjoyed financial success and some personal happiness, a series of tragedies followed. In 1854, a typhoid and cholera epidemic killed his parents, Samuel and Phoebe Weller, and most other members of the Weller family in Larue County, Kentucky. While W.L. and Sarah Weller welcomed son William Larue Weller Jr. in 1856, W. L. Weller's brother and business partner, Charles, was robbed and murdered in Clarksville, Tennessee, while on horseback collecting bills during the Civil War.

After Charles was murdered, W. L. Weller's oldest son George left to fight with the Confederate army in northern Georgia. Weller's young brother John, whom he raised like a son after the typhoid epidemic stole their parents, accepted a commission as a captain in the Confederate army's Fourth Kentucky Infantry Regiment, also known as the "Orphan Brigade." Capt. John Henry Weller served alongside men like Capt. Edward Ford Spears, grandson of Revolutionary War veteran and early Kentucky distiller Jacob Spears. Captain Weller was wounded in the battle of Chickamauga, a battle that pit brother against brother for Kentuckians. While John Weller's Orphan Brigade pledged allegiance to the Confederacy, his father's Louisville Legion, which had been reorganized as the Fifth Kentucky Infantry, fought for the Union at the Battle of Chickamauga. After the war, Gen. William Tecumseh Sherman later said that "no single body of men can claim more honor for the grand result than the officers and men of the Louisville Legion of 1861."[37] When both John and George returned from Confederate army service, they joined the family whiskey business.

The renamed W. L. Weller & Son distillery fared well after John and George came home from being at war. In 1871, the men moved into a larger space on Louisville's Second Street, but it too was destroyed by a "spectacular blaze" in 1873. According to the *Courier-Journal*, a vapor leak from their column still caught fire from a lamp and the still exploded. Fortunately, despite suffering a $55,000 loss, the Weller men recouped a portion of the loss through insurance and rebuilt once again. They purchased a custom-built, thirty-six-foot-high copper still with thirteen chambers and used it to distill high alcohol "cologne spirits."[38] Their flagship brands Mammoth Cave and Cabin Still were some of the most popular whiskeys in America when Weller's son William Larue Weller Jr. briefly left his job as a clerk at the distillery to join the Louisville Legion in 1878. When W. L. Weller Jr. completed his service, he rejoined his father, brother, and uncle, all veterans, and the business was renamed once again to W. L. Weller & Sons.

In 1893, the aging W. L. Weller Sr. hired two young salesmen, Alex T. Farnsley and nineteen-year-old Julian "Pappy" Van Winkle to help grow the company. Under their direction, Weller's company eventually merged with the A. Ph. Stitzel Distillery and developed a bourbon whiskey recipe featuring "wheat," instead of rye, as the secondary grain. Popular "wheated" brands like Old Fitzgerald, Rebel Yell, and W. L. Weller followed and enjoyed commercial success.

In the fall of 1895, when the Grand Army of the Republic hosted its annual "encampment" for Civil War veterans in Louisville, veterans were treated to whiskey and various pieces of whiskey merchandise.

Among other souvenir items, the men were given a pamphlet entitled "Louisville of To-Day." The pamphlet boasted that Louisville's own W. L. Weller & Sons wholesale liquor dealers

> enjoy an international reputation for the superiority of its old Kentucky rye and bourbon whiskies. . . . Here is carried the finest stock of old Kentucky whiskies to be found in town, or in fact anywhere. The firm handles only straight goods, the selected distillings of leading concerns, all of which have become thoroughly mellowed and aged before being put on the market. Absolute purity and finest quality are the guarantees accompanying all goods sold by this honorable old house, which sells exclusively to the trade, and covers every section of Kentucky, Indiana, West Virginia, Virginia, North Carolina, Alabama, Georgia, Florida, Mississippi, Louisiana, Texas, Arkansas, Indian Territory, etc., etc. Seven travelers are employed, and the sales of the house are annually enlarging.[39]

While the pamphlet was full of puffery, the Weller business was indeed popular, financially successful, and rapidly expanding.

In 1896, William Larue Weller retired to focus on philanthropy, leaving the business in the able hands of his sons George and William Jr., his younger brother John, Alex Farnsley, and Pappy Van Winkle. The men ably guided Mr. Weller's distillery and brands through Prohibition by securing a medicinal whiskey license, and they led the industry after repeal with products uniformly considered to be some of the finest bourbon whiskeys ever made. Today, the Buffalo Trace Distillery in Frankfort honors W. L. Weller's life and career by producing several "wheated" bourbons, W. L. Weller Special Reserve, Old Weller Antique, and the highly sought after William Larue Weller, with a label that briefly mentions his service to the Louisville Legion.

7

Thomas Hughes Handy

Nothing can resist the desperation of troops who regard not their own lives, but victory.

> Confederate major Joseph Lancaster Brent after sinking the USS *Indianola* and appointing Lt. Thomas H. Handy "prize-master"

Thomas Hughes Handy was born in Somerset County on the eastern shore of Maryland in 1839. At the age of eight, Handy moved with his family to New Orleans, Louisiana. In March 1862, he volunteered for service with a Confederate outfit known as the Crescent Artillery Battalion. During the Civil War, he was captured twice, court-martialed and acquitted, wounded in action, and decorated for gallantry on multiple occasions. He fought at the battles of Fort St. Philip (New Orleans), Vicksburg, and Fort DeRussy, and was involved in the sinking of the federal ironclad USS *Indianola*. He was seriously injured after being shot and thrown from a horse, but he survived his wounds and returned to New Orleans after the war. In 1869, Handy entered the retail liquor business and eventually purchased the Sazerac Coffee House, where the Sazerac cocktail was born. Today, the successor of Handy's business, the Sazerac Company, owns the Buffalo Trace and Barton 1792 distilleries, among many others.

In 1847, John Scarborough Handy relocated his family from the eastern shore of Maryland to New Orleans, Louisiana, a city in the midst of economic boom. The Handys, of Scottish descent, were shipbuilders and farmers and had attained great wealth along the Wicomico River in Maryland.[1] Over forty Handy men fought in the Revolutionary War, two of them as regimental commanders, and they established a large plantation near the city of Salisbury, Maryland following the war. Despite deep connections to the Old Line State, John Handy left Maryland for other opportunities in distant New Orleans. Once settled, he enrolled his young son Thomas Hughes Handy in public schools and trained him in caring for livestock and planting crops. As Thomas grew, he also grew to love his new hometown, a city that depended heavily on "the blessing of African slavery" as the state secession commissioner called it.[2]

In late January 1861, when Thomas H. Handy was twenty-one years old, the Louisiana Legislature voted overwhelmingly to secede from the United States. Citizens of Baton Rouge and New Orleans celebrated in the streets by lighting pine torches as the ordinance was read declaring Louisiana to be its own sovereign nation. Knowing that war was imminent, Louisiana's governor Thomas Overton Moore mustered a ragtag militia to occupy the nearby federal arsenal and the two forts guarding New Orleans, Fort Jackson and Fort St. Philip. Moore appointed Mexican-American War veteran Col. Braxton Bragg to command them. Louisiana eventually pledged its allegiance to the Confederate States of America in preparation for what they hoped would be a short war and lasting independence. Men across Louisiana enlisted to fight.

Thomas H. Handy was one of the men who volunteered. In early 1861, Handy was working in New Orleans for a Maryland-born liquor importer named Sewell Taylor.[3] After Taylor died in March of that year and Louisiana seceded from the United States, Handy volunteered for service in Capt. T. H. Hutton's Company A of the Crescent Artillery, a Confederate "water battery."[4] Handy was commissioned a second lieutenant and ultimately spent three years in combat. His wartime experience began with an ill-fated attempt to defend New Orleans in 1862.

When Louisiana seceded, President Lincoln, who considered the Mississippi River to be the backbone of the rebellion, moved immediately to control the river and capture New Orleans. He mobilized the federal navy, which flooded the river with ninety Revolutionary War–era ironclads. The federal navy's main effort steamed south on the river, fighting engagements along the way to the Crescent City. When federal troops and sailors arrived at the Confederate-held forts, Second Lieutenant Handy was on the wall of Fort St. Philip to defend his beloved city, the largest in the fledgling Confederate States of America.

On April 18, 1862, the Union navy began shelling the adjacent forts. Handy's commanding officer, Capt. T. H. Hutton, and his men were responsible for counter-battery at Fort St. Phillip, but Hutton and Handy found it difficult to rally their inexperienced artillerymen to fight back. As the commander of both forts recorded on April 18, "lack of shelter, food, blankets, sleeping quarters, drinkable water, along with the depressing effects of days of heavy, unanswered shelling were hard to bear."[5] When combined with sickness and ever-present, corrosive fear, the conditions were a drain on morale. Those factors contributed to a mutiny at the Fort Jackson garrison and the surrender of Fort St. Phillip. Every member of Captain Hutton and Thomas H. Handy's artillery company was captured. Handy endured a transfer to Fort Warren in the Boston Harbor.[6]

Lieutenant Handy was not a captive for long. In July 1862, he was transported back south to Richmond, where he was exchanged for a federal prisoner named George A. Bennett of the Fourth New Jersey Infantry.[7] After he was moved to Fort Monroe, Virginia, Confederate officials charged Lieutenant Handy with insubordination and mutiny.[8] The basis for, and the results of, his court-martial are unknown. In any event, he was not dismissed from military service, as he later rejoined Hutton's Crescent Artillery in Louisiana.

At the time of his return to the battlefield, Handy's men were about thirty miles south of Vicksburg, Mississippi, defending shipments of Confederate supplies along the Red River. To disrupt the shipments, Union commanders sent the powerful but flawed USS *Indianola* to attack. On the night of February 24, 1863, Hutton and Handy's artillery battery boarded the Confederate ship *Webb* and prepared a preemptive attack. Maj. Joseph L. Brent, the son of a U.S. congressman and a future Confederate general, "immediately selected Lieutenant Handy, a junior officer in whom [Brent] had confidence, and put him in command of the troops upon the Webb."[9]

Major Brent, Captain Hutton, and Lieutenant Handy knew that the USS *Indianola*'s weakness was her armament. She was optimized for bombarding fixed fortifications but not for firing at fast-moving steamboats like the CSS *Webb*. The valiant, and perhaps reckless, Lt. Thomas Handy attacked with vigor. Handy furiously fired the *Webb*'s thirty-two-pound gun at close range, causing flames to envelop in his own porthole.[10] As he fired eighty-pound shells at the enemy, Handy simultaneously directed the *Webb* to ram the *Indianola*, whose crew was not able to load and fire its eleven-inch Dahlgren guns fast enough to fend off disaster.

In a letter to Louisiana's assistant adjutant, Major Brent wrote that "the sharp bow of the *Webb* penetrated as if it were going to pass entirely through the ship. . . . Whilst the *Webb* had her bow knocked off to within fourteen inches of the water line, her splendid machinery was unhurt."[11] After the collision, Handy's men chaotically boarded the *Indianola*, looting and plundering everything in sight. Upon restoring order and moving the federal sailors onto the *Webb*, Major Brent "immediately appointed Lieutenant Thomas H. Handy prize-master."[12] Handy and his enthused rebels found their prize "filled with a valuable cargo."[13] In addition to the boatload of new supplies, over one hundred officers and men from the USS *Indianola* became Handy's prisoners, sweet revenge for a man who was a prisoner of war himself the previous summer.[14]

While his performance aboard the *Webb* was extraordinary, Lieutenant Handy exhibited great bravery and skill on several subsequent occasions. In the summer of 1863, Handy took command of the troops aboard the Confederate ship *Grand Duke* during a vicious river battle with the federal ironclad *Albatross*. During the artillery barrage, the *Grand Duke* had her steering apparatus and "mechanical contrivances" completely shot away.[15] With *Grand Duke* lying helpless in the river, a suggestion was twice made by "one having authority," likely Captain Hutton, that the boat run up the white flag of surrender. Lt. Thomas Handy was infuriated. "Not while there is a man to pull a lanyard!" he responded.[16] The *Grand Duke* fought on to a stalemate.

A month later, Handy was thrown from a horse and shattered his leg, an injury from which he never fully recovered. Handy was admitted to the Confederate General Hospital in Shreveport, Louisiana, and later wrote in his journal that he "had the misfortune to fracture [his] thigh on the 7th of August 1863—the union of which has never taken place. "After a failed operation that winter, the surgeon noted, "He is so much reduced that there is no probability of union taking place."[17] Indeed, Handy lived the remainder of his life with one leg three inches shorter than the other.[18]

Despite the mangled leg, Handy returned to the battlefield for a final showdown with Union forces. He found himself in command of Captain Hutton's company when it prepared for its final major engagement, at Fort DeRussy, Louisiana. Records reflect that Captain Hutton was under arrest pending a court-martial, possibly for his display of cowardice aboard the *Grand Duke*, and he was absent for the defense of Fort DeRussy.[19] As a result, Thomas H. Handy was selected to command an element of just over three hundred rebels as ten thousand federal troops made their way down the Red River. Handy and his ragtag battery of Louisianans, Texans, and some foreigners fired the first shots and held the federals at bay for twelve hours.

Around 6:30 p.m. on March 14, 1864, Brig. Gen. Joseph Mower, who had been wounded in the neck and taken prisoner by Confederate troops at the Battle of Corinth, ordered his men scale the walls of the fort, giving the badly undersupplied Confederates no choice but to surrender. For the second time, Lieutenant Handy was captured by federal troops. The Union army's inventory of captured weapons taken after the fall of Fort DeRussy showed a total of just 173 rifles and smoothbore muskets.[20] Over one hundred of Handy's men were without firearms to defend the fort. In the end, despite a tactical defeat at Fort DeRussy, the Union's Red River Campaign failed to accomplish its objective due to poor planning and mismanagement.

Gen. William Tecumseh Sherman called the campaign "one damn blunder from beginning to end."[21]

Handy's Union captors mercifully permitted him to travel back to Shreveport for medical attention. He was admitted and treated for the thigh fracture and a gunshot wound. On May 1, 1864, he was discharged from the hospital, but not before he submitted his resignation from the Confederate army. In January 1865, less than four months before the end of the Civil War, all of the men in Hutton's Crescent Artillery were exchanged for federal prisoners and permitted to return to their homes.

Upon returning to New Orleans, a city where men came together for both business and bourbon whiskey, Handy accepted a position as a clerk for John B. Schiller at the Sazerac Coffee House.[22] The Sazerac was already well known for its importation of French brandy and the use of Antoine Peychaud's bitters in its beverages. Schiller hired Handy to serve as the Sazerac's bookkeeper, but in 1871, Thomas Handy bought Schiller out. In advertisements, Handy noted that his liquor stock included "old superior Sazerac Brandy[,] . . . choice Bourbon and Rye Whiskeys, from the best known distillers, held by us to mature."[23] Handy also served fine champagne, wines, beer, Caribbean rum, Irish and Scotch whiskys, and his own line of aromatic bitters.

While Handy was running the Sazerac Coffee House, he engaged in a number of other activities in New Orleans. He served as a member of the school board and as a livestock inspector. His riskiest venture was as a railroad entrepreneur. Handy's Canal Street City Park & Lake Shore Railroad Company built a railroad line that ran from Basin Street to the Spanish Fort amusement park on the shore of Lake Pontchartrain, but it saddled him with debt. Despite having to file for bankruptcy, Handy was elected as the civil sheriff in the newly created Ninth Ward of New Orleans in 1876. The following year, in his capacity as the city's civil sheriff, he secured government employment for nearly five thousand Confederate veterans.[24]

In December 1878, Handy sold his company to a Frenchman named Vincent Micas, who rebranded the establishment the "Sazerac Barroom." Handy maintained property ownership of the building, however, and stayed on with the Sazerac as one of Micas's employees. Micas made a splash in New Orleans as the "sole proprietor of A. A. Peychaud's Celebrated American Aromatic Bitter Cordial" and Sazerac brandy.

Thomas Handy worked for Micas until August 1880, when he opened the new firm Thomas H. Handy & Co. just a few blocks down the street. For several years, Handy and Micas competed directly against one another, and they both offered Sazerac brandy and aromatic bitter cordials. In March 1882, Micas moved his wholesale and retail liquor establishment and "Sazerac Barroom" out of the building still owned by his rival Handy. After Micas moved to the other side of Canal Street, workers demolished the old building.

Several months after the original Sazerac was torn down, Thomas Handy built and opened a new establishment at the same location. In October 1882, the newly constructed Sazerac House, "with all the modern improvements," held its grand opening.[25] Patrons marveled at the new saloon's size, carved walnut bar, and beautiful fixtures. Eventually, Micas's rival saloon was lost, whiskey and all, to bankruptcy. New Orleans was left with just one Sazerac House, Thomas H. Handy's, which provided countless "Sazerac" cocktails to men making political and business deals in New Orleans. The Sazerac began as a brandy cocktail, but several accounts indicate that it was Handy who substituted rye whiskey, the traditional base in the modern cocktail.

Despite Handy's stature in New Orleans, his rebel spirit made the occasional appearance. In 1889, despite his position as an elected sheriff and community leader, Handy was arrested for knowingly violating New Orleans's prohibition on Sunday liquor sales. His crime was an act of principle though, intended to highlight the fact that he was "selling alcohol openly from his establishment while everyone else was selling theirs behind a curtain."[26]

In 1893, at the age of fifty-four, Handy died at his summer residence at Long Beach, Mississippi. Following Prohibition, his former secretary Christopher O'Reilly took control of the business, which he chartered as the Sazerac Company. Today, Sazerac owns the A. Smith Bowman, Glenmore, Barton, Fleischmann, Medley, Mr. Boston, and Buffalo Trace distilleries, among many others. Sazerac credits Handy's hard work and dedication as the foundation for its success. To honor his life and legacy, the Buffalo Trace Distillery produces Thomas H. Handy, a highly sought-after uncut, unfiltered straight rye whiskey.

On the evening of March 14, 2014, the 150th anniversary of the capture of Fort DeRussy, a group of Civil War reenactors, led by Louisianan author Steve Mayeux, met to fire blank rounds from working antique cannons and drink Thomas H. Handy rye whiskey in honor of the Confederate lieutenant turned businessman. Mayeux, a Marine Corps veteran and author of *Earthen Walls, Iron Men: Fort DeRussy, Louisiana, and the Defense of Red River,* had not fired a cannon since the 1970s when he was a tank platoon commander at Camp Lejeune, North Carolina. An excerpt from Mayeux's journal captures the moment well: "A little after five, we took our bottle of Thomas Handy whiskey and went to pick up Randy and Susan Decuir and went out to the fort. Angelo Piazza was out there with his cannon crew, and they must have fired over fifteen rounds. . . . After the shooting, at about sundown, we stopped for a little while to remember the men who defended the fort and drank a toast with Thomas H. Handy whiskey."[27]

8

Paul L. Jones Jr.

My dear, you will scarcely believe how indifferent soldiers become to Danger.

Samuel McKittrick on June 27, 1864, following the Battle of Kennesaw Mountain

Paul L. Jones Jr. was born on September 6, 1840, in Lynchburg, Virginia, to Paul Sr. and Mary Watkins Jones. In October 1861, Paul and his old brother Warner joined the army of the Confederate States of America. Paul was commissioned a second lieutenant in Company G of the Thirty-Third Tennessee Regiment, a unit that saw action at the Battles of Shiloh and Chickamauga, and General Sherman's 1864 siege of Atlanta. During the Battle of Kennesaw Mountain, Paul's brother Warner, then the regimental commander, was killed instantly when a bullet struck him in the head. Following the war, Paul Jones Jr. began rectifying whiskey in the Atlanta area. Around 1884, Jones moved to Louisville, Kentucky's "Whiskey Row," where he became a leader in the industry as the president of J. G. Mattingly Distillery. While precise details about the origin of the brand name are elusive, Jones is credited with registering the trademark Four Roses in 1888. Today, Four Roses sells nearly a million cases of bourbon whiskey worldwide.

In 1854, when fifty-year-old Mary Watkins Jones died, her husband Paul L. Jones was left to care for four children, Warner, Sallie, Josephine, and Paul Jr. while also operating a stagecoach business in western Virginia. Paul Jones did what many widowers do and found another wife as quickly as possible. He married Lavinia Cary Pankey in August of 1854, sold his business, and moved the entire family from Lynchburg, Virginia, to rural Obion County, Tennessee, just south of the border with Kentucky.[1] By 1858, Jones was working in the logging industry, which took him and his new wife to Alabama in 1860, just before the eruption of civil war.

Warner Paul Roland Jones and Paul L. Jones Jr. did not move to Alabama with their father and stepmother.[2] In 1860, the brothers stayed in Obion County to assemble a regiment of soldiers from across western Tennessee.[3] Many Tennesseans were deeply grieved when South Carolina seceded from the Union, but many of them also believed that the northern states acted unconstitutionally in refusing to enforce fugitive slave laws. While the Jones men did not own slaves, they likely believed that secession was well within their constitutional rights.

Between 1860 and 1861, Warner and Paul Jr. left their jobs as lawyer and miller, respectively, and began drilling with other men from western Tennessee for an inevitable clash with federal troops. In 1861, they were commissioned as officers in the newly assembled Thirty-Third Tennessee Regiment. Warner was appointed a captain and the commander of Company G, and Paul Jr. was his adjutant.[4] Warner ultimately became the colonel of the regiment and gave his life in its defense.[5] Paul also fought, but he survived the war, reunited with his father, and founded one of America's largest distilling operations and most popular bourbon brands.

On October 18, 1861, the Thirty-Third Tennessee was formally mustered into service with the army of the Confederate States of America under the command of Col. Alex William Campbell, a lawyer from Jackson. In early 1862, Campbell's regiment moved from Tennessee to Columbus, Kentucky, along the Mississippi River, just across from Missouri, where Gen. Ulysses S. Grant was also preparing men for combat. Grant's first action in the Civil War occurred at that site when

Confederate general Leonidas Polk attempted to run a large anchor chain across the river from Columbus to Belmont, Missouri, to block federal vessels from transiting soldiers and supplies.[6]

In response to Polk's provocation, General Grant attacked the Confederate Second Division, including the men and officers from the Thirty-Third Tennessee Regiment. The Tennesseans were only partially armed with shotguns and hunting rifles, but they survived the wild skirmish.[7] Throughout the spring of 1862, the Thirty-Third Tennessee begged, borrowed, and stole weapons, as it fully expected a second meeting with Grant. General Polk obtained a loan of flint and steel muskets for the regiment in April 1862, just before the Battle of Shiloh.[8]

According to the *Military Annals of Tennessee*, "the regiment received its baptism of blood on the sanguinary field of Shiloh."[9] Many of the rebels in the Thirty-Third Tennessee grew up near Shiloh and fought valiantly during what they considered an invasion of their beloved state. During the twelve-hour battle, the Tennesseans, including Warner and Paul Jones Jr., were held in reserve while the Fifth Tennessee Regiment moved forward to meet Brig. Gen. Benjamin Prentiss's men at a place nicknamed the Hornet's Nest. When the leading rebels advanced into a depression on the battlefield, federal troops poured artillery and musket fire into their lines. The Thirty-Third Tennessee remained stationary and held its fire in an effort to avoid shooting their brothers in the backs. When Colonel Campbell called to the regiments in front of him to charge, they declined. According to General Polk's report to Confederate leadership in Richmond, "[Campbell] then gave orders to his own regiments to charge, and led them in gallant style over the heads of the regiments lying in advance of him, sweeping the enemy before him, and putting them completely to rout."[10]

The Tennesseans captured General Prentiss and more than two thousand of his troops. They also captured the federals' modern weapons "and left their own flintlocks in place."[11] Despite the astonishing victory and new firearms, the cost in blood was high. The regiment suffered 20 killed, 103 wounded, and 17 missing.[12] One of the severely wounded was the regimental commander, Colonel Campbell, who was incapacitated for months. When Campbell was evacuated to convalesce in Jackson,

Warner Jones was promoted to colonel and assumed command of the Thirty-Third Tennessee. His younger brother Capt. Paul Jones Jr. remained with Company G.

In May 1862, the regiment marched south from Shiloh to Tupelo, Mississippi, and back to Chattanooga, where it was reorganized under Gen. Braxton Bragg's Army of the Mississippi. In October 1862, nearly a year after its formation, Col. Warner Jones led the men during the "Battle for Kentucky," at Perryville, one of the bloodiest engagements of the war and the most significant fought in the commonwealth. General Bragg hoped an incursion into Kentucky would divert Union attention from the Southern strongholds at Vicksburg and Chattanooga and encourage Bluegrass State volunteers to join the rebel cause.

When Confederate leadership discovered federal sharpshooters occupying a high hill, the Thirty-Third was ordered to charge it, dislodge the enemy, and hold the position at all costs. As the attacking force from Tennessee passed through open fields and meadows, Union general Thomas Crittenden's artillery and cavalrymen opened fire and charged. Thirty-three Confederate men were lost to Union shells and sabers, but somehow the regiment achieved its mission. Jones's men remained on the hill until one or two o'clock in the morning, when they were ordered to retreat. Col. Warner Jones was commended for his "bravery and warrior-like abilities."[13] Over thirty thousand men fought at Perryville, and over seventy-six hundred ended up as casualties. While Perryville was a tactical victory for the South, it was a strategic win for Union forces, as Bragg reluctantly withdrew to Tennessee.

Following General Bragg's retreat, the Thirty-Third and Thirty-First Tennessee Regiments were consolidated under the command of Maj. Gen. Alexander P. Stewart, a West Point educated artillery officer from Rogersville, Tennessee. Col. Warner Jones remained in command of the Thirty-Third Tennessee, and Capt. Paul Jones Jr. was selected to serve on General Stewart's staff. After retreating from Perryville, the Tennesseans stayed in Shelbyville, Tennessee, until December 1862, when they traveled to Murfreesboro for the Battle of Stones River.

By that point in the war, Union soldiers had occupied Nashville for nine full months, turning the Tennessee capital into a chaotic bastion of drinking and prostitution. On Market Street, "people were kept in a constant state of alarm all night by the breaking of fences, firing of pistols, and the most hideous noises."[14] The common cause of the turmoil was whiskey, specifically a saloon on College Street. According to Nashville's *Dispatch* on December 2, 1862, "poison is dealt out to soldiers at all hours of the day and night[,] . . . stolen property is sold and whiskey bought daily and almost hourly."[15] Union general William Rosecrans dismissed a large number of officers for drunkenness, but his action did little to relieve the misery for residents of Nashville. Federal troops outnumbered its citizens two to one by Christmas Day 1862. The holiday came and passed for soldiers in the field, and on December 27, 1862, General Rosecrans ordered his formation to maneuver toward Murfreesboro in the constant, cold drizzle. Rosecrans planned an attack for the morning of December 31, but Gen. Braxton Bragg and his army of angry rebels were well prepared to defend their state's honor in the terrible cold.

As the sun began to rise on December 31, Confederate skirmishers quietly emerged in the foggy half-light, formed into battle lines, and smashed into the Union line as the federal troops ate breakfast and drank coffee near their pup tents and campfires. Union soldiers attempted in vain to resist the rebel onslaught, but it was so sudden and the slaughter so great that most of them retreated in confusion. A second wave of Confederate attackers, led by Maj. Gen. Benjamin Franklin Cheatham, took advantage of the retreat and attacked. Capt. Robert D. Smith of the Second Tennessee Infantry Regiment wrote that the fighting was "more desperate than anything I ever witnessed."[16]

Warner and Paul Jones and the Thirty-Third Tennessee Regiment, led by Brig. Gen. Alexander P. Stewart, also attacked "with a splendid cheer."[17] Several hours into the fighting, men from the Thirty-Third Tennessee came across federal artillerymen dragging two guns from a grove of cedars. The Tennesseans "dispersed the guns' crews with a well-aimed volley and overran them."[18]

As the battle raged and rebels expended ammunition, however, the Yankees took advantage of the chaos. The rebel advance lost coordination and momentum as units intermingled, key leaders were wounded or killed, and supplies ran out. When the First and Fourth Tennessee Regiments were called up to storm a federal battery on a ridge, a separate Union artillery battery hidden in the woods opened up a raking fire on their right flank. Col. H. R. Feild ordered the Tennessee men to lie down and hold their fire. Feild and several other Confederate officers mistakenly concluded the fire was from their own men and attempted to stop the onslaught by conspicuously waving flags and their arms. After several minutes of being blasted from the woods, the Confederates finally realized their mistake and "swooped down on those Yankees like a whirl-a-gust of woodpeckers in a rainstorm."[19]

In the aftermath, several soldiers blamed the confusion on whiskey. "John Barleycorn was general-in-chief," wrote Sam Watkins. "Our generals, and colonels, and captains, had kissed John a little too often. They couldn't see straight. . . . They couldn't tell our own men from the Yankees."[20] Thomas Malone said he saw generals "manifestly somewhat excited by drink."[21] Union soldier Charles Doolittle, who stayed on the field to render aid to wounded Confederates, was attacked by men who "had been drinking."[22] Doolittle wrote that "the whiskey served to increase their hatred and bitterness." Indeed, even General Cheatham drank so much whiskey on December 31, 1862, that he fell from his saddle, further straining his relationship with the teetotaler Bragg, who was seen "foaming at the mouth like a mad tiger."[23] As Samuel Martin wrote in *General Braxton Bragg*, despite a brief stint of hard drinking as a West Point cadet, the general was totally intolerant of others' weaknesses for liquor.[24]

While some men surmised that whiskey fueled rebel anger, the battlefield at Murfreesboro "was frozen, the wind was strong, and rain beat hard against the field and glades."[25] P. R. Jones from the Tenth Texas Cavalry Regiment recalled that "whiskey was passed down the line . . . not given to the soldiers to inspire courage, but to warm them up after long exposure to the rain and cold weather."[26] The battle and the freezing conditions continued into New Year's Day as both Rosecrans and Bragg refused to retreat. The Union army expected more men and supplies, though, and General Bragg worried that the rising Stones

River would split his army. The Confederates begrudgingly withdrew to Tullahoma, Tennessee.

In the end, over twenty-four thousand men were wounded or killed at Stones River, including four general officers. No major Civil War engagement saw a higher percentage of men wounded or killed. One-third of Gen. John Breckinridge's Kentucky "Orphan Brigade" was lost in a counterattack on January 2, 1863. While General Bragg claimed that "God had granted [the Confederacy] a Happy New Year," President Lincoln praised his generals for what he considered a Union victory.[27] The battle boosted Union morale, and nearby Nashville remained a Union supply depot for the duration of the war.

Following the battle, Confederate major general Stewart wrote that "many of the enemy's dead, and some of our own, were left on the field unburied. . . . I cannot close this imperfect sketch without expressing my obligation to the gentlemen who served on my staff, and who made themselves intelligently useful and efficient, regardless of danger."[28] He explicitly recognized "Lieutenant Paul Jones, Jr., of the Thirty-Third," who he noted "preferred to be in the field."

According to Col. John Lindsley's *Military Annals of Tennessee*, the Thirty-Third Tennessee Regiment archives were lost sometime in 1863.[29] Detailed accounts of the regiment's next actions are relatively scant, but the men were present for the fateful Battle of Chickamauga in September 1863, during which thirty thousand men were killed or wounded in action, including William Larue Weller's younger brother John. The regiment moved for a short time to the town of Sweetwater, Tennessee, and fought at the Battle of Missionary Ridge in November 1863. On the eve of that battle, General Grant's staff began drinking whiskey and threw "quite a disgraceful party," which the future president had to personally break up at four o'clock in the morning.[30] During the next day's combat, eleven thousand men were killed or wounded.

Following Missionary Ridge and the resulting loss of Chattanooga, the Thirty-Third Tennessee retreated again, moving just south to spend the winter in Dalton, Georgia. The Army of Tennessee had been routed in its home state, thousands of men were killed, and several key commanders were relieved. General Bragg dismissed Gen. John Breckenridge for being unfit for duty and for drunkenness.[31] Bragg submitted his own resignation, which was quickly accepted by President Davis. As the Confederate leadership reorganized in 1864, the Union army planned a grand offensive deep into rebel territory, focused on ending the conflict.

In May 1864, Gen. William Tecumseh Sherman commenced a brutal operation to destroy the rebels' war-sustaining infrastructure. Sherman began his Atlanta Campaign by following the Western and Atlantic Railroad line south toward the city. Lying in wait for Sherman was Bragg's replacement, Confederate general Joseph Johnston and his men, including Warner Jones's consolidated Tennessee regiment. As Sherman's skirmishers clashed with Confederates attempting to halt the advance to Atlanta, Gen. Leonidas Polk was struck directly by an artillery shell. It ripped through his chest, killing him instantly, before exploding against a tree. The Tennesseans mourned the man that General Johnston called their "first captain."[32] They also sought to avenge his death.

On June 27, 1864, Sherman's forces made what would be its last frontal assault of the war. Over five thousand well-entrenched rebels on Kennesaw Mountain, near Marietta, were prepared to fight to the death. The battle began with a massive exchange of artillery. W. J. Worsham wrote that "the bursting shells and deadly missiles from the guns . . . made the old mountain seem like a grand volcano."[33] At eight o'clock in the morning, the Union infantry began its attack. Despite thick vegetation and rocky slopes, the federals made it to within a few yards of the main rebel line, but a slaughter ensued. "The fighting was desperate and beyond description."[34] In less than three hours, over three thousand men were killed. "This is surely not war, it is butchery," wrote one Ohio sergeant who survived the shooting.[35]

Sherman was forced to retreat from Kennesaw Mountain, but skirmishes continued as federal forces moved to flank Johnston's line over the next several days. On June 30 near Marietta, Georgia, a federal sharpshooter's minie ball impacted a log, ricocheted, and struck Col. Warner Jones in the temple, killing him instantly.[36] Within days, his thirty-four-year-old body was buried in Atlanta's Oakland

Cemetery. General Stewart wrote that Jones was a "true man . . . of dash, coolness, courage."[37] On the night that Warner Jones was killed, General Sherman wrote to his wife, "I begin to regard the death and mangling of a couple thousand men as a small affair, a kind of morning dash."[38] Less than one year later, the men of Jones's Tennessee regiment formally surrendered at Greensboro, North Carolina, and were paroled.

Paul Jones Jr. returned home to Tennessee and found his home "in ruins and the family destitute. His family's wealth, which before the war had been considerable, had been invested in Confederate bonds and was gone."[39] Jones Jr. and his father moved from Tennessee to Atlanta, Georgia, and took responsibility for Warner's young family. When they arrived in Atlanta, Jones and his father began selling tobacco and whiskey.[40] Some historians believe that Jones began working for the R. M. Rose Company, a distillery established along Little Nancy Creek in Vinings, Georgia, by Civil War veteran Rufus Mathewson Rose. Others believe that the Jones men were working independently.[41] The scantness of records makes it impossible to determine, but Jones and Rose had more in common than just whiskey. Rufus Rose was also a Confederate army veteran.

While Rose was raised in Connecticut and studied medicine in New York City before the war, he moved to Georgia to work as a druggist and met a southern belle. When the war began, Rose enlisted in the Confederate army and joined the Tenth Georgia Regiment as a foot soldier. He was transferred to the medical department to serve at the hospital on the College of William and Mary campus in Virginia. Rose later moved to a Confederate laboratory in Macon until the war's end.[42] In 1867, he established the distillery in Vinings.

Dr. Rose promoted his products in the Atlanta papers as "the oldest, richest and best wines, liquors and brandies."[43] Rose focused some advertisements on Atlanta women by inviting ladies into their store where they could purchase "wholesome and beneficial" pure medicinal whiskey.[44] Sometime in the late 1860s, the Georgia bourbon whiskey Four Roses made its debut.

When Georgia went "dry" for two years in 1883, however, the Rose

Company left for Chattanooga, Tennessee. In 1884, Paul Jones Jr. moved to downtown Louisville's bustling "Whiskey Row," where he purchased, rectified, and sold wholesale whiskey under the label Jones Four Star. By that time, Jones's nephews Warner and Saunders worked for him as a clerk and bookkeeper. In 1888, Paul Jones Jr. apparently purchased the rights to the brand name Four Roses. While historians disagree on several essential facts related to the origin of the Four Roses brand, the company claims August 1888 to be its birth month and Paul Jones Jr. to be its founder.

According to the modern Four Roses label, Paul Jones Jr. became smitten by the beauty of a southern belle and sent her a proposal. She apparently replied that if her answer was "yes" she would wear a corsage of four roses on her gown to the upcoming grand ball. While the legend ends in roses and marriage, in reality, Paul Jones Jr. lived unmarried in Louisville's Galt House until his death in 1895. Another version of the Four Roses story holds that Rufus Rose named the brand in honor of his four daughters, a curious tale considering that Mr. Rose only had two children (a daughter, Laura, and a son, Randolph). The most plausible explanation is that the original brand name was a reference to Rufus Rose, his brother Origen, and their sons.

One thing is clear. Paul Jones Jr.'s Louisville-based whiskey rectifying company quickly became one of America's largest, and his Four Roses bourbon whiskey was some of the country's most popular. Jones developed a series of progressive advertising techniques to promote the whiskey. He advertised in newspapers, he sold products in glass bottles, and he printed his company name on bar trays and saloon signs from coast to coast.

In the 1890s, as Civil War veteran Joseph Greenhut's Whiskey Trust controlled the price of whiskey stocks, Jones looked to escape the rectifying business and purchase a distillery of his own. When the J. G. Mattingly distillery ran into financial difficulties in 1889, Jones bought it for $125,000 at auction. For the next six years, he served as the Louisville distillery's president and expanded distribution of the brands Paul Jones, Four Roses, Jones Four Star, Old Cabinet, Old Cabinet Rye, Small Grain, West End, and Swastika (an inoffensive Native American good luck sign at the time). While his primary focus was whiskey, Jones used his wealth and prominence to engage in other endeavors. While distillery president, Jones simultaneously served as the director and vice president of the American National Bank and the president of the Louisville Fair and Driving Association. He was also a founding member of Louisville's Douglas Park Racetrack.

However, at the age of fifty-five, Jones developed a kidney ailment known as Bright's disease, which progressed quickly and caused him severe pains. He died on February 24, 1895, leaving the company in Saunders's hands. There was some discussion of burying his body in Atlanta's Oakland Cemetery near his beloved brother and father. Ultimately, he was laid to rest in Louisville's Cave Hill Cemetery.

In 1901, Saunders Jones sold the company and its brands to the Whiskey Trust, but he continued to manage the J. G. Mattingly distillery, mill, and fermenting house, a boiler house, and a cattle barn. The property also held five warehouses, all of them brick with slate or metal roofs. The property caught fire in 1903, but the warehouses containing sixty thousand barrels of whiskey were spared.[45]

Following Prohibition, Mr. Jones's company purchased the "Frankfort Distillery" in Shively with mashing capacity for thirty-one hundred bushels per day. The Frankfort Distillery, which grew to become an empire of plants in various Kentucky locations, continued to sell Paul Jones, Four Roses, Old Oscar Pepper, Shipping Port, Wheel House, Mattingly & Moore, and many other popular whiskey brands. In 1938 the Paul Jones Company installed an enormous Four Roses electric light display in New York City's Madison Square Garden, solidifying the brand as an American classic.

During World War II, the distillery was sold to Seagram's for $42 million. Seagram's also purchased the Old Prentice Distillery in Anderson County, Kentucky, which it later renamed Four Roses. In 2002, the Japanese beer company Kirin purchased that Four Roses Distillery for $165.6 million. At that time, Four Roses was selling six hundred thousand cases of bourbon annually. More recently, Kirin launched a $55 million distillery expansion, which will double production capacity of the historic brand Jones launched after the Civil War.

9

George Thomas Stagg

I will die right here.

> Col. Samuel Woodson Price, Twenty-First Kentucky Infantry Regiment commander, to Gen. William Rosecrans at the Battle of Stones River

George Thomas Stagg was born on December 19, 1835, in Garrard County, Kentucky. His great-grandfather James Stagg was a captain in the New Jersey Militia during the Revolutionary War. In 1858, Stagg married Elizabeth "Bettie" Doolin and started a family with her in Richmond, Kentucky, where he worked as a clerk in a shoe store. When the Civil War erupted, Stagg, a religious man opposed to slavery, enlisted in the Union army and experienced prolonged combat with Companies D and I of the Twenty-First Kentucky Infantry Regiment. After the conflict, Stagg moved with Bettie and his children to St. Louis, Missouri, where he sold whiskey made by distiller Col. Edmund Haynes Taylor Jr. While in St. Louis in 1876, Stagg exposed the illegal "Whiskey Ring," a noble decision that brought him notoriety in the business. Stagg later acquired two of Colonel Taylor's Kentucky distilleries and rose to prominence as one of the country's most successful whiskey businessmen.

The week after Christmas 1861, the officers and men of the Twenty-First Kentucky Infantry Regiment were officially mustered into federal service at Green River Bridge, Kentucky, the site of an early rebel attack.[1] The backbone of the newly formed Twenty-First Kentucky was a group of soldiers from an elite state guard unit known as the "Old Infantry," commanded by Capt. Samuel Woodson Price, a painter from Nicholasville.[2] His captaincy was a post of honor, as the unit traced its lineage to before the War of 1812 and fought at the Battle of River Raisin with William Henry Harrison and in Mexico with Cassius Clay.[3] Volunteers from across the commonwealth brought the unit to full strength.[4]

Standing in Company D was the wide-eyed 1st Lt. George Thomas Stagg, a twenty-six-year-old officer who left a job selling shoes in Richmond, Kentucky, to defend the Union.[5] George Stagg was new to the army, but he was raised on stories about his many ancestors who fought for independence. Thirteen Stagg men fought in the Revolutionary War. Maj. John Stagg was General Washington's private secretary at Valley Forge.[6] George T. Stagg's great-grandfather Capt. James Stagg commanded a company in New Jersey's "Flying Camp," an irregular reserve force established by Congress in the summer of 1776.[7] After the war, when Capt. James Stagg's home in Hackensack, New Jersey, was burned by retreating British troops, he began a journey over the Appalachian Mountains to Harrodsburg, Kentucky. In 1791, James Stagg acquired the farm where his great-grandson George was raised, approximately 125 miles from the site of the Twenty-First Kentucky Infantry's first wartime encampment.[8]

In February and March 1862, Lieutenant Stagg and his troopers marched south and east to the town of Creelsboro, Kentucky, in preparation for combat in Tennessee. During the trek, regimental commander Col. Ethelbert Ludlow Dudley, a Harvard-educated physician, contracted typhoid fever and died. Following the tragedy of Colonel Dudley's untimely death, the Twenty-First marched further south through Nashville, Shelbyville, and Tullahoma under the command of Samuel Woodson Price, who was hastily promoted to replace Dudley as colonel of the regiment. In October 1862, Lieutenant Stagg and his company pursued Confederate general Braxton Bragg's Army of Mississippi back to Perryville, Kentucky, the site of a massive engagement between the Army of the Ohio and Bragg's Army of Mississippi. Stagg's men were held in reserve at Perryville, but two months later, he and his men were forged in fire at the Battle of Stones River.[9]

When the Twenty-First Kentucky approached Murfreesboro, Tennessee, in late December 1863, their initial challenge was the bone-chilling rain, sleet, and fog. Upon their arrival, however, Stagg's Company D was greeted by harassing rebel artillery fire. Driven by adrenaline, the troops advanced along the Nashville Pike, repulsing attacks as they maneuvered. The fighting intensified on a farm to the west side of Stones River. The men were positioned near a key river crossing on McFadden's Farm with orders to defend the ford at all costs. In the midst of combat, Maj. Gen.William Rosecrans, affectionately called "Old Rosy" by his men, emerged on his horse with an unlit cigar clenched between his teeth. He approached Colonel Price and demanded, "Will you hold this ford?" "I will try, sir," the young Kentucky colonel replied. "Will you hold this ford?" Rosecrans asked again. "I will die right here," Price affirmed.[10]

In a battlefield report, Lt. Col. James Evans later noted that Twenty-First Kentucky men, especially the commanding officer of Stagg's Company D, acted with "great coolness and bravery" in the chaos of Stones River, but dozens of men were killed.[11] Confederate soldiers were able to flank the Kentucky regiment, and they poured destructive fire into its lines. As one Texas rebel later wrote about the battle, "the Yanks tried to make a stand whenever they could find shelter of any kind. All along our route we captured prisoners, who would take refuge behind houses, fences, logs, cedar bushes and in ravines."[12]

After surviving Stones River, George T. Stagg was promoted to captain. He temporarily served as an aide to Gen. Ambrose Burnside during the liberation of East Tennessee, but he returned to his own regiment's Company I as Colonel Price led the men to Chickamauga. The Twenty-First Kentucky fought several skirmishes around Chickamauga, the site of some of the hardest fighting of the Civil War but avoided the heavy combat it experienced at Stones River. As Colonel Price later wrote, "short rations, wearisome marches through weather cold and bleak, when poorly clad, in many instances feet lacerated for the want of shoes, was all borne with heroic endurance and cheerfulness."[13] He praised his men for their "daring deeds of bravery."[14]

There was little rest for the Twenty-First Kentucky after skirmishing around Chickamauga. The regiment saw action at Missionary Ridge and Shellmound in the winter of 1863. The spring of 1864 was spent marching to Georgia, where the men fought around Marietta and at the Battle of Kennesaw Mountain, where Colonel Price was wounded in action. General Sherman employed the regiment during the murderously hot summer of 1864 in the siege of Atlanta. The Twenty-First Kentucky skirmished constantly that fall before it traveled back to Tennessee to fight ragged rebels at Franklin and Nashville.

While maneuvering under heavy rebel artillery fire between the Granny White and Franklin Pikes in December 1864, Lt. Hugh A. Hedger and Private C. B. Thompson from Captain Stagg's company were struck and killed. In response, acting commander Lieutenant Colonel Evans ordered a furious six-hundred-yard charge across a cornfield. "Every man, it seemed, tried to get the lead" as they ran toward the enemy, yelling.[15] The Confederates fired back wildly as the Kentuckians closed the gap, but their fearful shots went over the soldiers' heads. Stagg's company overcame the rebels' earthworks and began the gruesome duty of hand-to-hand combat, stabbing the enemy with bayonets and clubbing them with rifle butt-stocks. Alongside elements of the Ninety-Sixth Illinois and Forty-Fifth Ohio Infantry Regiments, the men of the Twenty-First Kentucky captured several rebel cannons as remaining enemy soldiers fled. Only three men from the Kentucky regiment were wounded in the valorous charge.

After a crushing Union victory, the Twenty-First Kentucky pursued Confederate general John Bell Hood for over a week to the banks of the Cumberland River, a mission that spanned Christmas 1864. As Union forces engaged in several hard-fought rear-guard actions, the Kentucky men raced to Huntsville, Alabama, to cut off General Hood's retreat. They remained in Alabama until March 1865, a month before General Lee's surrender at Appomattox Courthouse. After being transferred to New Orleans that June, the regiment was mustered out of service in

December 1865, four years after its initial assembly by the Green River Bridge. According to Brig. Gen. Jefferson C. Davis, "no regiment exhibited a higher state of discipline and efficiency in the whole army than the Twenty-First Ky. Infantry."[16] In the end, Stagg's regiment lost 218 men to combat and disease.

George T. Stagg returned to Kentucky where he rejoined his wife, Bettie, and their two children. Uninterested in selling shoes after the war, Stagg moved his family west to St. Louis and seized an opportunity to sell whiskey with local businessman James Gregory. Doing business as "Gregory & Stagg, Commercial Merchants and Distillers Agents," the men purchased straight and rectified whiskey from across the Midwest, which they distributed throughout the United States, particularly in the eastern markets.

During the early 1870s, Stagg and his business partner became agitated by widespread corruption among distillers and federal tax officials in St. Louis. In 1875, Stagg contacted senior members of the Federal Internal Revenue Service to report the fraudulent activities rampant in the industry. The resulting investigation led to the prosecution of hundreds of distillers and tax officials across the country. When Elverton R. Chapman, head of the Stamp Division for the Federal Internal Revenue service, testified in Washington about the scandal, he credited George T. Stagg with providing "the most valuable assistance that we got in St. Louis." According to Chapman, "Mr. Stagg is entitled to more credit for the exposure of the St. Louis whiskey ring than any other man that lives."[17]

Following his exposure of the Whiskey Ring, an embarrassment for the nation's most senior officials, including President Grant, Stagg's notoriety grew rapidly. He and Mr. Gregory enjoyed more success selling whiskey than ever before. By 1877, their firm owned every single barrel of whiskey produced by the nation's top distiller, Col. Edmund Haynes Taylor Jr. Colonel Taylor became so indebted to the firm of Gregory and Stagg that he ceded control of his beloved Old Fire Copper (O.F.C.) and Carlisle distilleries in Kentucky to fulfill his obligations. While reluctantly working for Stagg, Colonel Taylor rebuilt the O.F.C. distillery, originally constructed in 1869, by adding copper fermentation tanks, state-of-the-art grain equipment, column stills, and a steam heating system still used in warehouses today.

Capitalizing on Taylor's popularity, Stagg registered the "O.F.C." trademark and established the E. H. Taylor Jr. Company in 1879, originally incorporated with five thousand shares. Stagg owned nearly 70 percent of the company while Colonel Taylor owned a single share. As a result of their lopsided financial arrangement, the relationship between George Stagg and Colonel Taylor devolved. By 1885, the men wanted nothing more than to part ways. In exchange for his single share of stock in the company, Stagg loaned Colonel Taylor enough money to develop another distillery on McCracken Pike in nearby Millville. Stagg also agreed to remove the colonel's name from the O.F.C. and Carlisle distilleries, but later reneged on his promise and inserted Taylor's script signature onto the labels of bourbon made there. A series of lawsuits and appeals followed, which completely destroyed the relationship between Stagg and Colonel Taylor, who proceeded to find success at the Old Taylor distillery in Millville, where he built a castle-like welcome center in 1887.[18]

Despite the ugly split with Colonel Taylor, George T. Stagg's business continued to perform well, for a time. It made $125,000 in profit in 1889, but overproduction and the costs of maintenance and litigation placed the company in financial jeopardy. Stagg turned to Walter Duffy, a former Union officer during the Civil War and the owner of the Rochester Distilling Co., for an infusion of capital. By the 1890s, Walter Duffy's annual profits were in the millions. He aggressively marketed his "pure malt whiskey" as a heart tonic and remedy for pneumonia, dyspepsia, malaria, and hemorrhages. Duffy focused his marketing efforts on aging veterans, whom he occasionally used as spokesmen. He concocted a story that "the formula was worked out fifty years ago by one of the world's greatest chemists."[19] Dr. Harvey Washington Wiley, a Civil War veteran and renowned chemist, adamantly disagreed. Wiley urged his colleagues to denounce the brand and argued that Duffy's Malt Whiskey was "one of the most gigantic frauds of the age and a flagrant violation of the law."[20]

Throughout the early 1890s, Duffy and his associates quietly purchased

Stagg's stock in the company and eventually gained complete control of his distilleries. Stagg, in poor health, longed for his family. "I am scarcely in Saint Louis. I have not been there, perhaps, for more than a few days at a time for a year and a half, or two years."[21] Not long after losing control of the company, George T. Stagg died at the relatively young age of fifty-eight. His distillery, included in the National Register of Historical Places as the George Thomas Stagg Distillery, stands alone as the only one in America to produce industrial alcohol for the War Department during both World Wars. Today, the warehouses Stagg and Taylor used to age whiskey after the Civil War hold more bourbon than any other site in America. Two of the distillery's most popular brands are named for Stagg and Taylor.

1. *The Whiskey Rebellion*, ca. 1795, depicts President Washington on horseback at Fort Cumberland, Maryland, before the federal army's march to Bedford, Pennsylvania. Washington's men confronted a band of several hundred angry farmer distillers, including dozens of Revolutionary War veterans. Courtesy of the Library of Congress.

2. *Isaac Shelby*, ca. 1816, painted by Matthew Harris Jouett, the son of Jack Jouett, a Revolutionary War hero and early Kentucky whiskey distiller. Courtesy of the Library of Congress.

3. William Larue Weller fought in the Mexican-American War with Kentucky's First Regiment of Infantry, the "Louisville Legion." After the war, in 1849, he established a successful whiskey rectifying operation in Louisville and employed his brother and sons, all of whom fought in the Civil War. Courtesy of the Sazerac Company Archives at Buffalo Trace Distillery.

4. Thomas H. Handy fought during the Civil War as part of a Louisiana-based Confederate artillery battery. During the war he was captured twice, court-martialed, wounded, and decorated for heroism. After the war, in 1869, he purchased the Sazerac Coffee House in New Orleans and enjoyed great success selling whiskey and cocktails. Courtesy of Handy family.

5. George T. Stagg fought for the Union with the Twenty-First Kentucky Infantry Regiment. In the 1870s Stagg became one of America's most successful whiskey producers and helped to uncover the infamous and illegal Whiskey Ring. Courtesy of the Sazerac Company Archives at Buffalo Trace Distillery.

6. *Opposite:* George T. Stagg. Courtesy of the Sazerac Company Archives at Buffalo Trace Distillery.

7. *Above: KO at Manassas* depicts Confederate soldiers enjoying plundered Union whiskey near Manassas Junction in August 1862. The painting is on display at KO Distilling, a veteran-owned craft whiskey distillery in Manassas, Virginia. Courtesy of Nathan Loda and KO Distilling.

8. Bill Wilson struggled with alcohol after discovering it as a lieutenant in the army. In 1935 he founded Alcoholics Anonymous. He is pictured here (*back row, center*) as a member of the Norwich University rifle team. Courtesy of Norwich University Archives, Kreitzberg Library, Northfield VT.

9. Elmer T. Lee (*front row, second from left*) served as a B-29 radarman in the Sixteenth Bomb Squadron and delivered bombs to Japanese targets until the end of World War II. When he returned home from Guam he completed his degree and landed a job at the George T. Stagg Distillery. Courtesy of 315th Bomb Wing Association.

10. In October 1943 Jimmy Johnson left his job at the George T. Stagg Distillery to enlist in the army. He deployed to the island of Guam to help construct airfields for B-29 crews like Elmer T. Lee's. Courtesy of the Sazerac Company Archives at Buffalo Trace Distillery.

11. Jimmy B. Johnson Jr. and Elmer T. Lee reinvigorated the bourbon whiskey industry with the release of Blanton's: The Original Single-Barrel Bourbon. Courtesy of the Sazerac Company Archives at Buffalo Trace Distillery.

12. Paul, Charlie, Bill, and Bob Willett all served during World War II and worked in various capacities at their family's Bardstown, Kentucky, distillery. Courtesy of Willett Distillery.

13. *Above:* Curtis G. "Bud" Culin worked for Schenley Distillers Corporation until he enlisted as a tanker. He was wounded in the D-Day invasion, remained in France, and invented a hedgerow-cutting device that earned him the Legion of Merit and personal recognition from Generals Omar Bradley and Dwight Eisenhower. Courtesy of the Cranford Historical Society.

14. *Opposite:* In 1942 Julian Van Winkle Jr. left his job as the treasurer of Stitzel-Weller Distillery to join the army. He commanded Company A of the Forty-Fourth Tank Battalion during the Battle of Leyte, Philippines, was wounded in action, and was awarded the Silver Star Medal for heroism. He named his tank "Old Fitz" after Stitzel-Weller's flagship bourbon whiskey. Courtesy of Sally Van Winkle Campbell.

15. Col. Frank B. Thompson fought in both world wars and served as the president of Glenmore Distillery for sixty-five years. Courtesy of Kentucky Historical Society.

16. Col. Frank B. Thompson became a living symbol of Glenmore's Old Kentucky Tavern label. Courtesy of the Sazerac Company Archives at Buffalo Trace Distillery.

17. Ernest W. Ripy Jr. served as the third master distiller at the Anderson County, Kentucky, facility known today as Wild Turkey. Provided by the author.

18. The "Band of Brothers" from Easy Company, 506th Parachute Infantry Regiment, celebrated victory over Hitler by drinking his champagne, wine, and whiskey on V-E Day. Courtesy of the U.S. Army.

ARMY SERVICE FORCES
OFFICE OF THE COMMANDING GENERAL
WASHINGTON 25, D. C.

JUN 7 1945

Mr. Lewis S. Rosenstiel, Chairman of the Board
Schenley Distillers Corporation
350 Fifth Avenue
New York, N. Y.

Dear Mr. Rosenstiel:

I want personally to express to you the appreciation and admiration all of us here feel for the part your company has played in the victory over Germany.

What you and others in the great American production team have accomplished is already having its effect on Japan. Yet in some ways the job ahead of us will be the most difficult of the war. While our production requirements are less than for a two-front war, they are still heavy. I know you share our determination to meet them in full so that our troops may finish their job as quickly as brave men can.

What especially concerns me is that our new programs contain increases as well as reductions. While some plants will be released for return to peacetime work, we will be placing even heavier loads on some others. We need the help of industry to insure that, as reconversion takes place, we do not fail to get the war materiel we still urgently need.

Industry has done a great job. Half the war is over. Like the men in the Pacific, it's up to us to finish it!

Cordially yours,

BREHON SOMERVELL
General, Commanding

This high tribute is intended for you... each and every member of the Schenley organization. The credit is yours, and you rightly deserve it.
Lewis Rosenstiel G.B.

19. Following victory over Germany, Gen. Brehon B. Somervell, the commanding general of the Army Service Forces, personally wrote to Schenley Distillers Corporation chairman Lewis Rosenstiel to express appreciation and admiration for the company's role in defeating the Nazis. Courtesy of the Sazerac Company Archives at Buffalo Trace Distillery.

20. Tom Bulleit served as a navy corpsman in Vietnam in 1968. After a long career practicing law he fulfilled a lifelong dream and established the Bulleit Distilling Company. Courtesy of Tom Bulleit.

21. Dave Pickerell served in the army for eleven years before leaving the service for the chance to make whiskey. Courtesy of Dave Pickerell and the U.S. Military Academy. U.S. Army photo.

22. During World War II, Bill Mannshardt served as an electrician's mate first class aboard the USS *Saratoga* supporting operations in the Pacific. He saw combat near Guadalcanal, the Eastern Solomon Islands, Wake Island, Tarawa, the Marshall Islands, and Iwo Jima. Courtesy of the Mannshardt family.

23. Lance Winters served as a nuclear engineer in the U.S. Navy for eight years prior to joining St. George Spirits. He is pictured here on the USS *Enterprise*, not far from St. George Spirits' current location in Alameda, California. Courtesy of Lance Winters.

24. George Washington rye whiskey is produced at the George Washington Distillery and Gristmill in Mount Vernon, Virginia. Army veteran Dave Pickerell oversees the production based on Washington's original recipes and methods. Courtesy of David Cole.

25. *Young George Washington.* Courtesy of Nathan Loda. Painting commissioned by and displayed at the Farmers & Distillers restaurant in Washington DC.

26. Buffalo Trace Distillery in Frankfort, Kentucky, produces several whiskeys named for military veterans. Photo by author.

27. Bulleit bourbon whiskey is produced by the Bulleit Distilling Company in Louisville, Kentucky. Photo by author.

28. 4 Spirits bourbon is produced at the veteran-owned 4 Spirits Distillery in Corvallis, Oregon. It is named in honor of four Oregon National Guard soldiers killed in action: Lt. Erik McCrae, Sgt. Justin Linden, Sgt. Justin Eyerly, and Sgt. David Roustum. Courtesy of 4 Spirits Distillery.

29. Armored Diesel bourbon is produced at the Boundary Oak Distillery in Radcliff, Kentucky. It is named in honor of Gen. George S. Patton and his infamous wartime cocktail recipe. Courtesy of Boundary Oak Distillery.

30. Marine Corps veteran Zach Hollingsworth produces Have a Shot of Freedom bourbon whiskey to honor American heritage and provide veterans with employment opportunities. Courtesy of Have a Shot of Freedom Whiskey Company.

31. The American Freedom Distillery in St. Petersburg, Florida, produces Horse Soldier bourbon in honor of the Fifth Special Forces Group's participation in the 2001 invasion of Afghanistan. Courtesy of American Freedom Distillery.

32. Barton 1792 Distillery produces Military Special, a four-year-old, 80 proof bourbon, sold in U.S. military post exchanges for nine dollars. Photo by author.

33. Patriarch Distillers' Soldier Valley bourbon, packaged in a patented glass World War II canteen replica bottle, won a Double Gold Medal at the 2014 San Francisco World Spirits Competition. Courtesy of Patriarch Distillers.

34. Rob Dietrich, the master distiller at Denver's Stranahan's Colorado Whiskey, is a veteran of the Tenth Mountain Division. In Vail the 10th Mountain Whiskey & Spirit Company pays homage to the division's rich history. Photo by author.

35. In 2012 veterans John Collett and Jack Landers founded the Three Rangers Company to bottle rye whiskey to benefit their Three Rangers Foundation. Photo by the author.

10

Julian Proctor Van Winkle Jr.

The War of Japan was lost in the Campaign of the Philippines, and the Campaign of the Philippines was lost in the Battle of Leyte, and the Battle of Leyte was lost in the skirmish on Breakneck Ridge.

Gen. Tomoyuki Yamashita

Julian Proctor Van Winkle Jr. was born in Louisville, Kentucky, in 1914. He served as the commander of Company A, Forty-Fourth Tank Battalion during the decisive Battle of Breakneck Ridge in the Pacific Theater of World War II. Despite being shot in the hand and abdomen, Van Winkle continued to fight through pain, torrential rain, and Japanese resistance until he was forced to recover in Dutch New Guinea. Following his return from the war, Van Winkle rejoined his father, Julian "Pappy" Van Winkle, at the Stitzel-Weller Distilling Company where he hired several army buddies as salesmen. In 1964, Van Winkle Jr. succeeded his father as the president of Stitzel-Weller, a position he held for eight years. Following its sale in 1972, he continued to purchase Stitzel-Weller whiskey for the Old Rip Van Winkle brand. His son, Julian Van Winkle III, joined the family business in 1977 and ultimately developed the famed Pappy Van Winkle Family Reserve line in the mid-1990s.

When Japanese forces invaded the Philippines in early 1942, Gen. Douglas MacArthur, the American commander in the islands, was ordered to escape to Australia. He left reluctantly but vowed to return. By the time he did two and a half years later at the head of a powerful armada, the Japanese had determined to defend the Philippines to the death. They dug in on the island of Leyte, prepared for a fight that would determine the fate of the Japanese empire. At the center of MacArthur's bloody 1944 return was Capt. Julian Proctor Van Winkle Jr., a thirty-year-old tank commander from a well-known Kentucky whiskey family.

As a young man, Van Winkle attended the Woodberry Forest School in pastoral Madison County, Virginia. When he turned eighteen in the summer of 1932, he went to work at the W. L. Weller & Sons Distilling Company, where his father, Julian "Pappy" Van Winkle, had worked as a salesman since 1893. Pappy was hired by Mexican-American War veteran William Larue Weller and ultimately purchased Mr. Weller's company in 1915 along with Alex Farnsley. By the time Julian Jr. showed up to do odd jobs at the company's Story Avenue plant in downtown Louisville, Weller & Sons was selling medicinal whiskey made by the A. Ph. Stitzel Distillery and hoping for the end of Prohibition.[1]

After shuttling back and forth to the post office a dozen times, the teenage Van Winkle quit and traveled to California for vacation. Fortunately for Julian Jr., his youthful decision to quit mid-summer was not career-ending, as he was rehired the following summer to do various jobs for Pappy, Mr. Stitzel, and distiller Roy Beam. The six-foot-four Julian worked in the bottling house and bulked up by rolling full forty-eight-gallon barrels around the warehouses in preparation for Princeton University, where he would play football. Fortunately for all of them, Prohibition was repealed the winter of 1933, Julian Jr.'s first year in the Ivy League. On Derby Day in 1935, Pappy Van Winkle and Alex Farnsley formally merged with Arthur Philip Stitzel's Louisville distillery and established the Stitzel-Weller Distilling Company in the city's Shively district.

Van Winkle continued his summertime work rotations for Stitzel-Weller until his graduation from Princeton in 1937. Having matured and gained an appreciation for the physical aspects of the whiskey business, he was promoted to treasurer sometime in 1938. By then, Pappy hired master distiller Will McGill to run production, and business was booming due to the success of the Old Fitzgerald and W. L. Weller bourbon brands. But everything changed in early December 1941, for Stitzel-Weller and the nation, when Japanese fighter squadrons attacked the quiet Hawaiian naval base at Pearl Harbor. Van Winkle suspended life as he knew it and volunteered.

Compelled by patriotism and a sense of duty common among his generation, he reported to Fort Knox, Kentucky, on February 20, 1942. According to his contract with the army, he left "civil life," including his wife, Katie, "for the duration of the War, plus six months, subject to the discretion of the President."[2] As he humbly explained in a letter to his father, "three years or four is really not so much out of a man's life time. . . . [Ten or twenty] years from now we will have forgotten the more sanguine part and remember only that during the war our nation progressed."[3]

After in-processing at Fort Knox, Van Winkle reported to Camp Campbell, Kentucky, where he trained for several months. The Princeton graduate was commissioned a lieutenant in 1943 upon the completion of additional officer's training and placed in command of Company D, Forty-Fourth Armored Regiment, a Watertown, Tennessee–based National Guard unit that was attached to the Twelfth Armored Division "Hellcats" in preparation for combat. Van Winkle led his men through all of the standard army training—marching, running, rifle ranges, and tank maneuvers. After completing basic training, the unit was transferred to Tennessee for a final exercise. Upon completing the exercise to the satisfaction of the upper echelon, the Forty-Fourth Armored Regiment was re-flagged as the Forty-Fourth Tank Battalion. Van Winkle was promoted to captain and assumed command of Company A, a significant honor and responsibility for the well-respected officer.

In one of his first official acts as Company A commander, Captain Van Winkle lifted a restriction placed on Sgt. Raymond "Red" Cartier by the previous commander. Van Winkle knew about the fight between

Cartier and another platoon's sergeant, and he knew that Cartier acted in defense of a younger soldier. According to Cartier, "later that day, as the trucks were being loaded with GIs who had passes for Nashville, Capt. Van came over to me and asked if I had been to Nashville during maneuvers. I had to say no, because all during maneuvers I had been restricted to the company area for fighting. Capt. Van reached into his pocket, and came out with a 20 dollar bill and said, 'Cartier, get cleaned up, get a buddy, you're going to Nashville with those two officers. . . . The 20 is a loan.' It was the end of the month. He must have guessed that I was broke."[4] Almost two years later, after fighting and bleeding together in the Philippines, Van Winkle would select Cartier to serve as his first sergeant.

In the winter of 1943, the Forty-Fourth Tank Battalion moved from Kentucky to Camp Barkeley, Texas, for several months of grueling tank exercises. The men trained hard, but they also had fun. Off-duty time was spent in Abilene, a dry town, but "after a few inquiries," the men found alcohol.[5] Captain Van Winkle did his best to keep the men focused, even though the battalion's final destination was still unknown.

In March of 1944, the Forty-Fourth was transported by rail from Texas to Portland, Oregon, while the rest of the Twelfth Armored Division deployed to the Atlantic theater. The Forty-Fourth was designated a "separate battalion" and placed under the command of Lt. Col. Thomas Ross and given orders to deploy to the Pacific theater. The battalion spent about two weeks preparing (and partying) in Portland and Vancouver, Washington, until it departed Portland for New Guinea aboard the ten-thousand-ton Dutch freighter USAT *Kota Baroe*. At 2300 hours on March 22, 1944, the men departed Portland in the pouring rain.

After a trying fifty-one-day trip, the battalion landed at tropical Milne Bay near an outpost the Americans dubbed Camp Washington. Upon its arrival, the Forty-Fourth Tank Battalion became the first tank outfit in the Southwest Pacific and the first tank battalion in Gen. Walter Krueger's Sixth Army, the headquarters element in MacArthur's amphibious assault force. The men adopted the nickname "Wolf Pack" after learning the signature wolf call used by the Dutch crew that carried them across the Pacific.[6]

When the Forty-Fourth Tank Battalion came ashore in Dutch New Guinea, Indonesian nationalists were battling Japanese forces for control of the island. Van Winkle noted in a letter to his family that the native islanders were "very, very efficient as scouts and soldiers. They speak a pidgeon English very simple to learn, are wonderful in the jungle, make good pack carriers and are actually very smart people."[7] As the locals fought, so did the Americans. All four companies in the battalion saw action in close combat support with various infantry units on New Guinea and the many islands off the Filipino coast. As preparations were being made for a large-scale invasion of Leyte Island, Van Winkle's Company A was reorganized under the command of Col. William J. Verbeck's Twenty-First Infantry Regiment.

As Van Winkle and his men advanced from island to island, he found time to write to his father. Despite the conditions and arduous duty, amazingly, he made a point to stay abreast of Stitzel-Weller and whiskey industry happenings. He promised Pappy that he "spent almost all day yesterday going over the Stitzel-Weller August statement," which he noted "certainly looked good despite the vast decrease in some of the accounts." Captain Van Winkle also asked about rising taxes, the distillery's efforts to provide alcohol to the War Department, and whether their Old Fitzgerald Bourbon was "finally on sale in L.A."[8]

Throughout the summer and fall months of 1944, torrential rain battered Captain Van Winkle and his men. Still he wrote, and he remained optimistic: "Dear Dad, we have a steady rain for three nights and two days. Sometimes so hard that it wakes you up. . . . This is real adventure dad, an A-1 high-class fiction material and I only wish I could tell you all the things I know about the projected plan. It is fascinating of course and an undertaking of the greatest magnitude. It has undoubtedly been in the works for months although I understand the schedule has been stepped up considerably. We are all totally sure that it will be another MacArthur success."[9]

The main assault on Leyte finally began on October 17, 1944. The U.S. Navy's Third Fleet engaged Japanese forces in an effort to secure a beachhead for Krueger's Sixth Army. The naval battle in Leyte Gulf lasted four days and is still considered to be the largest naval engagement in human history. When General MacArthur waded ashore, he announced, "People of the Philippines, I have returned!"[10] Behind him was an amphibious attack force consisting of four divisions, a ranger infantry battalion, and the Fifth Air Force—more than 320,000 warriors. Naval assets provided indirect fire support from Leyte Gulf.

Van Winkle's tank company landed on Leyte Island on October 20 on a mission to clear a path for Colonel Verbeck's dismounted infantrymen. When Company A hit the beach on Leyte, thousands of rockets were streaming from ships offshore pounding enemy positions.[11] From that first day, it was grim, savage combat, often hand to hand, up and down slick, muddy ravines and rainswept valleys. Sometimes the Americans attacked, sometimes the Japanese, with the struggle sweeping back and forth and in and around the spurs and ridges until it was hard to tell front line from rear, Japanese position from American.[12]

Despite the mid-November typhoon in the Philippines, Colonel Verbeck, a recipient of the Silver Star, four Bronze Stars, and two Purple Hearts, ordered a full frontal assault of the area known as Breakneck Ridge for its ugly, rugged terrain. Verbeck relentlessly attacked well-defended Japanese positions with mortars, tanks, and maneuvering infantrymen. The Americans attacked despite pounding rain, high winds, falling trees, mudslides, and intense Japanese resistance. There was courage, determination, pain, and dying on both sides. For ten days, Breakneck Ridge saw some of the bitterest fighting of the campaign. During the battle, Captain Van Winkle and his men destroyed at least twenty-five Japanese machine gun positions.

Colonel Verbeck directed Van Winkle's Company A to punch through Japanese positions on the ridge to clear a way for his infantry battalions behind it, although the conditions made the task impossible. According to official reports, tanks became bogged down on steep, slippery heights. Even on more level terrain the going was often too muddy for the heavy vehicles. Rifleman had to guard the tanks on all sides. Otherwise, the Japanese would rush from concealment to slap magnetic mines, grenades, or other demolitions against the vulnerable tracks on the tanks. One of Captain Van Winkle's tanks got stuck when it went off the edge of a road. Another crew came to fire a 75-mm shell into the stalled tank vehicle to prevent its use by the Japanese.[13]

During the third week of the assault, Captain Van Winkle earned his Purple Heart. According to a corporal in his company, the gung-ho Captain Van Winkle exited the safety of his tank,[14] appropriately named *Old Fitz* for Stitzel-Weller's most popular whiskey, and "personally directed [his company's] operations under heavy fire."[15] Captain Van Winkle "was standing there, with his M1 rifle in his left hand. His right hand was on his hip. A sniper hit him on his right hand, the bullet going through his side and out his back."[16] Van Winkle's tankers heard him scream, "Damn, that stings!" The men were unable to get to him, as they were busy firing at the sniper. By the time they did get to him, he was sitting on a water can. The company fought on without its commander for six days until it finally cleared a way for Colonel Verbeck's First Battalion.

On November 18, 1944, the Forty-Fourth Tank Battalion's commander, Lt. Col. Thomas Ross, persuaded Van Winkle to move to a medical aid station in Dutch New Guinea. Ross also offered to send Van Winkle back to the United States, an opportunity he declined. In a journal entry, a restless Van Winkle reflected, "the thought of the boys banging away without me running the show is unbearable. I have not made many regrettable mistakes in my life but getting shot was certainly one of them."[17] Lieutenant Colonel Ross appointed Captain Van Winkle the battalion's "acting intelligence officer," a position he begrudgingly held on paper for several months while in recovery.[18]

In a letter to his father, Captain Van Winkle wrote from Dutch New Guinea, "You asked why I was not in my tank. I can only say that there are times when reconnaissance must be made on foot before planning the next move. Tanks have some limitations in this respect when on questionable terrain. Naturally I try to do this work on foot only when necessary and that goes double in the future. After all, infantry are always on foot so that makes us 95% safer than they are. . . . Next time I'll be an 'old soldier' and my job will be tempered by old man experience."[19] Pappy had reason to doubt his son's promise to be more cautious. According to First Sgt. "Red" Cartier, Captain Van Winkle "was a doer. . . . He felt the faster we hit them, and with everything we had, the faster this war was going to be over with."[20]

Throughout his recovery, Van Winkle shuddered at the notion of being sent home or stuck on the battalion staff. He adored his men and knew he belonged with them in the field. He recorded his emotions in a journal entry on January 10, 1945, the day after his men participated in S-Day, the amphibious invasion of Luzon, writing, "What a terrific attachment one gets to a group of men and an organization. The pride that it gives a man to be a leader of men is tremendous. They depend on you. Conway [the surgeon] will decide on me tomorrow. I have died a thousand deaths for fear I'll go to the states. I will go to any length to remain here."[21]

Tragically, during Van Winkle's recovery, his temporary replacement was killed in action. The highly respected Lt. Leo Frederick Reinartz Jr. was killed on Leyte just nine days after Captain Van Winkle was wounded. During an advance, Reinartz exited his tank in an effort to warn other American tankers about a Japanese ambush. As he ran, artillery rounds exploded behind him. Fragments struck his back and ended his young life.[22] He was awarded the nation's second-highest award for valor, the Distinguished Service Cross, for his bravery. Reinartz was the first commissioned officer in the battalion to be killed in action, but he was not the last. The battalion ultimately lost thirty-two men, including the Wolf Pack commander himself. Lt. Col. Tom Ross was cut down by Japanese rifle fire on the first day of February 1945 on the island of Luzon.[23]

When the recovering Captain Van Winkle learned that Lieutenant Colonel Ross had been killed in action, he took a flight from New Guinea to Dagupan Airfield in the Philippines and hitchhiked south on the island of Luzon, intent on regaining command of his men.[24] He rejoined Company A just in time to take part in MacArthur's main invasion of Manila. Van Winkle and his tankers were some of the first Americans to enter the capital city, where undersupplied but fanatical Japanese soldiers lay in wait among a massive civilian population.

On February 3, 1945, at 4:00 a.m., the reenergized Captain Van Winkle was ordered to push into Manila and destroy any Japanese fighting positions along the route. His company was about a half mile behind the tip of a "flying column" of tanks consisting mostly of First Cavalry Division units. "Buildings and Jap trucks were burning all along the way," he wrote to his wife, Katie.[25] Just before dark, the men made their way into the outskirts of the city as elements of the column fought near the Bilibid Prison, where nearly one thousand prisoners of war were held captive.

On February 4, the Forty-Fourth Tank Battalion arrived at Santo Tomas University in Manila, where several thousand civilians, most of them Americans, had been interned since 1942. Several miles west of the university, other American tank units liberated prisoners of war who had suffered through the Bataan Death March.

As Captain Van Winkle observed, "on one side there was still a fight going on . . . and in front of the main dormitory, people were singing and shouting and doing everything possible to express their joy at their deliverance."[26] Van Winkle noted that the people were pitiful and emaciated. "For the past six months, their rations had been systematically reduced until they were dying at the rate of six a day. They were rationed only 700 calories (mostly rice) per day and many have said that in another 30 days half would have been dead."[27]

On February 5, Captain Van Winkle's men exchanged pot shots with a group of fifty Japanese soldiers near the Education Building at Santo Tomas University, but the engagement was short. Japanese lieutenant colonel Toshio Hayashi agreed to release his hostages and was allowed to rejoin Japanese troops to the south of Manila, carrying only individual arms. The Japanese soldiers were unaware the area they requested was the now American-occupied Malacañan Palace, and when they arrived, they were fired upon and several were killed, including Hayashi.

On February 6, General MacArthur announced that Manila had fallen. Sporadic fighting continued for several weeks, but by March 1945, it was clear that MacArthur had made good on his promise to return. American forces on Luzon had control of all of the island's economically and strategically important locations. Japanese losses in the Philippines totaled 205,535 dead compared to 8,310 Americans killed.[28] For his wounds and heroic actions, Pappy's son was awarded the Purple Heart and Silver Star Medal, the nation's third-highest award for valor. In a letter to his father, Van Winkle reflected on his experience: "Perhaps it is almost justice dad that we should have to go through war every so often to pay for the peace years—so filled with plenty and pleasure as compared with the other people on the earth. That sounds harsh but it is true that war brings forth in people a certain vitality, spirit and a mettle that lies dormant in the serene years."[29]

Several months later following the Japanese surrender, a U.S. Military Commission convened in Manila to try Japanese general Tomoyuki Yamashita for war crimes. Yamashita had commanded the Japanese Imperial Army's Fourteenth Group on Leyte and was charged with "permitting his men to commit brutal atrocities and other high crimes against people of the United States and of its allies."[30]

One of the American generals appointed to the commission was Maj. Gen. James A. Lester, a 1915 West Point graduate and World War I veteran. General Lester spent a total of six years in the Pacific and directed forces against Yamashita, "the Butcher of the Philippines," while in command of the Twenty-Fourth Infantry Division. At a break in the proceedings, which continued for two months, General Lester looked down at General Yamashita and asked, "When did the Japanese lose the war?"

According to Lester, the accused Japanese officer turned to him and replied, "the War of Japan was lost in the Campaign of the Philippines, and the Campaign of the Philippines was lost in the Battle of Leyte, and the Battle of Leyte was lost in the skirmish on Breakneck Ridge."[31]

In late 1945, Julian P. Van Winkle Jr. finally returned to his old Kentucky home, where he rejoined Pappy at Stitzel-Weller. Pappy hired Charles "King" McClure when Julian Jr. left for the Pacific to handle sales and marketing operations. When Julian Jr. returned from the war, he immediately went back to work as Stitzel-Weller's vice president (with King as secretary-treasurer). Together, they were known as "The Father, the Son, and the Holy Ghost."[32] Stitzel-Weller was fully operational once again.

One of Van Winkle's first moves as vice president was to hire two army buddies, Robert E. "Bob" Lee and Ivan Parks. Van Winkle spotted the proud southerner Lee selling used cars in Tupelo and immediately hired him. Parks had been Van Winkle's aide in the Philippines and quickly became one of Stitzel-Weller's top salesmen. While Parks, who was also wounded in action, spent many days among the Van Winkle family during those years, the topic of war rarely came up.

Stitzel-Weller also hired Norman Hayden, a veteran of the U.S. Air Force Training Command, who joined the company to do odd jobs like babysit Julian's young children, drive Pappy to and from work, and even take King's dog out. Hayden ultimately stayed at Stitzel-Weller / Old Fitzgerald for forty-four years, becoming its plant manager. Hayden was notorious for drinking his bourbon uncut and unfiltered, a habit that was well before its time.

Throughout the post-WWII years, Julian Jr. worked for and learned everything he could from Pappy, overseeing production and sales of Old Fitzgerald, Belle of Bourbon, Cabin Still, Cascade, Old W. L. Weller, Old Elk, and Rebel Yell. After the war, Stitzel-Weller opened for tours so the public could watch master distiller Will McGill turn corn, wheat, and malted barley into unfinished bourbon whiskey. The whiskey would rest in thicker-than-average oak barrels for as long as it took to fully mature. Head cooper George Durkalski, a World War II veteran himself, constructed, charred, and repaired the barrels and managed warehouse operations.[33] He "was a man of patience, thoroughness, and pride."[34]

Bourbon business boomed in the postwar years. Stitzel-Weller expanded from twelve to nineteen warehouses to accommodate increased production. Whereas other distilleries diluted products to 90 and 80 proof to fulfill demand, the Van Winkles continued to bottle 100 and 107 proof bourbon. Pappy believed strongly that Stitzel-Weller should make a premium product and keep it in short supply. They notably sold cases of Old Fitzgerald to other war veterans named Eisenhower and Kennedy, who preferred it to any other whiskey.[35] They operated pursuant to the philosophy "We make fine bourbon at a profit if we can, at a loss if we must, but always fine bourbon."

Following Pappy's retirement in 1964, Julian Jr. was anointed the president of the company his father had joined as a nineteen-year-old salesman. He served as president of Stitzel-Weller for eight more years but "would never ask anyone to do anything he wouldn't do himself."[36] According to Norman Hayden, Julian Jr. "operated like he was still a tank commander."[37] During his time as the company president, Van Winkle kept himself in shape. "He did Army exercises every morning, jumping jacks, and bicycle, and sit-ups. . . . Whenever he was feeling particularly in need of space and sweat, he'd call up one of his buddies, and they'd go out in the woods near the house and chop trees. You could hear them out there-whooping and hollering and laughing— telling stories."[38]

During Julian Van Winkle Jr.'s tenure as president, Stitzel-Weller produced expressions of Old Fitzgerald that men still dream about. One U.S. marine named Bill Cowern recently recalled,

> In 1967–1968, I was a Marine helicopter pilot in northern I Corps, South Vietnam. I was fortunate enough to get R&R to Hawaii in February of '68, to meet up with my wife. On the flight back to Vietnam, we stopped to refuel in Guam and I bought a bottle of Very Old Fitzgerald for $15 or $20 in the duty free shop there on base. I had always remembered it as being labeled 25 years old but it could be that 50 years has dulled that memory. Regardless when I returned to the base I was assigned to, in Dong Ha, I opened the bottle when we were under mortar attack one night and could not believe what a smooth soothing whiskey it was. Like nothing I had ever tried before, or since. We had slit trenches under our wooden hooches and trap doors in the floors to allow us to be below ground during attacks. It became a routine for four of us that we would have a half jigger of the bourbon whenever we were under attack. After a while we used to joke about how we wished they would attack. The bottle lasted about one month, but I, obviously, have never forgotten it.[39]

Unfortunately, by that time, bourbon's popularity leveled off in the United States. Times were tough for most distilleries, as expenses rose and sales declined nationwide. Many distilleries began lowering the proof of their products or merging with companies that produced other types of alcohol. Even Stitzel-Weller, in an effort to adapt, released an

86.8 proof Old Fitzgerald bourbon. The company also moved away from bulk sales and toward selling bourbon by the case, but it did not help.

In the summer of 1972, at the behest of other stockholders within the family, Stitzel-Weller Distilling Company was sold to the Norton Simon Company for $19.5 million.[40] Stitzel-Weller was renamed Old Fitzgerald. It was such a difficult time for Van Winkle that he could not bear to talk about it. But Julian Van Winkle Jr. was not finished. He subsequently created a company called J. P. Van Winkle and Son, and began independently selling bourbon in porcelain decanters. He created the Old Rip Van Winkle brand, contracted to buy Stitzel-Weller whiskey, and bottled it himself.[41] He kept the business alive primarily in the hopes that his son, Julian III, would join the family business. In 1977, Julian Van Winkle III did join his father, but their time together was short. Van Winkle Jr. died on a cold November night in 1981 after a short battle with cancer. He was sixty-seven years old. His coffin was covered with a large American flag, a small recognition of heroic service at Breakneck Ridge, an experience he rarely discussed.

11

Elmer Tandy Lee and James B. Johnson Jr.

War is hell, but it is double hell in the skies.

Gen. Frank Armstrong to the officers and men of the 315th Bomb Wing upon his assumption of command at Fairmont Army Airfield, 1944

Elmer Tandy Lee was born near Frankfort, Kentucky, in 1919. He joined the U.S. Army Air Corps in December 1941, commissioned as a B-29 radarman, and deployed to the island of Guam in the spring of 1945. While stationed on Guam, Lee participated in several vital bombing missions against Japanese military infrastructure. James B. "Jimmy" Johnson Jr. was also born in Frankfort, Kentucky, in February 1916. In October 1943, he left his position as a "warehouse yard person" at the George T. Stagg Distillery to enlist in the U.S. Army. He also served on the island of Guam as part of an all–African American aviation engineer battalion that built airfields for B-29 crews. After the war, Lee and Johnson returned to the United States and went to work at the George T. Stagg Distillery. They stayed for more than thirty years. Lee, who became the master distiller, is widely recognized as the man who saved the bourbon industry from near demise in the 1980s by developing the original single-barrel bourbon with Johnson's expert assistance.

In the years leading up to World War II, the U.S. Army Air Corps sought intelligent company-grade officers to serve as pilots, navigators, flight engineers, bombardiers, and radarman aboard B-29 Superfortresses. While noncommissioned officers were eligible to fill some of the positions, senior leaders within the War Department thought it more appropriate that specially trained commissioned officers operate the state-of-the-art technology in the B-29.[1] The Superfortress was a four-engine, propeller-driven heavy bomber developed in the late 1930s by Boeing. It featured a pressurized cabin, a computer-operated fire control system, and four machine gun turrets that could be operated by a single gunner. Additionally, some B-29s were outfitted with advanced radar systems, like the AN / APQ-7 Eagle radar, an all-seeing eye in the sky. Throughout the war in the Pacific, several thousand lieutenants from across the U.S. Army Air Corps were screened and selected to operate these advanced systems from above, identifying targets and directing payloads to the enemy, especially the Japanese. One of those lieutenants was Elmer Tandy Lee.

Lee was born on a tobacco farm near Peaks Mills, Kentucky, in 1919 to Ernest Franklin and Ann Shields Lee. He was a child of the Great Depression and recalled growing up with few material things. Despite dire financial straits for the Lees, and most families in 1930s Frankfort, he enjoyed a happy childhood playing outdoors, hiking, riding his bicycle to school, swimming, and playing baseball each summer. In 1936, Lee graduated from Frankfort High School and secured a job at the Jarman Shoe Company factory, where he oversaw the manufacturing of men's dress shoes.[2]

In 1938, Lee enrolled in the University of Kentucky's School of Engineering part-time, but the drumbeats of war echoed in the distance. By 1940, Americans were preparing for a possible war against the Axis. Lee's employer submitted a bid to produce boots and shoes for the military. Jarman's annual report from that October announced "the company, of course, holds itself in readiness to handle any possible requests from the Army."[3] The same report also reflected deep concern that a draft would deplete its relatively young workforce.

On November 26, 1941, while Elmer Lee was working at the Jarman factory, the Japanese carrier strike force *Kido Butai* set sail from Hitto-kapu Bay, arriving in Hawaiian waters on Sunday, December 7, 1941. Around 8 a.m. Hawaiian time, the first wave of attacks was directed on the U.S. Pacific Fleet based at Pearl Harbor and on outlying airfields. By the end of the day, 21 American ships were either sunk or crippled, 188 aircraft were destroyed, and over 3,500 American personnel were killed or wounded in action.[4] Japan followed with a formal declaration of war.

Like many of his peers, Lee enlisted before the month of December 1941 came to a conclusion. The soft-spoken Kentuckian explained, "I just went before I was drafted. That way I got to select the service that I wanted to go in which was the Air Force. At that time they called it the Army Air Corps. . . . I went through several school and training sessions before I wound up going overseas to Guam on a B-29 crew to bomb Japan."[5]

Lieutenant Lee's initial training included "operational and nav-igational weather, radar, group intelligence functions, briefing and interrogation, minelaying procedures, and bombardment" and occurred at several locations across the continental United States.[6] For the grad-uates of the 315th Wing training program, the reward was an immense amount of personal pride in being a member of an elite B-29 Superfor-tress outfit. When Second Lieutenant Lee graduated from the rigorous B-29 program, he was selected to serve as a radarman for the 315th Bombardment Wing's 16th Bombardment Group. The news media and the Army Air Corps repeatedly heralded "Very Heavy" B-29 units like Lee's.[7]

In the autumn of 1944, the men and officers of the 16th Bomb Group reported to Fairmont Army Airfield in Nebraska for a massive training exercise. "We were there for work and we worked hard. Ask any line man shivering from the sub-zero winds sweeping across the flat plains of Nebraska while he was trying to work on a B-29," remembered Preston Crans, a 16th Bomb Group veteran. On December 7, 1944, the unit received its official colors and standards.[8] Col. Samuel Gurney accepted the colors on behalf of Lee's group, which received deployment orders for overseas movement to the Pacific theater of operations on

December 22, almost three years to the day after Lee signed his enlistment contract. Between March and May 1945, the 16th Bomb Group's Flight Echelon followed a route from Sacramento to Oahu to Kwajelein to Guam, where mostly African American aviation engineer battalions worked feverishly to complete construction of Northwest Field, aircraft hangars, and living facilities for the crews.

When asked whether he was "scared at all" upon arriving on Guam, Lee stated, "Oh, yes, everybody's scared that's in the service in harm's way. If they tell you they're not scared, they're not being truthful."[9] Men dealt with the natural fear by talking and drinking. They discussed airplanes, war, Japan, women, and good whiskey. They drank rationed beer and whiskey smuggled in from home or sent by family members.[10] Not long after arriving, Lee and his crew were tasked to fly a series of missions from Northwest Field to destroy oil refineries and petroleum production facilities in Utsube and Kudamatsu, Japan. On some missions, the enemy was nonexistent, while on others anti-aircraft batteries littered the skies.

Hundreds of Superfortresses attacked Japan "again and again day and night, week after week, month after month."[11] B-29 crews dropped incendiary bombs, ignited the hottest fires to ever burn on earth, and they killed one hundred thousand people. Whenever there was weather in the skies, radarman Elmer T. Lee would take over the job of dropping bombs from his crew's bombardier. Only two months after Lee's crew began its air campaign against Japanese oil production facilities, however, another B-29 crew from nearby Tinian Island took off bound for Japan. On August 6 at 8:15 a.m. Hiroshima time, a nuclear bomb known as "Little Boy" was released from the aircraft. A minute later, it detonated.

The great destruction of the atomic attack on Hiroshima and the second in Nagasaki did not immediately spur Japan to surrender. On August 14, 1945, subsequent American bomber attacks were ordered. Hundreds of B-29s from Guam, Saipan, and Tinian, loaded with powerful Torpex bombs, delivered the last attacks of the war over the city of Koromo. The Japanese surrendered unconditionally the next day. Elmer Lee returned home to Kentucky and was honorably discharged from the U.S. Army Air Corps in January 1946.

When he returned from Guam, Lee enrolled full-time at the University of Kentucky and used the GI Bill to complete a bachelor's degree in chemical engineering. When he graduated in 1949, Lee inquired about an engineering position at the George T. Stagg Distillery near his home in Frankfort. That fall, he walked into the distillery and met with plant superintendent Orville Schupp, who was optimistic about the young veteran's chances. The distillery's president at the time, Col. Albert Bacon Blanton, however, spoke briefly with Schupp and turned Lee down. "Son, we're not hiring any hands today," he told the company's future master distiller.[12] With Schupp's encouragement, Lee showed up for work the next Monday anyway and stayed for thirty-five years.

Between 1949 and the mid-1960s, Elmer Lee advanced from plant engineer to plant superintendent and eventually plant manager and master distiller. In his early years at the Stagg Distillery, Lee recalled, it was a "booming operation" that employed nearly 250 people.[13] One of those employees was James B. "Jimmy" Johnson Jr.

Johnson Jr. was born on Leestown Road in Frankfort in 1916. He started working alongside his father, James, the well-respected foreman at the Stagg Distillery, in 1936. Before the war, Johnson was a "warehouse yard person," responsible for plugging leaky bourbon barrels and hauling aged barrels to be dumped for bottling, but in October 1943, he left his job to enlist in the segregated U.S. Army.[14]

Twenty-seven-year-old Johnson Jr. left the distillery to follow his cousin Jack's lead and enlisted as a construction technician. He completed enlistment paperwork at the Fort Benjamin Harrison Reception site in Indiana and immediately shipped to Chanute Field in Illinois for six weeks of basic training. Fortunately for Johnson and other distillery workers who left for military service, the Schenley Distillers Corporation, which purchased the Stagg Distillery in 1929, kept many men who enlisted on the payroll for the duration of the war.[15] Johnson drew a week's pay from the company every month he spent in the army, an unusual benefit for an African American man during WWII.[16]

In the winter of 1944, Johnson completed technical training and was assigned to an aviation engineer battalion. He received deployment orders to Guam with a mission to clear extremely thick vegetation and build runways for B-29 bomber crews. He arrived on Guam June 20, 1945, just a month after the island's Northwest Field opened to Lt. Elmer T. Lee and B-29 crews from the 315th Bombardment Wing.[17] Johnson and fellow construction soldiers immediately went to work, day and night, to complete a second airstrip and the administrative buildings around it.

Johnson and his men hauled rocks, dug ditches, laid culverts, erected bridges, cleared bamboo jungles, and fought erosion. Johnson and other men assigned to construct airfields in the Pacific worked in jungles and on mountains, through monsoon rains and alternating heat and cold, and often without the equipment they deserved. The work of the 823rd Aviation Engineer Battalion, for example, was hampered by the fact that its six bulldozers, the only available machines with sufficient power and traction to clear the jungle, arrived without blades. The engineers borrowed a single blade from a nearby British unit until theirs were delivered five months later. In addition to the expected dangers and challenges of working in a jungle combat zone, African American units faced the difficulties of segregation, substandard living and recreational facilities, and suspicion or outright hostility from other units.[18]

After work was completed on Guam's second airfield, the bombing campaign accelerated. In the summer of 1945, Johnson was promoted to technician fifth class (referred to as corporal) and was transferred briefly to the island of Okinawa. He was tasked to guard Japanese prisoners of war who were captured on Guam during the initial invasion. Johnson stood guard as a sentry at a temporary prisoner of war camp. In 2008, at the age of ninety-two, Jimmy Johnson recalled how he treated the Japanese POWs well, although, with a laugh, he noted he had to guard them "with an empty gun." The prisoners gave him improvised artwork as a sign of their appreciation for his fair treatment. "They went back and tore up a sheet . . . and there was one in the bunch that was an extremely good drawer, and he drew something on that sheet pertaining to Japan. . . . Where they needed something green, they got green grass, if they needed tan, they got tan coffee stains, needed some black, they got black coal dust. And they were natural beauties, and I carried them home."[19] While Johnson was guarding POWs on

Okinawa, "Little Boy" was released over Hiroshima. Corporal Johnson sailed home on March 14, 1946. He was honorably discharged on April 1, 1946, at Camp Atterbury, Indiana.

After the war, Johnson immediately regained his job in the Stagg Distillery warehouses alongside his father, from whom he learned to understand the effects different warehouses had on barrels of aging whiskey. As a "leak hunter / stopper," he mastered the ability to repair leaking or damaged barrels while the whiskey remained inside, a very valuable skill. While Johnson was hunting for and plugging leaky barrels in the warehouses, new engineer Elmer Lee was rotating through different distillery operations under the tutelage of Kentucky Bourbon Hall of Fame distiller Albert Geiser, learning how to manage the warehouse, the bottling facility, and the front office. Lee, who always drank bourbon in moderation, grew to respect and love the product and built strong relationships with his fellow distillery employees, like the Johnson men.

In his first ten years at the distillery, the whiskey industry had to reinvent itself. The George T. Stagg Distillery had been in the business of making medicinal whiskey and industrial alcohol for decades by the time Elmer Lee and Jimmy Johnson returned from Guam. In the 1950s, high demand for beverage alcohol led to major changes across the industry. The Stagg Distillery constructed a huge new still house complex and boiler house. It demolished many of its pre-Prohibition buildings to make room for new, modern warehouses. Lee and Johnson were present for the distillery's transition from railroad to truck transport. They were there to celebrate Colonel Blanton's retirement in November 1952, and they helped roll out the two-millionth barrel of whiskey produced at the distillery since repeal in 1953. The distillery featured several popular bourbon brands like Ancient Age, Echo Springs, Cream of Kentucky, Old Stagg, Carlisle, Three Feathers, and Buffalo Springs.[20] Lee and Johnson were mainstays at the distillery, helping to produce and roll out the three-, four-, and five-millionth barrels made since repeal in 1961, 1971, and 1981, respectively.[21]

Unfortunately, however, by the late 1970s, bourbon was in serious decline. During the Vietnam War, younger American drinkers rejected bourbon whiskey and replaced it with clear spirits like vodka, gin, and tequila. Between 1973 and 1975, more than one hundred American whiskey brands reduced the proof of their products from 86 to 80 and some began advertising "light whiskey" to appease the changing market.[22] In 1976, two hundred years after whiskey replaced rum as the nation's beverage of choice, vodka caught and surpassed whiskey in sales.[23] In 1979, Hiram Walker closed its one-thousand-employee distillery in Peoria, Illinois, and in 1983, the last Maryland rye whiskey distillery shut its doors.[24] Many of the employees were Vietnam veterans and suddenly unemployed. According to Elmer Lee, by the early 1980s, business was going "downhill fast."[25]

In late December 1982, the distillery property and one brand, Ancient Age, were sold to the Ancient Age Distilling Company. After the sale, well-known executives Ferdie Falk and Robert Baranaskas approached Elmer T. Lee in desperate need of a winner. Bourbon whiskey's sales, and its standing in American society, were continuing to plummet, but Falk and Baranaskas, a former U.S. Army drill sergeant, "knew how to make a buck."[26] The men wisely put their trust in the aging master distiller when they asked him to develop something novel. Lee, Falk, and Baranaskas considered all of the Japanese auto executives who purchased the most expensive whiskeys on business trips to Kentucky. They chose to reject the industry trend of weaker whiskey and developed an unfiltered, premium brand for the booming foreign whiskey market, where single-malt Scotch whiskys were performing well.

Instead of blending barrels, Lee began filling bottles with bourbon dumped from the highest-quality single barrels in the metal Warehouse H. Warehouse H, constructed after repeal in order to age whiskey faster, got warmer during the summer days than did traditional wooden warehouses and was steam-heated during the winter, further aiding the bourbon's maturation in the wood.

From single barrels selected from Warehouse H, Elmer Lee created Blanton's: The Original Single-Barrel Bourbon, in 1983. Very quickly, Blanton's popularity spread at home and in export markets like the United Kingdom and Japan. As hoped, Lee's former enemies happily paid top dollar for his "single-barrel" bourbon whiskey, and as other super-premium bourbons came to market, Kentucky distilleries regained their glory, and their financial investment in the product.

In what one author called "the whiskey equivalent of a Hail Mary pass," the World War II veteran Elmer T. Lee won the bet that single-barrel whiskey would reverse bourbon's downward spiral.[27] Falk and Baranaskas went on to create other single-barrel bourbons like Rock Hill Farms and Elmer T. Lee in honor of their master distiller. When other distilleries took note of Blanton's success, they moved to imitate it with other "super-premium" releases. Inspired by Lee, Jim Beam master distiller Booker Noe introduced "small-batch" bourbons like Knob Creek, Basil Hayden's, Booker's, and Baker's. Brown-Forman's master distiller Lincoln Henderson introduced the elegantly packaged Woodford Reserve. In relatively short order, Lee's emphasis on high quality pulled the bourbon industry out of its darkest days and into the renaissance of today.

Encouraged by the success of Blanton's, the Sazerac Company of New Orleans purchased the plant in 1992 and changed its name to Buffalo Trace Distillery in 1999. After Elmer Lee retired from his position as the Buffalo Trace Distillery master distiller, he continued to visit the distillery to taste and select the best barrels for the increasingly popular Elmer T. Lee single-barrel bourbon brand and to meet with old colleagues and friends. Former Buffalo Trace general manager Richard Wolf fondly remembers sitting with Elmer and listening to him share his encyclopedic knowledge of the distillery and its history. Mr. Wolf, who served as a U.S. Marines artillery officer in the 1980s, recalled climbing to the top of the stillhouse with Elmer, who suffered from emphysema in his older age. Despite losing his breath with each flight of metal stairs, Elmer insisted on making the ascent so he could enjoy the view and share a story. "He was a great distiller and man," Wolf recalled. "He remembered everyone's name and cared deeply about the work they did."[28] Elmer Lee died on July 16, 2013, at the age of ninety-three. To honor him, Buffalo Trace Distillery released a commemorative 93 proof single-barrel bourbon and donated the profits to Lee's local Veterans of Foreign Wars Post #4075 in Frankfort, Kentucky.

Johnson officially retired from the distillery in 1978, but he remained active at the distillery, coming back in 2008 to roll out the six-millionth barrel produced since Prohibition ended. In 2009, the Buffalo Trace Distillery dedicated the James B. Johnson Jr. Room, located within the employee clubhouse. In 2011, Jimmy B. Johnson Jr. died after a battle with cancer. To fulfill a promise, his son Freddie Johnson left a position at AT&T to carry on the family tradition of work at the distillery. Freddie is now a cherished tour guide at Buffalo Trace, the distillery he played behind as a child with his grandfather and father.

12

Richard J. Newman

Well, they say you never hear the one that hits you, and it's true. The next thing I knew, I was in a field hospital behind the lines.

Dick Newman

Richard J. Newman was born in St. Louis, Missouri, in 1932. He served as a private first class in the First Marine Division's Recon Company during the Korean War. He was badly injured in the frigid winter of 1953, when a Chinese mortar explosion shredded his leg, leading to its amputation below the knee. After recovering and leaving the Marine Corps, Newman used the GI Bill to attend the University of Pennsylvania. He entered the liquor industry and rose through the ranks of Austin Nichols Distilling Co. and the Buckingham Corporation. In retirement, Newman helped revitalize the historic brand Michter's with Joe Magliocco of Chatham Imports.

Following the Second World War, defeated Japan was forced out of the Korean peninsula, a territory it had governed since the early twentieth century. In August 1945, American military officers arbitrarily divided the Korean peninsula at the 38th parallel. At a conference in

December 1945, the Soviet Union agreed to administer governance north of the line while the U.S. Army Military Government in Korea agreed to administer the territory south. The newly created United Nations facilitated Korean elections in the summer of 1948, but the Soviets and North Koreans rejected their legitimacy. By the fall of 1948, North Koreans established their own government amid rising tension and sporadic violence.

Inspired and armed by the Soviet Union and China, the North Koreans set out to reunify the country under communist rule. Top Chinese and Russian leaders agreed to provide North Korea with training, troops, and all the mechanized and infantry equipment needed to stage a largely unprovoked war with South Korea. On the night of June 24, 1950, ninety thousand North Korean troops assembled at the border, prepared for battle. At dawn, a heavy artillery bombardment began, followed by an invasion of tank-led troops.[1]

In speaking with his National Security Council, President Harry S. Truman expressed the belief that "communism was acting in Korea, just as Hitler, Mussolini and the Japanese had ten, fifteen, and twenty years earlier."[2] The president was certain that if South Korea fell, Communist leaders would be emboldened to override nations closer to home. Truman believed he could intervene in Korea without provoking direct hostilities with Russia or undermining America's commitments elsewhere. Thus, by the end of June 1950, the bourbon-drinking commander in chief deployed air and naval forces to support the South Korean government.[3]

From the very onset of hostilities U.S. Marines participated in some of the most intense fighting of the war, defined by amphibious assaults, violent patrols, and constant shelling. Gen. Douglas MacArthur deployed the First Marine Division to slip behind enemy lines and invade Inchon. Marines from the First Reconnaissance Company were tasked to maneuver through no-man's-land into enemy territory, specifically to gather intelligence about North Korean People's Army and Chinese Communist forces. In so doing, the marines collected vital information about enemy locations, strengths, and troop movements, ambushing specific areas and taking prisoners for interrogation. Their work came at a bloody cost.[4]

Throughout the "Forgotten War," indirect fire inflicted heavy marine casualties. If a marine stayed in Korea long enough, the odds were he would get hit. On January 15, 1953, U.S. Marine Corps private first class Richard "Dick" Newman was firing his Browning automatic rifle on a North Korean hill when a Chinese mortar round exploded behind him and destroyed his leg. Shrapnel mashed his arm and riddled his side and face. Newman eventually woke up on the hospital ship *Constellation*, shocked that he was missing his leg and angry that the doctors shaved his mustache to remove shrapnel from his lip.

Dick Newman was the son of a World War I veteran who warned him not to join the U.S. Marine Corps. He grew up comfortably in St. Louis, Missouri, and enjoyed a disorderly adolescence. When President Truman ordered U.S. forces to Korea, however, he ignored his father's warning and enlisted. Twenty-year-old Dick Newman "wasn't very gung-ho," but he and a friend decided that joining the marines was the "macho thing to do."[5] Newman reported to Parris Island, South Carolina, in early 1952, where he met his drill instructor, whom he considered a bona fide psychologist. On the first day of training, the drill instructor called a formation and announced, "Listen, you idiots, one of you clowns has the crabs. Never mind who. I am going to take you down to the delouser and each one of you is going to get his balls sprayed. And that's the way it's going to be for the next ten weeks. If one of you screws up, everyone is going to pay the price. Forget that individualistic bullshit. You jerks are going to act like a team. . . . Might save your life if you get to Korea."[6]

Fortunately, Newman graduated from basic training, and he never found out whether anyone actually had the crabs. When Private Newman reported to Camp Lejeune, North Carolina, he was assigned to the Second Marine Division's Reconnaissance Company, a newly created group of specialized scouts and marksmen. Newman and his fellow marines spent the next several months practicing grueling amphibious assaults on Virginia Beach and honing their marksmanship skills.

Newman hated the training regimen so intensely that he wrote to his congressman requesting to go overseas. Within weeks, his wish was granted, and he shipped to Camp Pendleton to await a flight to Korea.

While waiting on the West Coast, Newman and other replacement marines threw a party in San Diego, keenly aware of what awaited them overseas. The young men hung a sign from their hotel banner that said, "Welcome. Big Party. Come On Up as Long as You Are Female."[7] He recalled there being plenty of whiskey.

Shortly after his final night of revelry in California, Private Newman boarded a five-thousand-man ship headed for Japan. All around him, seasick men were vomiting, which inevitably caused other men to puke. "It was a treadmill going nowhere," he said.[8] When the vessel finally came ashore in Okinawa, Newman quickly found his way into town, where he met several women and a bottle of Canadian Club. He was late returning to the ship where the officer of the day noticed the suspicious bulge in his jacket. "Got any liquor?" the officer asked. "Hand it over, marine." "That was the end of my Canadian Club. I think the sonofabitch drank it himself," Newman lamented.[9]

Several days later, the ship landed at Inchon and Private Newman reported to the First Marine Division's Recon Company on the front lines. Things were far less formal than what Newman had become accustomed to in training. Recon marines all went by first names. The officers removed their insignia. The unit was all volunteers and full of foreign nationals motivated to fight communism. There were several refugees from Central Europe who had come to America after communists took over their native countries. The 144 men, of a dozen nationalities who spoke many languages, became known as the "Pocket Foreign Legion." They were disciplined combat veterans and full of the genuine camaraderie that the threat of death will quickly encourage. Newman recalled that the outstanding officers even shared their liquor with their marines between missions. Indeed, many marine officers and senior noncommissioned officers carried whiskey in their left canteens.[10] In frigid conditions, whiskey was sometimes the only liquid available.

Dick Newman saw his first combat action shortly after he joined the recon company in country. On Christmas Eve 1952, while they were out on a typical patrol, the enemy had their loudspeakers going full blast—all propaganda: "They'd play Christmas songs and tell [the marines] they'd all be going home in burial bags."[11] The patrol kept getting closer to the Chinese and then "wham, they opened up."[12] Men on both sides of Newman were hit. Newman later wrote that he "peed his pants," but he fired back with a grease gun doing the best job he could.[13] He was scared every moment, but he didn't want to let his buddies down. "It happens so fast you lose your perception of time. No matter how long it lasts, it's impossible to judge correctly the time that has elapsed during a firefight."[14]

Newman experienced several combat patrols in late December 1952 and early January 1953 as recon marines hunted the enemy in support of the Seventh Marine Division. Just a few months after his first firefight, Newman experienced his last. On January 15, 1953, Private First Class Newman donned his equipment for a routine patrol, but for reasons unknown to him, superior officers brought more men along than was normal. Cooks, bakers, clerks, "everyone who could walk" headed out in the daylight in a skirmish line.[15] U.S. pilots accompanied the patrol, bombing and strafing the Chinese with conventional ordnance and napalm. Not long after the mission commenced, a terrified Newman and several of his squad mates were pinned down in a ravine, but they followed orders when an officer yelled, "We're going up that hill!"[16]

Newman was carrying an automatic rifle in the cradle of his arm, firing it as he moved up toward the enemy. The last thing he remembers before the world went dark was the sound of mortars exploding. In a flash, Private First Class Dick Newman became one of the 523 Marines wounded or killed in Korea in the month of January 1953. Marine casualties that month alone included 42 KIA, 5 MIA, and 4 deaths from other causes.[17] In the same month, marines killed 694 enemy fighters and wounded 1,846 more; yet January 1953 was considered slow.

Months later, while recovering in the Oak Knoll Naval Hospital in Oakland, California, Newman met a friend who had been "clobbered by a land mine" during the mission.[18] His friend described what happened that day. It turned out the cooks, bakers, and clerks were along on patrol to be stretcher-bearers. There was one, a Polish kid from

Detroit named Leo Suchy, whom he had never gotten along with, who turned out to be the one guy to see him go down. No one wanted to leave the ravine they were cornered in, so Private Suchy picked up a rifle and yelled, "You better get up here and pick up Newman! If you don't, I'm going to open up on you!"[19] Dick Newman was dragged back to the ravine and put on a stretcher to be carried back a mile or so to the field hospital, and he never saw Suchy again.

Dick Newman lost his leg from the knee down, but he returned home intent on going back to school. As a disabled veteran, he qualified for the GI Bill, and graduated from the University of Pennsylvania with a bachelor's degree in business. Newman eventually married and landed a sales job with National Distillers & Chemical Corporation, where he managed distribution for several popular whiskey brands. As a young businessman, Newman was responsible for distributing Old Crow, Old Taylor, and Old Grand-Dad bourbons among several others. In the 1970s, when Jim Beam acquired National Distillers, Newman briefly went to work for the behemoth Seagram's. After proving his worth there, he was recruited to work for the Austin Nichols Distilling Company, where he managed the Wild Turkey bourbon portfolio.[20]

Thanks to Newman's creative and aggressive marketing efforts, Wild Turkey sales increased despite the downward trend in bourbon sales nationally. In April 1980, a twenty-pound wild turkey "just flew in" to the west lawn of the White House, puzzling National Park Service officers and President Jimmy Carter, an avid turkey hunter. The wild turkey spent several days stalking the executive grounds, even pecking the ground outside the Oval Office. While the president surmised that "the turkey may have been sent by the National Wild Turkey Federation," a group he met with several weeks earlier, members of the press had a strong hunch that "a certain Kentucky distiller which markets a certain product with a certain name" was behind the stunt.[21]

In New York, reporters pressed Dick Newman, who adamantly denied his company's involvement. Newman said, "I can state unequivocally that to the best of my knowledge neither our company nor its public-relations firm had anything to do with releasing the turkey on the White House lawn." Newman added that "wild turkeys should be maintained in their natural habitat, although it's lovely to see one on the White House lawn. . . . We're just delighted that it happened. . . . Ben Franklin wanted to make the wild turkey the national bird."[22] When the reporters left, he lit up a cigarette and laughed.

Later in 1980, Newman was hired to be the president and CEO of the historic Buckingham Corporation in New York. While at Buckingham, Newman oversaw the importing and distribution of Cutty Sark Scotch whisky, America's favorite Scotch at the time. Early in his tenure at Buckingham, Newman created a new marketing department and cleaned up "bloated inventories" of Cutty Sark. Newman "influenced his people to put in extra time and come up with new ideas," and he focused on building for the future.[23] In 1981, Buckingham saw a 300 percent increase in profit from the year before.[24] In November 1981, in a move that came as a shock to many, Buckingham was acquired by the Beatrice Company. In one of his first moves, Beatrice chairman James Dutt called Newman and asked him to stay with the company. Under Newman's leadership, profits continued to rise.

In 1984, however, Beatrice decided to get out of the liquor business and put Buckingham on the chopping block. The eventual buyer, Whitbread, merged Buckingham and Julius Wile Sons & Co., to form the Buckingham Wile Company. After the sale and merger, producers of two popular Buckingham accounts, Mouton Cadet Bordeaux and Finlandia (a vodka maker), defected to another distributor. Following the loss of their business, three quarters of the Buckingham staff was laid off. Newman was one of the few that stayed on, as executive vice president, but he soon left Buckingham Wile for a smaller consulting firm.

After ten years of full-time consulting, Dick Newman retired from his firm, but he was eager to stay busy. Newman continued to work with a small company that imported and distributed Angostura bitters and rum, among other items. When the importer Newman was advising went bankrupt, he found himself in serious need of an importer for a shipment of Angostura rum stuck on a barge in the Atlantic Ocean.

Newman called Joseph J. Magliocco, a young and talented Harvard educated attorney who had worked for former Four Roses executive R. C. Wells at his family's New York City liquor company, Chatham

Imports. After Magliocco agreed to import the rum on an emergency basis, Angostura hired Chatham to be its exclusive importer.[25]

Early in his career, Magliocco, who had managed Chatham's Michter's whiskey account for New York and Connecticut, grew to appreciate the Lebanon County rye whiskey crafted by Dick Stoll, a celebrated master distiller and former navy combat air crewman. It was a dark time for brown spirits, however. In February 1990, Michter's employees abandoned the historic Pennsylvania distillery, including approximately forty thousand barrels of straight whiskey. Some of the whiskey was redistilled into "gasohol," some of it was sold, and other barrels were stolen from the Schaefferstown warehouses.

Not long after, Newman and Magliocco, who developed a friendship, started "kicking around the idea" of resurrecting the historic Michter's brand.[26] Newman would often visit Chatham offices in New York, usually with a cigarette in his hand, to talk about potential business plans.

Around 1997, Magliocco purchased and registered the abandoned Michter's trademarks and prepared to revitalize the old brand he once marketed. He consulted his friend Dick Newman, who recommended that the "new" Michter's operate in Kentucky to take advantage of his strong network and resources available only in the commonwealth. Newman put Magliocco in touch with old friends at big distilleries to get the company off the ground. Magliocco and Newman visited the abandoned Old Crow and Old Taylor distilleries on McCracken Pike near Versailles, but ultimately decided on the construction of a new facility when the timing was right. Today, Magliocco's Louisville-based Michter's Distillery is producing its own whiskey and recently joined the Kentucky Distillers' Association as its newest Heritage Member.

When Dick Newman died of lung cancer several years later, Magliocco was surprised, not because it was completely unexpected—Newman was a heavy cigarette smoker for most of his life. Rather, it was because Dick Newman never complained. According to Magliocco, "He was always positive, always smiling. He was just a really good guy, a born gentleman."[27]

13

Thomas E. Bulleit Jr.

The thing I am most proud of in my life—other than being a husband and a father—is my service as a corpsman with the Marine Corps in Vietnam.

Tom Bulleit

Thomas E. Bulleit Jr. was born into a family of soldiers and raised in Louisville, Kentucky. His father enlisted in 1943 and served in Gen. George S. Patton's Third Army during World War II. While fighting on a tank crew during the Battle of the Bulge, Bulleit Sr. suffered a traumatic brain injury and lost an eye to shrapnel. Two of Bulleit's uncles also served in World War II, his grandfather was an army major in World War I, and Bulleit men fought on both sides of the American Civil War. As a young man, Bulleit worked summer rotations at Louisville's Bernheim Distillery and imagined a life in the bourbon whiskey industry. After graduating from the University of Kentucky in 1966, he tabled his dream of becoming a distiller to enlist as a hospital corpsman in the U.S. Navy. In 1968, he deployed to the Republic of Vietnam, an experience that "made him a man." When he came home from war, Bulleit used his GI Bill to attend the University of Louisville School of Law and spent the next twenty-six years as a tax attorney. In 1987, while still running a robust law practice, he founded the wildly successfully Bulleit Distilling Company, which sells nearly a million cases of whiskey annually and recently broke ground on a $115 million facility in Shelbyville, Kentucky.

The year 1968 was a pivotal one for American forces in Vietnam. In January, North Vietnamese and Viet Cong forces launched the Tet Offensive, a string of surprise attacks against military targets, the U.S. embassy in Saigon, and other government centers in South Vietnam. Gen. William Westmoreland, commander of the U.S. Military Assistance Command, Vietnam (MACV), was stunned by the enemy's cunning and success. The MACV response led to some of the most intense fighting of the entire conflict. Sixteen thousand Americans lost their lives by the end of the year.[1] Also in 1968, American troop numbers hit an apex of 536,100, and soldiers from the U.S. Army's First Battalion, Twentieth Infantry Regiment committed an infamous massacre at the village of My Lai.[2]

In the United States, confidence in military and civilian political leadership dwindled. The percentage of Americans who believed that the United States made a mistake by sending troops to Vietnam rose from 25 percent in 1965 to 45 percent in early 1968.[3] Mass demonstrations devolved into riots in places like Chicago, where the Democratic Party held its convention to nominate a candidate to replace President Lyndon Johnson. In April, Martin Luther King Jr. was killed in Memphis, and in June, Attorney General Robert F. Kennedy was assassinated. The relentless national draft continued to deposit men into the murderous jungles of Southeast Asia.

Thomas "Tom" E. Bulleit Jr., the son of a combat-wounded World War II veteran of General Patton's Third Army, watched the chaos in Vietnam from his home in Louisville. Fresh out of the University of Kentucky, Bulleit carefully considered his options. First, he dreamed of a life as a whiskey distiller. Growing up, he spent several summers working in Louisville's Bernheim Distillery, where his uncle was a master distiller, an endeavor he appreciated. Next, he weighed the more practical option of pursuing a law degree, which would almost guarantee him a deferral from the draft. Finally, he considered military service. Bulleit sought the counsel of his father, who encouraged him to post-pone his bourbon ambitions, join the U.S. Marine Corps, and pursue a law degree when he returned from the combat zone.

After several of his close friends were conscripted and left for various basic trainings, Bulleit voluntarily enlisted in the U.S. Navy. Impressed by the Navy Hospital Corps' proud tradition of providing medical support to marines, he enlisted as a corpsman in 1967 knowing that it meant he would accompany marines into firefights and expose himself to combat and bloodshed. In early 1968, upon completion of his basic and job-specific training, Tom Bulleit quickly received orders to deploy. Just several months into his military service, he reported to Vietnam and was attached to a battalion from the First Marine Division north of the Da Nang airbase.

Operational tempo for the Marine Corps units in the vicinity of Da Nang was on the upswing when Bulleit arrived. The number and intensity of foot patrols increased, as did the frequency and ferocity of enemy attacks. Due to high casualties among grunts, marine commanders employed administrative personnel like clerks, cooks, and drivers on missions to capture and kill enemy fighters and take Viet Cong and Communist-held villages by force. Rockets and mortars disrupted daily life even when men were not on patrol, and took a physical toll on the marines, their bases, and their equipment. Hospitalman Petty Officer Third Class (HM3) Bulleit and other corpsman were inundated with relevant work.

In the imperial city of Hue, marines engaged in urban combat, fighting gun battles from street to street supported by M50 Onto tanks. Hundreds of Americans were wounded and killed in the month-long offensive. Under the command of the intrepid Col. Stanley S. Hughes, a World War II and Korean War veteran and recipient of the Silver Star and two Navy Crosses, the under-strength marine battalions accom-plished the mission, but sniper fire took a devastating toll. Tom Bulleit recalled that enemy snipers targeted medics and corpsman, easily iden-tified by the red crosses on their helmets. Over two thousand army medics and navy corpsman were killed in action during the Vietnam

War. Upon taking the city's provincial headquarters from the Viet Cong, exhausted men from Company H, Second Battalion, Fifth Marines hoisted an American flag in the courtyard despite a MACV directive that forbade its display without a South Vietnamese flag beside it.

After the Hue offensive, enemy ground fire destroyed an inbound C-123 supply plane near Khe Sanh, killing forty-eight Americans, mostly marines. Six thousand marines on Khe Sanh remained under siege and cut off by two North Vietnamese divisions for over two months. As a result, the First Marine Division moved forces south to conduct Operation Pegasus, a thirty-thousand-man mission to clear the area and relieve their besieged brothers. The battle of Khe Sanh witnessed the most intense air bombing campaign in the history of warfare, not to mention some of the fiercest ground engagements.

Tom Bulleit remembers being on top of a mountain, near a French bunker, and thinking, "How can men come to this? How can we so strongly believe in our cause that we come to this?"[4] The Vietnam War transformed HM3 Bulleit from a boy into a man. During the course of the Vietnam War, twenty members of the First Marine Division earned Medals of Honor for conspicuous bravery on the battlefield. The First Marine Division was twice awarded the Presidential Unit Citation for gallantry in action in Vietnam and received the Vietnamese Cross of Gallantry with Palm and the Vietnamese Civil Action Award.

Toward the end of his combat tour, Hospitalman Petty Officer Third Class Bulleit caught a ride to the Da Nang airbase and completed the Law School Admission Test per his father's guidance. Despite what he calls a horrendous undergraduate performance at the University of Kentucky, Bulleit performed well enough on the LSAT, which he took with his government-issued pistol by his side, to be accepted into the University of Louisville School of Law. After a year in the combat zone, Bulleit returned home to Kentucky.

After putting his hard-earned GI Bill to use, Bulleit earned a Juris Doctor from Louisville in 1971 and began practicing law, focused primarily on corporate bankruptcy and tax issues. In 1976, he completed an advanced degree in Taxation Law at Georgetown University's Law Center. Over the next three decades, Bulleit built a successful practice, but he never abandoned a desire to work in the whiskey business. In 1987, while still fully engaged in the practice of law, Tom Bulleit pulled the trigger on his dream of forming the Bulleit Distilling Company.

Bulleit began by buying stocks of bourbon whiskey from Kentucky distilleries and bottling them under an orange label bearing his family name. A savvy businessman, he capitalized on a family legend about his great-great-grandfather, Augustus Bulleit. Augustus, a French immigrant who likely lived in Kentucky and Indiana, was involved in the liquor trade in the early nineteenth century. In 1860, he vanished while traveling on a flatboat to deliver bourbon whiskey to New Orleans. The intriguing story inspired the company's marketing strategy, but the product stood on its own. The Bulleit Distilling Company bought and sold bourbon with high rye content, giving the whiskey a spicier flavor than could be found in most available products. Through engaging marketing, handsome packaging, and a dogged effort to sell the spirit, Tom Bulleit found quick success.

A break came in 1997 when the massive liquor company Seagram's purchased the Bulleit Distilling Company. Soon after, the London-based Diageo, formed in 1997 through the merger of Guinness and Grand Metropolitan, purchased the Bulleit Bourbon portfolio from Seagram's. Bulleit has been part of the Diageo family ever since.

Tom Bulleit experienced a personal and professional challenge in 2005 when he was diagnosed with colon cancer. Despite the difficult treatment and side effects, Bulleit continued to work every day for the company he formed in his mind as a young man. He found inspiration in memories of his father, who never missed a day of work despite massive headaches caused by his war injuries.

In the last several years, the company introduced Bulleit ten-year-old bourbon, Bulleit rye whiskey, and a barrel-strength version of its standard bourbon offering. The additions are some of the most appreciated whiskeys available today, particularly among mixologists. Whereas Bulleit sold thirty-five thousand cases of whiskey in 2007, the company sold six hundred thousand in 2014 and projects to sell one million cases in a year in the near future.[5] Diageo recently announced a $115 million investment in a new Bulleit distillery to be built in Shelby County, Kentucky.

In 2009, Tom Bulleit was inducted into the Kentucky Bourbon Hall of Fame along with two members of the Beam family, renowned whiskey writer Chuck Cowdery, and President William Howard Taft. While Tom Bulleit gladly displays proof of his Hall of Fame induction, the thing he is most proud of, other than being a husband and a father, is his service as a young corpsman in 1968.

14

David Steven Pickerell

People want historic things, authenticity. And the fact is, the first American cocktails had rye in them. The whiskey rations during the Revolutionary War were in rye. If you want to be authentic, you need rye on the bar.

Dave Pickerell

David Steven Pickerell was born and raised in Greene County, Ohio. In 1974, Pickerell accepted an appointment to attend the U.S. Military Academy at West Point, where he studied chemistry and played football. After graduating from West Point in 1978, he was commissioned a second lieutenant in the Armor Corps and became one of the U.S. Army Cavalry's preeminent logistics officers. While an army captain, Pickerell obtained a master's degree in chemical engineering from the University of Louisville and began teaching chemistry at West Point. Following his stint on the faculty, Major Pickerell resigned his commission to dabble in the spirits industry at Kentucky's Ro-Tech Inc. Five years later, he was the master distiller at Maker's Mark, a position he held for fourteen years. Today, Pickerell is the "Johnny Appleseed" of the whiskey industry and regularly consults for popular craft distilleries like F.E.W., Corsair,

Garrison Bros., Hillrock Estate, Rock Town, Willett, WhistlePig, Woodinville, and the reconstructed George Washington Distillery and Gristmill in Mount Vernon, Virginia.

After the United States' armed forces withdrew from Vietnam in 1973, the military experienced a decade of decline and discredit. The American public shunned the two million men and women who returned from Vietnam, a conflict that saw fifty-eight thousand Americans killed and over three hundred thousand wounded. Most Vietnam veterans returned home to empty airports and scornful looks. Such disdainful treatment exacted an undeniable toll on men and women who experienced the trauma of combat. More Vietnam vets committed suicide after the war than had died in it.

In the years following the war, the U.S. Army struggled to transition to an all-volunteer force. Recruiting efforts were hampered by Hollywood's portrayal of soldiers as rage- and drug-driven maniacs. Discipline in the shrinking force plummeted, and morale hit an all-time low. "The Army in the 1970s was a terrible organization," admitted Conrad Crane, a retired officer and chief of historical services at the Army's Heritage and Education Center.[1] Even the official service history acknowledges that "the Army emerged from Vietnam cloaked in anguish. . . . It was an institution fighting merely to maintain its existence in the midst of growing apathy, decay, and intolerance."[2] The nation's 1976 bicentennial celebration was dampened by an overwhelming conclusion that gains made in Vietnam, paid for in blood and $167 billion, were simply not worth it. The year 1976 also happened to be when Russian vodka surpassed whiskey as the nation's top-selling spirit.

David S. Pickerell, a poor kid with a dogged work ethic from Fairborn, Ohio, made a difficult, albeit sensible, decision in 1974 to pursue a commission in the U.S. Army. After graduating seventh in his class at Park Hills High School, "Pick" accepted an appointment to attend the U.S. Military Academy at West Point. As an adolescent, Dave Pickerell attended public schools in Fairborn, "a dirty suburb of Dayton."[3] Naturally curious, he would bother his father with questions as they drove around their blue-collar town on Sunday afternoons.

Dave wrote, "From my little kid perspective, we drove until we got lost, then found our way home. Given the area where we lived, we would always pass a factory or two. When we did, I would just pepper dad with questions like 'why is that tank there?' 'What is all that smoke coming out of the chimney over there?' 'What is that piping for?' Pretty soon, Dad would say, 'The only person who understands all that is a chemical engineer.' I'm not sure whether he was aiming me at a career in chemical engineering or just trying to get me to shut up. Either way, it worked."[4]

By the time Pickerell was old enough to register memories, he was completely dedicated to a life as a chemical engineer. By the time he was ten years old, he knew his family was so poor that "someone else was going to have to pay for [his] college education."[5] Fortunately, Pickerell was not just a smart kid; he was also a big, strong one. Knowing that a full athletic scholarship was more likely than an academic one, he began playing all kinds of sports. His goal was never amusement but rather to put himself in a position to afford higher education.

By his sophomore year at Park Hills High School, it was evident that Pickerell was good enough to run track or play football at the collegiate level. By his senior year, he was first team All-State in football and held all of the Park Hills records in shot put and discus. The two schools most interested in Pickerell's athletic ability were West Point and the Citadel in Charleston, South Carolina. As he considered the future, Pickerell chose the school with the best reputation for academic excellence and accepted a hard-earned congressional appointment to the New York military academy, founded in 1801 by Thomas Jefferson.

In the summer of 1974, Pickerell drove from western Ohio to West Point and in-processed. As a member of the last batch of American men to be assigned a draft number for Vietnam (his was #144), he was administratively awarded the National Defense Service Medal, even though the war had virtually ended. Cadet Pickerell, a member of the 1974 Army football team, focused intensely on his studies, determined to become a chemical engineer. "There was a promise that if you graduated in the top 5% of your class, you had an automatic offer for a Master's degree. When I attended West Point, they did not offer chemical engineering, so I majored in chemistry and took nuclear engineering—that's as close as I could get to a chemical engineering degree. I really wanted to be top 5% so the Army would pay for a Master's in chemical engineering and complete my dream," he recalled.[6]

Pickerell found himself surrounded by other talented and motivated cadets. There were cadets who transferred from other top colleges, those he considered true geniuses, and plenty of other extremely focused hard-workers. To compete, Pickerell studied obsessively, to the detriment of his college football career and personal life. He said, "I was on the edge of losing it. I was absolutely miserable."[7] On the gridiron, the Army Black Knights stumbled through a 3-8 season under first-year coach Homer Smith, the former UCLA offensive coordinator who replaced Tom Cahill, the man who recruited Pickerell. After the season, Pickerell remembers "sitting in a computer lab on a beautiful Saturday afternoon, all by myself, looking out on the Plain at all the cadets having fun. I was nearly in tears."[8]

After that agonizing Saturday afternoon of studying indoors, for the sake of his own survival, the young cadet ceded his dream of being in the top 5 percent of his class. He began granting himself Saturdays and Sundays to relax and interact socially with other cadets. His class rank dropped to the top 8 percent the next semester, but his mental state improved as he focused on new goals. After his first and only football season, Cadet Pickerell was released from the team, a blessing of even more time to learn on his own terms. Feeling as if a weight had been lifted from his shoulders, he discovered intramural soccer, handball, racquetball, lacrosse, and a slew of new friends.

Following his first Christmas break, Cadet Pickerell won a bet with his classmates over who could grow the most facial hair, a stunt that earned him four punishment tours. It also earned him a handful of cash from his competing comrades. While discipline was never an issue for him at West Point, Pickerell loosened up and started having fun.

During the summer after his second year, Cadet Pickerell reported to the Eighty-Second Airborne Division at Fort Bragg, North Carolina, where he interned as an acting platoon leader in the Fourth Battalion, Sixty-Eighth Armor Regiment, the last unit to drop an M551 Sheridan tank from an airplane. Despite not having gone to Airborne School at that time, he participated in a mass tactical jump and was "prop-blasted" (i.e., initiated—or hazed, depending on how you look at it) before the use of alcohol during the initiation was forbidden. It took him two days to recover from his hangover.

When he returned to New York, Cadet Pickerell focused on what he wanted to be after graduating and commissioning. He sought out what he considered to be the biggest challenge available—service as a cavalry officer in the Army's Armor Corps. In the operating environment of the post-Vietnam Cold War, the cavalry offered the biggest challenge, biggest units, big tanks, and more autonomy and responsibility than the other branches did.

In the spring of 1978, David Pickerell earned a bachelor of science degree with a concentration in chemistry from the U.S. Military Academy. He was commissioned as a second lieutenant in the Armor Corps. That summer, he reported to the Cavalry Officer's Basic Course at Fort Knox, Kentucky, just down the road from where he would launch an epic career in the whiskey business eleven years later.

After completing the basic course at Fort Knox, Lieutenant Pickerell attempted Ranger School twice but was injured both times. He was assigned as an Armored Cavalry platoon leader in the First Squadron, Tenth Cavalry Regiment, a Fourth Infantry Division outfit at Fort Carson, Colorado. Many of the men in his squadron were Vietnam combat veterans, but they welcomed the new lieutenant into their ranks. Between 1978 and 1981, Lieutenant Pickerell served as an assistant operations officer, platoon leader, troop executive officer, and assistant logistics officer. Continuing his tradition of attempting new sports, Lieutenant Pickerell took up skiing and martial arts while stationed at Fort Carson. In 1981, he was crowned Colorado's heavyweight champion in karate and kung fu after winning the state's all-styles open tournament.

Pickerell departed the Fourth Infantry Division in 1981 and returned to Fort Knox, Kentucky, where he completed the Armor Officer's Advance Course in 1982. After a promising stint at the Tenth Cavalry Regiment in logistics, he was selected to attend the Quartermaster's Officer Course at Fort Lee, Virginia. He graduated with the highest academic marks in the history of the course.[9]

Having thoroughly enjoyed the commonwealth of Kentucky as a lieutenant, the freshly promoted Captain Pickerell returned to Fort Knox in 1982 for an assignment as the primary logistics officer for the Second Squadron, Sixteenth Cavalry Regiment. While assigned to the squadron, Captain Pickerell was selected to command the largest cavalry troop in the army. For two years, he was responsible for two hundred scouts, twenty-three M3 Stuart tanks, and twelve M1 Abrams tanks. Captain Pickerell and his men pushed the tanks to the limits of their capabilities, briefed high-ranking officers on their performance, and rewrote the army's training and doctrine manuals on tank warfare. He was awarded a Meritorious Service Medal for his training manuals, which were later employed in the Gulf War.

In 1986, Captain Pickerell left Fort Knox for a two-year opportunity he had dreamed about since childhood. The army paid for him to attend the University of Louisville's School of Engineering where he finally obtained a master's degree in chemical engineering. While a student, Captain Pickerell published "Excess Volumes of Mixing: The Benzene + Trichloroethylene System," a brilliant display of his mastery of complex chemistry. The thesis was so well received that he was promoted again and offered a position as a professor of chemistry at West Point.

From 1987 to 1989, Pickerell taught cadets at his alma mater. When he completed his teaching obligation in 1989, Major Pickerell resigned his commission for an intriguing opportunity in Louisville. He was offered a position as a chemical engineer at a small company called Ro-Tech Inc., where other talented chemical engineers helped build new distilleries and still components for Kentucky's, Tennessee's, and Canada's biggest whiskey companies. Pickerell accepted the job at Ro-Tech and immediately began consulting for exotic distilleries in Scotland, the Dominican Republic, Mexico, and China.

Five years into his Ro-Tech experience, Pickerell was working on-site at the historic Maker's Mark distillery in Loretto, Kentucky. Distillery president Bill Samuels Jr. approached him and quickly explained that the distillery was struggling to find a vice president of operations and master distiller. Before the conversation was over, Pickerell, a self-described "idiot savant" in distilling, was hired.[10]

Under Dave Pickerell's leadership in the 1990s, Maker's Mark initially increased production from 75,000 to 125,000 cases a year. Today, it produces over 1.3 million.[11] He impacted everything else the distillery did, including safety, environmental protection, tourism, and marketing. While serving as the Maker's Mark master distiller, Pickerell attended the Babson School of Entrepreneurial Studies in Massachusetts and traveled the world handling public relations for the company. If he wasn't traveling the world promoting his bourbon, he was working long hours at the distillery. Most days, Pickerell left his house before the sun rose and left work long after it set. He said, "It was intense, but I learned so many valuable things for doing that. I can't say enough about how wonderful Maker's was to me. They equipped me with a lot of things."[12] Pickerell stayed at Maker's Mark for fourteen years.

Since leaving Loretto in 2008, Dave Pickerell has served as the craft distilling industry's "Johnny Appleseed," spreading practical whiskey-making knowledge to countless new distillers.[13] He is, without a doubt, the movement's most prolific consultant. Through his company Oak View Spirits, he has designed stills, built dozens of distilleries, and helped innovative distillers produce a range of fascinating whiskeys.

Pickerell has worked with the Sons of Liberty in Narragansett, Rhode Island, which makes what he calls "an idiosyncratic malt whiskey" for beer lovers.[14] In 2013, the distillery's pumpkin whiskey won *Whiskey Magazine's* Best Flavored Whiskey in the World. Last year, their hop whiskey won North America's Best Flavored Whiskey.

In Virginia, he has worked at the Belmont, Copper Fox, and Ragged Mountain distilleries to produce several award-winning bourbon and rye whiskeys. In the Carolinas, he helped establish the High Wire and Asheville Distilling companies. He helped build Florida's Saint Augustine Distillery, which recently released their Double Cask bourbon, the state's first bourbon since Prohibition.

Pickerell has consulted for Louisiana Spirits, makers of Bayou Rum, which he predicts will explode in popularity. In Tennessee, he has advised successful moonshiners and cutting-edge whiskey-makers at Short Mountain, Ole Smoky, Popcorn Sutton, Corsair, Nelson's Green Brier, and Tenn South. He's done work at Rock Town Distillery, Arkansas's first legal distillery since Prohibition, and the Old Pogue Distillery in historic Maysville, Kentucky.

In his home state of Ohio, he helped Watershed Distillery develop their flavorful spelted bourbon. He helped the team at Kansas's Union Horse Distilling Co. (formerly Dark Horse) "bring something new to Kansas City."[15] They must compete, however, with the nearby J. Rieger and Co. distillery, which also retained Pickerell to revitalize an old brand.

In Washington State, he helped get the Woodinville Whiskey Co. off the ground. In Detroit, he worked with Two James Distillery. In Chicago, he worked with the Chicago Distillery. Elsewhere in Illinois, he helped Paul Hletko launch F.E.W. in Evanston, the Walters family build Whiskey Acres in corn-rich DeKalb, and the no-nonsense Blaum Brothers with their distillery in Galena. In Wisconsin, Pickerell helps the Driftless Glen distillery produce two thousand barrels of quality bourbon and rye each year. In Minnesota, there are the Panther and Far North Distilleries. In Texas, there are the Firestone & Robertson Distillery in Fort Worth and the Garrison Bros. in rural Hye, where air force veteran Donnis Todd produces the award-winning Cowboy Bourbon.

The poor kid from Ohio has come a long way. At the scenic WhistlePig Distillery in Vermont's Champlain Valley, Pickerell purchases, finishes, and blends 100 percent rye whiskey from distilleries in Indiana and Alberta, Canada. He also mashes and distills the highest-quality rye grown on the Vermont farm for future releases. When he is not in Vermont, Pickerell spends about a third of his time at New York's scenic Hillrock Estate Distillery, where he helps owner Jeffrey Baker produce one of the few solera-aged bourbons on the market.[16] He also spends a significant amount of his time and energy on George Washington's Mount Vernon estate, where he oversees production at the founding father's reconstructed distillery and gristmill. Each year, Pickerell dons eighteenth-century attire and mashes rye with volunteers who rely on him to transform General Washington's historic methods and recipes into good, clear rye whiskey. Without a doubt, Washington would be proud to know that Dave Pickerell is there, carrying on an American tradition.

15

Veterans in Craft Whiskey

There were tens of thousands of small-scale distilleries in early nineteenth-century America.[1] Whiskey-making was a national pastime for the Revolutionary War veterans whose pot stills lined the Monongahela and Ohio River Valleys. However, advancements in grain processing, still construction, chemistry, transportation, and finance slowly eliminated the need for the American farmer distiller. Just two years after the War of 1812 ended, Kentucky's newest veterans witnessed the construction of their state's first commercial distillery, known as the Hope Distillery, in downtown Louisville. Whereas an average farmer distiller could produce twenty gallons of whiskey on a good day, Hope Distillery could easily pump out twelve hundred.[2]

A generation later, the American Civil War demanded the seizure of many small stills, which were melted down and converted into cannons, fuze adaptors, and artillery shells. After the war, rapid industrialization and the development of efficient transportation networks further diminished the need for small-scale distilleries. High taxation caused many distillers to cease operations or run for the hills, although there were still nearly a thousand licensed distilleries when the United States entered World War I.[3] Some writers suggest that whiskey-drinkers of the pre-Prohibition era preferred "handcrafted" local farm whiskeys to the commercial products made in "factories."[4] Indeed, Louisville's large Hope Distillery failed not long after New England venture capitalists built it.

Just before the turn of the century, though, dozens of smaller distilleries were consolidated by decorated combat veteran Joseph Greenhut's Whiskey Trust. The trust bought as many as fifty-nine distilleries in Kentucky alone and closed many of them in order to concentrate operations in larger plants.[5] In the wake of the trust's demise, the temperance movement and national Prohibition destroyed the tradition of small-scale distilling in America altogether. Only six highly regulated distilleries continued to operate lawfully during Prohibition and only to fulfill prescriptions for medicinal whiskey.

In the decades that followed repeal, massive column stills retrofitted to produce industrial alcohol for the War Department satisfied the nation's need for beverage whiskey. As World War II veteran Elmer T. Lee noted, his title was "plant manager," not "master distiller," until the latest stage of his career, a reflection of the industrial approach to whiskey production.[6] While several well-known distilleries produced legendary bourbons between World War II and the Cold War, the industry suffered from a lack of innovation overall. As the biggest companies applied high-volume techniques in production, ancient "handcrafted" methods of distillation were lost. Americans eventually turned to spirits imported from other countries, like odorless and tasteless vodka. Fortunately, as army veteran and master distiller Dave Pickerell argues, taste is important again.[7] Small whiskey distilleries are important again too.

America's craft beverage renaissance began in the 1980s when Germain-Robin and Jepson Spirits introduced small-batch brandies distilled in alembic pot stills acquired from abandoned distilleries in Cognac.[8] The year after those distilleries were established, two more California distilling operations, Charbay and St. George Spirits, joined them.

In 1984, the founder of St. George Spirits, Jorg Rupf, hired U.S. Navy veteran Bill Mannshardt to oversee all distilling operations.[9] Mannshardt was a tough, even-keeled war veteran with a deep passion for making his own beer and wine. During World War II, Mannshardt served as an electrician's mate first class aboard the USS *Saratoga* supporting operations in the Pacific. He saw combat near Guadalcanal, the Eastern Solomon Islands, Wake Island, Tarawa, the Marshall Islands, and Iwo Jima. During the battle of Iwo Jima in February 1945, the *Saratoga* was badly damaged by Japanese bombs and kamikaze attacks. One hundred twenty-three men were killed, 192 were wounded, and 36 planes were destroyed in the attacks and ensuing blazes.[10] The battered *Saratoga* withdrew to Bremerton, Washington, for repairs. While on liberty, Bill Mannshardt took a train to Oakland, California, where he met and fell in love with Jeanne, with whom he had five sons.

After the war, Mannshardt spent thirty-five years working for the California telephone company, Pacific Bell. During his time at the company, he became acquainted with an Italian social club whose members made their own pasta, sausage, beer, wine, and grappa. Despite his German heritage, the Italians welcomed Mannshardt, and they facilitated access to grapes in Napa and Sonoma. His home-brewing and winemaking efforts evolved into liquor experiments. Mannshardt built a still in his basement and, as his son Ken recalled, "he proceeded to make some pretty crappy brandy."[11] However, over time, Mannshardt's brandy improved and his dedication to the hobby deepened.

When he retired from Pacific Bell, Mannshardt went to visit St. George Spirits after reading an article about the small distillery in a San Francisco newspaper. Soon, the former navy electrician's mate was spending much of his time at the distillery, helping Jorg Rupf properly wire stills, thermostats, and pump motors. Rupf and Mannshardt became fast friends and teammates, and ultimately Rupf appointed Mannshardt to be his master distiller. For twelve years, the men produced award-winning fruit eau de vies, or un-aged brandies, despite the general public's lack of attention. Toward the end of his career at the distillery, however, Mannshardt began experiencing serious knee pain. In 1996, after struggling to climb a ladder he built to get on top of the tanks, he called Rupf to retire.

Before Rupf found time to even think about replacing Mannshardt, a man named Lance Winters came by the distillery unexpectedly. Winters, a brewer at Fremont's Brewpub on the Green, was a former U.S. Navy nuclear engineer and wanted to produce spirits. He showed up to St. George with a bottle of homemade whiskey in his hand, which he considered his resume. When Rupf and Mannshardt tasted the whiskey, they hired him on the spot. Within a year of hiring Winters, St. George began producing whiskey to complement its line-up of extraordinary eau de vie. A concurrent rise of craft brewing pumped new capital and life into the small-scale beverage industry.

In 2004, St. George expanded into a sixty-five-thousand-square-foot airplane hangar on the former Alameda Naval Air Station in California. Coincidentally, Winters had worked at Alameda before, when he was stationed aboard the world's first nuclear-powered aircraft carrier, the USS *Enterprise*. While in the navy, Winters would gaze from the *Enterprise* toward the San Francisco Bay and think to himself that the only thing he was missing was a drink. Under Winters's direction, St. George launched several iconic spirits, including St. George Single Malt Whiskey, Baller Single Malt Whiskey, and an array of absinthe, gin, rum, and vodka products.

Around the time St. George moved into the Alameda Air Force hangar, Stranahan's Colorado Whiskey Company emerged in Denver, Colorado. Brewery owner and whiskey connoisseur George Stranahan, who served in the U.S. Army from 1954 to 1956, teamed up with a volunteer firefighter named Jess Graber after one of Stranahan's Aspen-area barns caught on fire. While watching the blaze, the men bonded upon the realization that they both loved making alcohol. Stranahan later permitted Graber to establish a still in one of his other barns. Graber developed what became Stranahan's American single-malt whiskey. In 2009, Stranahan's won *Whisky Advocate's* award for Artisan Whiskey of the Year, and Jim Murray declared Stranahan's to be the small-batch distillery of the year in his *Whiskey Bible*.

In 2011, after Proximo Spirits purchased Stranahan's Colorado Whiskey Company, the distillery hired Rob Dietrich to serve as its master distiller. Prior to launching his career as a whiskey distiller, Dietrich served in the Fort Drum, New York–based Tenth Mountain Division's Target Acquisition Detachment.[12] Dietrich specialized in forward observation but also served on highly trained Quick Reaction Forces capable of operating in difficult terrain and weather conditions. He served in Mogadishu, Somalia, during the *Black Hawk Down* fight of October 3–4, 1993. In 1994, he deployed again to Port-au-Prince, Haiti, as part of a security force during Operation Uphold Democracy. His fascination with fermentation and alcohol began as a young soldier when he tried to convert army-issued Kool-Aid into wine in Somalia.[13]

When St. George expanded and Stranahan's was launched, however, there were fewer than 50 craft distilleries (those that sell less than one hundred thousand proof gallons each year) in the United States.[14] By 2016, the number of craft distilleries had risen to 1,315.[15] Over the last several years, the overworked and underfunded Alcohol and Tobacco Tax and Trade Bureau processed hundreds of applications for additional distilling permits and new whiskey labels. Dozens of additional veteran-owned or -operated distilleries have emerged across the country to satisfy an ever-increasing demand for local, innovative American spirits.

In 2007, Dan and Charlie Garrison, proud navy brats, officially established the Garrison Brothers Distillery in Hye, Texas. In 2002, Dan Garrison was unemployed and searching for a job that would make him money and bring him joy. A lover of straight whiskey since the age of thirteen when he sampled his mom's bottle of Rebel Yell bourbon, Garrison began the process of making Texas's first bourbon whiskey around 2001. He traveled to Kentucky several times to meet with master distillers and tour historic bourbon distilleries, becoming friends with Maker's Mark's Bill Samuels Jr. in the process. Garrison began to seriously consider opening a Texas distillery in 2004, but did not obtain a permit until 2007 and did not hire any experienced whiskey-makers until 2008.

That year, a former U.S. Air Force mechanic named Donnis Todd showed up unannounced at the immature distillery. The fully bearded and tattooed Dan Garrison challenged Todd and asked him what he was doing on the property. Todd responded, "I'm Donnis Todd, and I want to make bourbon."[16] Even though Garrison had no money to pay Todd, a week later, the determined veteran was living in a condemned trailer without air conditioning or running water about a mile from the distillery.

Todd immediately applied his advanced knowledge of chemistry and home-brewing to help Garrison develop his recipes and methods. Today, Donnis Todd is Garrison Brothers' master distiller, and he employs a handful of other military veterans, who help him produce small-batch, single-barrel, and popular, limited-edition Cowboy bourbon whiskey. A large contingent of the staff at Garrison Brothers served in the armed forces, and the distillery recently chopped through administrative "red tape" to ensure its products are available to sailors, soldiers, airmen, marines, and coast guardsmen in Korea, Okinawa, and Germany, and on bases across the United States.

Garrison Brothers' Texas bourbon whiskey helped introduce the expanding market to high-quality, non-Kentucky bourbon whiskey. (Recall that, in accordance with Title 27 of the Code of Federal Regulations, bourbon must be made in the United States, but not exclusively in Kentucky.) In 2008, Bryan and Kari Schultz opened Roughstock Montana Distillery in Bozeman, Montana. Bryan Schultz fell in love with small European breweries while stationed overseas. When he came home from Germany and left the service, he planned to open up a brewery in his home state of Montana but was shocked to realize that Montana had no licensed distilleries.

He and his wife obtained the licenses and funding to open Roughstock. Today, they double-distill a mash of mostly Montana grains in custom copper pot stills at the base of the Bridger Mountain Range. Roughstock Montana Bourbon was the first legal whiskey made in Montana in over one hundred years. The Schultzes also produce Pure Malt single-malt whiskey, a single-barrel version of the Pure Malt, Montana, straight rye whiskey, spring wheat whiskey, and sweet corn whiskey.

Not to be outdone by the Texans and Montanans, U.S. Army veteran Paul Tomaszewski founded the MB Roland Distillery in Pembroke, Kentucky, in 2009, not far from Fort Campbell, where he once served as a platoon leader in the 101st Airborne Division. Tomaszewski was a West Point cadet on September 11, 2001, and found himself leading men in Iraq after commissioning as a second lieutenant in 2003. Between 2004 and 2005, Lieutenant Tomaszewski served in a cavalry troop for twelve months in Baghdad with the Eighty-First Brigade Combat Team. When he returned, he took leave to visit his brother, a U.S. Navy dentist stationed on a Marine Corps base in Okinawa, Japan. While perusing the Class VI (liquor store) at the Base Exchange in Okinawa, Tomaszewski bought a few bottles of good Scotch whisky. Fascinated by the smoky, single-malt beverage he sipped over ice with his brother, he began to research how to distill.

After leaving the Eighty-First Brigade, Paul had a "rendezvous with destiny" when he reported to 101st Airborne Division at Fort Campbell, Kentucky. He was assigned to the 1st Battalion, 506th Infantry Regiment, the same unit featured in the HBO series *Band of Brothers*. Again, Lieutenant Tomaszewski deployed to Iraq for a year as a platoon leader, this time to Forward Operating Base Falcon in Baghdad. After returning from war a second time, Paul met his wife, Mary Beth ("M.B."), and fell in love with her and her home state. After a brief stint as a company commander at Fort Benning, Georgia, he left the army in 2008 for the rich cornfields of Kentucky.

Fresh out of the army, Tomaszewski started looking for jobs. As the economy was in deep recession, the former combat commander found it difficult to land meaningful employment. Still interested in whiskey, he and M.B. spent their weekends visiting big Kentucky and Tennessee distilleries like Maker's Mark and Jack Daniel's. Eventually, they started visiting craft distilleries like Corsair and Willett. At some point, "it clicked."[17] With the money he saved up during deployments, Tomaszewski purchased a small Amish dairy farm in tiny Pembroke and began obsessively planning to build a whiskey distillery. He and M.B. drove all the way to New York and back visiting every micro-distillery they could find, which in 2008 was just nine.

He purchased a hundred-gallon pot still and a cheap aluminum hand crank mill with an electric motor, and he started making white dog and "black dog," which features tobacco-smoked corn in the mash recipe. Before long, M.B. Roland's portfolio expanded to moonshine, flavored moonshine, and, in time, Kentucky straight bourbon whiskey. These days, Paul and M.B. make their spirits with a six-hundred-gallon still, and each year, the bourbon white dog goes into bigger and bigger barrels for future releases. M.B. Roland hosts an annual concert on the farm, known as "Pickin' on the Porch," where the whole world is invited to come relax and sip on fine craft bourbon for an evening.

Craft whiskey's tipping point came shortly after as other small distilleries successfully experimented with unique recipes and project whiskeys. In 2010, Jerry Meyer, Tom Anderson, and Ralph Haynes opened the Pinckney Bend Distillery in New Haven, Missouri. Meyer, a retired U.S. Air Force lieutenant colonel, serves as the distillery's chief executive. Meyer's distillery produces rye whiskey, Rested American Whiskey, and several whiskeys finished in wine casks. Pinckney Bend recently launched a project through which it plants rare and hard-to-find heirloom varieties of corn (e.g., Tennessee Red Cob, Hickory Cane, and Pencil Cob) and distills the corn into whiskey.

Also in 2010, Willie Blazer founded Willie's Distillery in Ennis, Montana. Willie Blazer handcrafts Bighorn Bourbon along with an array of liqueurs and unique moonshines, including honey moonshine distilled from Montana grains and molasses, matured in oak for two years. Before he and his wife moved back to her home state of Montana to open the distillery, Blazer was a ranger and Green Beret in the U.S. Army, dashing around the world in support of operations in Panama, Malaysia, Iraq, and Afghanistan. He spent six years in Third Battalion, Seventy-Fifth Ranger Regiment and five years in the Nineteenth Special Forces Group. His operational detachments conducted missions in some of the most dangerous places on the planet. During a stint in the Montana Army National Guard, Blazer lived up to his name and joined a "hotshot" crew fighting wildland fires with the U.S. Forest Service. In 2005, while working as a contractor to support Hurricane Katrina relief operations, Blazer had a revelation: "Why not make moonshine, legally, in Montana?"[18]

Blazer poured every bit of energy he had into the business plan, assembled a team, and taught himself the art and science of whiskey-making. Recalling the lessons learned in the Ranger Regiment and Special Forces community, he remains mission focused and challenges his employees to adapt and innovate, a mindset the whiskey industry will benefit from for many years to come.

Ted Pappas, a Citadel graduate and U.S. Air Force veteran, founded

Big Bottom Distilling Company in Hillsboro, Oregon, in 2010. Pappas's initial focus was on the merchant bottling of specialty bourbons. Between 2011 and 2014, his 111 proof bourbon and bourbon whiskeys finished in port and zinfandel casks won Gold Medals at the Great American Distiller's Festival, San Francisco World Spirits Competition, and "The Fifty Best" Bourbon Competition, respectively. Pappas also helped establish the Oregon Distillers Guild to promote the common interests of licensed distilleries and prospective distillers in the state. Oregon now has sixty-nine distilleries, which produce more than four hundred different products.

For example, in 2011 Dawson Officer established the 4 Spirits Distillery in Corvallis, Oregon, in an old air force building. Officer is the descendant of a long line of military veterans. His grandfather served in World War II. His father served in Vietnam. He served with the 2nd Battalion, 162nd Infantry Brigade in eastern Baghdad, Iraq, from September 2003 to May 2005. During his deployment, four of his friends were killed in action. He established and named the distillery to honor Lt. Erik McCrae, Sgt. Justin Linden, Sgt. Justin Eyerly, and Sgt. David Roustum. Currently, 4 Spirits produces a bourbon whiskey, American whiskey, and single-malt whiskey, among many other spirits.

Officer donates a portion of the sales from 4 Spirits' Bourbon Whiskey to support local programs that help veterans and their families with reintegration support. Ten percent of the proceeds from each bottle sold are donated to combat veteran reintegration programs throughout Oregon, Washington, Idaho, Montana, Wyoming, and Michigan. 4 Spirits also started the first-ever combat veteran scholarship endowment at Oregon State University and hopes to expand reach to other universities throughout the northwest. The distillery recently expanded to a new, larger site in the Corvallis Business Park.

Also in 2011, U.S. Navy veterans Don and Ben Alexander founded Trinity River Distillery in Fort Worth, Texas, in the historic Ranch Style Beans plant. Trinity River produces Texas Silver Star whiskey, the only American whiskey made with rainwater collected through a complex harvesting system. That same year, Quentin Witherspoon founded his distillery in nearby Lewisville, Texas. Witherspoon joined the U.S. Marine Corps after high school and began a military career that would allow him to travel the world. While in Central Africa, Quentin began distilling spirits, using basic water distillation equipment. While stationed near Charleston, South Carolina, Witherspoon met fellow marine Ryan DeHart, a home-brewer. After leaving the Marine Corps, the men reconnected in Texas and hatched the idea for a distillery along with DeHart's wife, Natasha. Currently, the Witherspoon Distillery produces straight bourbon whiskey and single-malt whiskey "from grain to glass," controlling every step of the production process.

At Patriarch Distillers, founded in 2012, in La Vista, Nebraska, retired U.S. Army sergeant first class Richard Hagedorn and his team produce spirits to honor the service of U.S. military veterans. Like Quentin Witherspoon in Texas, Hagedorn uses local grain and water to produce small-batch bourbon, rye, and "Prohibition-style" whiskey. Prior to joining Patriarch, Hagedorn fought to liberate Kuwait with the 1st Battalion, 327th Infantry Regiment, part of Fort Campbell, Kentucky's 101st Airborne Division. On February 24, 1991, Hagedorn took part in the largest air assault in history when over three hundred helicopters lifted the "Screaming Eagles" and the French 6th Light Armored Brigade 110 miles into Iraq. Hagedorn and his men successfully enveloped the regular Iraqi Army units on the left flank of the coalition line and captured hundreds of enemy soldiers.

After coming home and transitioning into the Nebraska Army National Guard, he met and joined the distilling team in La Vista. Patriarch's Soldier Valley bourbon, packaged in a patented glass World War II canteen replica bottle, won a Double Gold Medal at the 2014 San Francisco World Spirits Competition. Following the competition, sales increased and the company began donating a portion of its profits to the Oklahoma-based Airborne Demonstration Team and the Nebraska-based Soundz of Freedom charity, nonprofit organizations that assist veterans in need.

At the Top of the Hill restaurant, brewery, and distillery, established in 2012, in Chapel Hill, North Carolina, Scott Maitland and Esteban McMahan provide their community with a place to eat good food, drink good beer and whiskey, and watch the University of North Carolina Tar Heels. Proprietor Maitland is a West Point graduate and former combat engineer platoon leader and, like Richard Hagedorn, served overseas during Operation Desert Storm. Business partner and spirits guide McMahan was a medical platoon leader in the Seventh Infantry Division and deployed to Panama for Operation Just Cause. Their distillery produces Eight Oak Carolina Whiskey and organic Carolina Moonshine Whiskey under the TOPO label.

The year 2012 also welcomed Whitmeyers Distillery in Houston, where brothers Travis and Chris Whitmeyer produce peach whiskey, Texas Moonshine, Texas Whiskey, single-barrel bourbon whiskey, and cask-strength bourbon whiskey. Following the September 11 attacks, the Whitmeyer brothers enlisted together in the U.S. Army Field Artillery. After basic training, they were both assigned to the First Infantry Division in Germany. While overseas, Travis Whitmeyer dated a local girl who lived on a small Bavarian farm. Her family had been producing brandies, schnapps, beers, and wine for generations. Travis spent many days with her family and fell in love with the process of producing spirits. In February 2004, the brothers deployed to Iraq for thirteen months, where they sketched out plans to start a distillery at home in Texas. Whitmeyers Distillery is the fulfillment of a dream developed in combat.

Also in 2012, John Collett and Jack Landers founded the Three Rangers Company to bottle rye whiskey to benefit their Three Rangers Foundation. As younger men, Collett and Landers served together at the Fort Benning, Georgia-based Third Battalion, Seventy-Fifth Ranger Regiment and compiled extraordinary combat service records. Collett and Landers first met in the ranger barracks over twenty years ago. Landers lived on the second floor, where he threw loud parties between training exercises and missions. Collett came by one day wearing a Grateful Dead T-shirt and holding two cases of beer. A brief conversation ("Wrong room?" "Nope." "Who you looking for?" "Someone to party with . . .") led to a lifelong friendship and a growing whiskey business.[19]

By that fateful day in the barracks, John Collett had already returned from Somalia, where he was wounded during the Battle of Mogadishu depicted in *Black Hawk Down*, a film he did stunts for later in life. On

October 3, 1993, he was a gunner with B Company and fast-roped into Bakara Market shortly after a ranger in his company fell seventy feet from a UH-60 Black Hawk helicopter. Collett witnessed a rocket-propelled grenade bring down another chopper, call sign Super 61. In the ensuing firefight, the most violent engagement American troops had experienced in two decades, he was hit by gunfire and shrapnel and earned a Bronze Star Medal for Valor for saving other men's lives.

Landers was a new ranger when he met Collett, as he began his career as a helicopter mechanic in an Iowa-based reserve unit in the early 1990s. In 1993, he volunteered for active-duty service as an artilleryman and graduated from the Ranger Indoctrination Program the same day elements of B Company returned from Somalia. While fate would have him miss Mogadishu, he experienced plenty of combat later in his career.

On September 11, 2001, having recently reclassified as an infantryman, he was serving as a squad leader in Third Battalion; there was hardly time to process the gravity of the day before he was underway aboard the USS *Kitty Hawk* bound for the north Arabian Sea. During the initial invasion of Afghanistan, Landers deployed to some of the most dangerous places on earth. Between rotations, he cross-trained as a medic and filled the senior medic role at Shkin firebase in eastern Afghanistan, a village considered to be the "evilest place in Afghanistan," on his last deployment to the country.

When the Ranger Regiment was employed in Iraq in 2003, Landers was a platoon sergeant on the west side of Haditha Dam. Had Saddam Hussein destroyed the dam as planned, the U.S. Army's Third Infantry Division would have been destroyed by millions of gallons of rushing water. Staff Sergeant Landers and his rangers seized the dam on the night of April 1, 2003, and repulsed counterattacks for the next thirty-six hours straight. Landers remained in the special operations community for the rest of his career, which was defined by many more high-intensity deployments. He retired as a master sergeant after serving in a series of special operations senior enlisted advisor positions.

In 2012, when his old friend John Collett called to gauge his interest in launching Three Rangers, Landers immediately agreed to help.

Collett had been distilling whiskey at the KOVAL Distillery in Chicago and developed a rudimentary business plan to sell whiskey in support of combat veterans in need. He asked Landers to join him, his friend Mark Palmieri, and other Ranger Regiment combat veterans Larry Moores, Clay Othic, and Marcus Hull. The men applied for distilling licenses and labels, and created the Three Rangers foundation. Through the sale of whiskey, which they hope to eventually produce in their own brick and mortar distillery, they assist homeless veterans with finding decent housing and fund behavioral health services for veterans suffering with posttraumatic stress.

Many other veteran distillers support veteran charities or contribute to their local communities. In 2013, Charles Florence opened the Indiana Whiskey Company in South Bend, Indiana. After graduating from Purdue University, Florence served as an infantry officer in the U.S. Army for twelve years. After being medically discharged in 2009, Florence started visiting the American Legion and Veterans of Foreign Wars to drink with other veterans of World War II, Korea, and Vietnam. It was during this time that he developed the idea to make a small-batch Indiana whiskey. Today, the Indiana Whiskey Company operates a traditional alembic-style copper pot still to transform Indiana grains and water into Just Whiskey, a wheated bourbon, Silver Sweet corn whiskey, and several flavored whiskey products. It plans to produce a rye and single-malt whiskey in the future.

Florence's distillery enjoys a strong relationship with the Department of Veterans Affairs' Vocational Rehabilitation and Employment program for northern Indiana. Distillery employees volunteer with and donate to the Miller Center for Veterans at the Center for the Homeless in South Bend, and the company hires transitioning veterans as interns. Three percent of all profits go to Veterans Support Programs and Organizations in Indiana.

In 2013, Jason Riley founded his distillery in Redlands, California. Riley graduated from Redlands High School in 1995 and spent five years as a helicopter machine gunner in the U.S. Marine Corps. He served in Africa, Kosovo, Haiti, and the Dominican Republic before leaving the service in 2000. Riley later worked as a State Department contractor employee in Afghanistan, where he met his business partner, Doug Kidd, a former army sergeant. After working in construction for several years, Riley invested his savings into the former headquarters for his contracting business, Crown Painting, which he transformed into a distillery. Riley handled all of the plumbing, wood, and concrete work himself while also teaching himself how to make whiskey with a small pot still.

Today, Riley operates a fifty-five-gallon spirit still, a hundred-gallon stripping still, and two hundred-gallon cooking and fermentation vessels to produce 1775 Whiskey (a nod to Marine Corps history), California Clear white whiskey, and Jeremiah Riley Bourbon, made with New Mexico blue corn and Wisconsin barley. Riley recently invented a way to save water by rigging two swamp coolers, a sub pump, and extra hoses and circulating water from the condenser to cool mash without blending water into it. Riley estimates that his "swamp thing" will save approximately 150,000 gallons of water every year.

Also in 2013, Bill Rogers, the son of a sailor, founded Liberty Call Distilling near San Diego. His business partner and head distiller, Steve Grella, joined the business after completing his service to the U.S. Navy aboard the USS *Carl Vinson*. The distillery's name is a nod to the navy's unofficial tradition of allowing sailors to get off of their ships to drink. The men operate a hundred-gallon column still to produce a solera-aged four-grain whiskey among many other spirits.

In 2014, Travis Barnes founded Hotel Tango Whiskey in Indianapolis, Indiana. Barnes enlisted in the U.S. Marine Corps after September 11, 2001, and served as a recon marine in the First Reconnaissance Battalion from 2002 to 2006. Barnes deployed three times to Iraq and still boasts of leading six men into combat on his first deployment and bringing them all home safely. Like most recon marines who deployed to Iraq during that timeframe, Barnes has war stories. The "best whiskey [he] ever tasted" was from a bottle he purchased in a small shack outside of Ramadi, Iraq; unfortunately, it was also the "worst diarrhea [he] ever blasted."[20] After spending time in Fallujah and Baghdad, Sergeant Barnes suffered a traumatic brain injury, came home, and was honorably discharged. He continued his education, all the way through Indiana University's Robert H. McKinney School of Law, where he met his wife, Hilary.

During law school, Hilary and Travis began seriously considering opening a business instead of pursuing traditional legal careers. "None of the big law firms were knocking down my door during second year of law school, so necessity became the mother of all inventions for me. I have always had an interest in distilling, and turned a hobby into a career," he said.[21] In November 2013, Barnes secured a license to make liquor and pitched the business plan to his law school study group. At an Indiana University Club private Scotch tasting, Barnes passed out samples of his liquor and found several investors.

Today, Hotel Tango Whiskey produces an American whiskey, Bravo Bourbon, Victor Vodka, Mike Moonshine, Lima Charlie Limoncello, Romeo Rum, Golf Gin, and Oscar Charlie Orangecello. Travis runs the distillery like a platoon and considers Marine Corps leadership traits in evaluating prospective employees. "Every man knows the job of the guy below and above him/her. . . . I owe everything to the Marine Corps for where I am today. It hasn't all been sunshine and roses since getting out, but I wouldn't have graduated college, law school, worked for a senator, and started my own business without the lessons I learned in the military."[22]

Also in 2014, Kevin Kurland founded the Smoky Quartz Distillery in Seabrook, New Hampshire. In 2008, while Kurland was in the U.S. Air Force and deployed to Iraq, he read a *Wall Street Journal* article about micro-distilling during a prolonged indirect fire attack. "That sounded a whole lot more fun than what I was doing at the time."[23] When Kurland came home, he left the air force and started the distillery with the help of his father and uncle, both veterans, who ran all of the necessary piping for the stills to operate. Today, Kurland's distillery produces V5 Small Batch Bourbon from 100 percent locally sourced organic corn.

In 2015, Ryan Cherrick, a Marine Corps veteran, opened Branded Hearts Distillery with air force veteran Josh Nichols in Reno, Nevada. Cherrick's current business partners are also military veterans. Branded Hearts produces wheat whiskey and bourbon whiskey made with oats. In Frederick, Maryland, Mark Lambert founded the forty-one-hundred-square-foot Dragon Distillery after serving in the U.S. Navy as an Arabic linguist and intelligence analyst. Lambert served on a number of surface and subsurface ships while stationed in Greece for five years and participated in Operations Desert Storm / Desert Shield. Lambert's Dragon Distillery currently produces Basilisk Bourbon Whiskey, among many other spirits. In Miami, Fernando Plata cofounded Big Cypress Distillery. In the 1990s, Plata served in the historic and highly decorated 504th Parachute Infantry Regiment, part of the 82nd Airborne Division. Plata served as a personal radiotelephone operator for Generals John Abizaid and David Petraeus. Today, he and fellow veteran Danny Garo produce Hell's Bay American whiskey, along with craft rum and gin.

Retired rear admiral Scott Sanders helped to establish the Tobacco Barn Distillery in Hollywood, Maryland, in 2015. In addition to producing its "navy-style" rum, the distillery now produces a Maryland bourbon whiskey, distilled from estate-grown corn. Before cofounding the distillery, Admiral Sanders served on active duty as an E-2C pilot with VAW-126 "Seahawks" and deployed to the Atlantic, Mediterranean, and Caribbean aboard USS *John F. Kennedy* from 1983 to 1986. He later reported for duty as the E-2C model manager and naval air forces Atlantic E-2C evaluator ashore before transitioning to reserve status in 1987.

Sanders spent much of his career focusing on maritime ballistic missile defense. He served as vice commander, U.S. Naval Forces Central Command, and the commander of Combined Task Force 151, where he led forty-four hundred sailors on nineteen ships from seven nations, in a coalition counter-piracy force operating off the coast of Somalia. He finished his career as the deputy commander for U.S. Second Fleet.

Admiral Sanders is not the only retiree to open a distillery. In 2015, Chad Butters and Jesse Tyahla established Eight Oaks Craft Distillery in New Tripoli, Pennsylvania. Butters, who grew up in an army family, flew UH-60 Blackhawk helicopters in the U.S. Army Reserve for twenty-five years, retiring as a chief warrant officer five. Upon his retirement, Butters chose Pennsylvania's Lehigh Valley, an agricultural hub with a rich whiskey tradition, to open the distillery. The first spirit the men produced in December 2015 was applejack, a spirit made and consumed by soldiers during the Revolutionary War. Today, Eight Oaks produces bourbon and Penna Rye whiskey among several other spirits.

Robert Copeland founded the Martin Greer Distillery in Alvarado, Texas, in 2015. Copeland served in the U.S. Army for twenty-four years, many of which were spent overseas in combat zones. Copeland spent a total of nine years overseas in locations including Afghanistan, Iraq, Haiti, Cuba, El Salvador, and Honduras. These days, he operates a custom built 110-gallon Rockypoint Copper still to make rum, moonshine, and Texas whiskey. David Reavis, a retired navy submarine electronics technician, founded the Three Brothers Distillery in Disputanta, Virginia, in 2015. The distillery produces George Rye Whiskey and Kablam white corn whiskey. Retired soldier Andrew Fairchok and retired airman Rodney Kaeding opened the Old Soldier Distillery in Tacoma, Washington, in 2015. The men produce traditional American whiskey, bourbon whiskey, and white corn whiskey under the Old Soldier label.

Like Old Soldier Distillery, several veteran-owned establishments incorporate patriotism and service into their operations and products. The veteran-owned clothing company Article 15 expanded into the whiskey space with their sourced Leadslingers bourbon, produced by the Scissortail Distillery in Oklahoma. Similarly, former recon marine Derek Sisson recently introduced Merica bourbon to the market, a whiskey sourced from MGP Ingredients in Indiana. Alex Mackiewicz and Alex Plitsas founded American Valor Spirits, a Connecticut-based company, in 2015. The men purchase American whiskey and bottle products under the Valor label at the Crown Valley Distillery in Missouri. Plitsas, an aerospace and defense industry executive, was once a junior volunteer fireman in New York. He performed search and rescue operations following the September 11, 2001, attacks, an experience that inspired him to join the U.S. Army Reserve. He served a tour of duty in Iraq, where he saw combat and received the Bronze Star Medal. He later deployed to Afghanistan as a Department of Defense civilian employee on a detail from the undersecretary of defense for intelligence. American Valor Spirits donates 10 percent of whiskey sales to first responder and military charities.

Jason Justice, whose father and grandfather both served in the military, founded the Justice Label Distillery in an old Sinton, Texas, Radio Shack building in 2015. Justice, an army logistics officer, deployed to Iraq in 2011 and is married to an army civil affairs officer. Inspired by his grandfather, a Vietnam veteran who served in all four branches of the military and dabbled in whiskey-making, Justice custom-built his distillery's two hundred-gallon stills. The distillery, which employs three veterans, currently produces a number of flavored moonshines and a series of Bronze Star Texas whiskeys, which is enhanced by charred pecan wood chips. Justice plans to release a cask-strength Bronze Star whiskey in 2018, followed by a straight whiskey, bourbon, and other whiskeys by 2020.

Several veteran-owned distilleries reflect relationships forged in the military. At Three Rivers Distilling Company in Fort Wayne, Indiana, military service is the bond that ties the men together. Three of the four owners, as well as four out of six employees, are active duty or retired military. The distillery produces Early Bourbon and a 122 proof un-aged corn whiskey in honor of northeast Indiana's military community.

Bill Karlson and John O'Mara met as students at the U.S. Merchant Marine Academy in Kings Point, New York. In 1982, both men earned commissions as ensigns in the naval reserve as well as U.S. Coast Guard licenses to sail as officers in the merchant marine. O'Mara left the service as a lieutenant, and Karlson left as a lieutenant commander. In 2015, they founded KO Distilling in Manassas, Virginia, where they produce straight bourbon whiskey, wheat whiskey, and rye whiskey under the Bare Knuckle label in addition to Virginia Moon white whiskey and other spirits.

At Old Line Spirits in Baltimore, Maryland, distillers Mark McLaughlin and Arch Watkins proudly walk through their twenty-five-thousand-square-foot warehouse, where hundreds of oak barrels silently mature their American single-malt whiskey. Mark and Arch met while serving as naval flight officers in the same electronic attack squadron, an experience that inspires their work today. After graduating from Villanova's navy ROTC program and the Citadel respectively, Mark and Arch were assigned to VAQ-129 on Whidbey Island, Washington. In 2005, they deployed to the Persian Gulf and flew missions from the USS *Theodore Roosevelt* in support of Operation Iraqi Freedom. Mark later spent time flying missions in the Pacific theater while Arch flew additional combat missions in Iraq and Afghanistan.

In 2010, Mark left the navy to attend business school in Charlottesville, Virginia. Arch completed an exchange program with the German Luftwaffe but eventually left active duty for a job at Johns Hopkins University in Baltimore. When Mark accepted a job in the investment banking industry in Maryland, he and his wife moved down the street from Arch in "Charm City." Both men continued to fly Prowlers for a navy reserve unit at nearby Andrews Air Force Base, but entrepreneurial spirits and a mutual love of whiskey led them to the next great adventure.

In 2014, Mark traveled to Seattle for a friend's wedding. He also attended the American Distilling Institute's Spirits Conference and Vendor Expo, intent on learning everything he could about opening a craft distillery with his friend Arch. While exploring the various vendor booths, Mark encountered an older gentleman named Bob Stillnovich. Mark learned that Bob was not only the proud owner of the popular Golden Distillery on Samish Island, Washington, but he was also a fellow combat veteran.

Bob had been drafted into the army in 1965. He completed officer candidate school, branched infantry, and shipped out to Vietnam as a second lieutenant. When another lieutenant in his battalion was shot during a helicopter assault, Bob was there to take control of a platoon in the Thirty-Fifth Infantry Regiment, and he fought for nearly eighteen months in the most dangerous jungles of South Vietnam. After his war ended, Bob came home and embarked on a career that included stints in high school physical education, seafood trading, developing restaurants, and whiskey-making. When he introduced himself to Mark, Bob and his partner, Jim Caudill, a U.S. Navy veteran, were looking to sell their five-year-old Puget Sound micro-distillery. Jim was gravely ill and Bob was interested in retiring, so he went searching for the right buyer.

When Mark returned to Maryland, he pitched the idea of purchasing Golden Distillery to his navy buddy and soon-to-be-business-partner, Arch. The men rode out to Washington State to inspect Golden's copper stills and Minnesota white oak barrels, taste Bob and Jim's single-malt whiskey, and learn everything they could about the Golden recipes and methods. In 2015, Mark and Arch purchased all of Golden's equipment and product and transported it to Maryland, where they developed the Old Line Spirits brand.

After buying Golden Distillery, Mark and Arch developed a partnership with Middle West Spirits in Columbus, Ohio, where they continue to learn the art and science of making whiskey in preparation for what they hope will be a long and prosperous career in the business. On the Old Line single-malt whiskey label, there are two small naval flags, "bravo" and "zulu," the military maritime signals for "well done." It is not only Mark's and Arch's vision for their distillery—it is also a message to fellow veterans Bob Stillnovich and the late Jim Caudill.

Former U.S. Navy divers Scott Nixon and Jason Pelle founded the Copper Collar Distillery in Santee, California, in 2016. Nixon and Pelle met in the navy and developed their business plan after deciding to leave the service. Both men used the GI Bill to continue educations, but they ultimately followed their entrepreneurial spirits and joined the San Diego Distillers Guild. Their distillery's name is a nod to the copper diving helmets navy sailors began wearing in the nineteenth century. Copper Collar currently produces vodka and rum and is planning to release a whiskey.

Calder Curtis founded Cockpit Craft Distillery in Colorado Springs, Colorado, in 2016. Curtis enlisted in the U.S. Air Force after graduating from high school and still serves as a reserve air force aircraft metals technologist. Calder has worked on F-117 Nighthawks at Holloman Air Force Base in New Mexico and C-130s at Peterson Air Force Base in Colorado and Afghanistan. After coming home from Afghanistan, he concluded definitively that office work was not for him and opened the distillery. Cockpit Craft pays homage to American aviation history through the production of fine spirits. The distillery currently produces P-51 Mustang Whiskey and P-38 Lightning Moonshine among others.

Pat Levy founded the Fairbanks Distilling Company in downtown Fairbanks, Alaska's historic city hall with his wife in 2016. Levy's father, stepfather, and older brother all served in the U.S. Coast Guard, so when he graduated from high school, naturally, he signed up to "save lives and property."[24] Between 1975 and 1979, Levy served as the navigator for a California-based search and rescue crew. He said, "Our aircraft would fly out at altitude to a new search location daily, drop down to 2,000 feet, shut down two of our four engines for extended search time, and search and search and search the high seas."[25] These days, Levy is making potato vodka and working with local farmers to purchase barley for whiskey.

Gary Grantham founded the White Mule Distillery in Purdy, Missouri, in 2016. Grantham decided to open the distillery during a 2013 deployment to Afghanistan in support of Operation Enduring Freedom. He was on R&R leave in Dubai when he made up his mind. After eight years in the army and losing a good friend in combat, he decided to move home to the Ozarks and make whiskey. Grantham and his wife, Misty, also an army veteran, hired their friend Mark, a retired helicopter door gunner, to assist them at the distillery. White Mule currently produces whiskey aged in used bourbon barrels and several moonshines.

U.S. Air Force veteran Hugh Thomas founded Gorget Distilling Company in Lugoff, South Carolina, with U.S. Army veteran Richard Butler. Gorget released a bourbon whiskey in December 2017 and plans to produce other whiskey products in the future.

Zach Hollingsworth, a U.S. Marine Corps veteran and Scott Brown, a U.S. Air Force veteran, founded the Have a Shot of Freedom Whiskey Company in Wilmington, Ohio, in 2017. Hollingsworth traces the company's roots to a 2011 Marine artillery barrage in Afghanistan when he heard a senior noncommissioned officer shout that "freedom has a flavor the protected will never know." The men currently purchase small-batch bourbon whiskey made in California and sell it through their website. They donate a portion of their profits to several charities, including the Semper Fi fund, the Hoody Memorial Fund, Operation Finally Home, and the American Legion.

Andrew Lang opened Leatherwood Distillery in Pleasant View, Tennessee, in 2017 as a tribute to his former Special Forces unit. Lang spent twenty-four years on active duty in the U.S. Army, retiring as a master sergeant. Lang served with the Fort Campbell, Kentucky–based Fifth Special Forces Group for sixteen years and deployed nine times to Iraq and Afghanistan. During a 2011 tour to Afghanistan, Lang met Afghan Masoud Rezai, and the men formed a friendship. In 2014, Lang was back in Afghanistan and reunited with Rezai, who later obtained a special visa to move to the United States. Today, Rezai works for Lang at the distillery. The men currently produce rum and five flavors of moonshine. In time, they will produce Tennessee straight whiskey.

U.S. Army Special Forces soldiers Scott Neil, Rob Schaefer, John Koko, and Tyler Garner founded the American Freedom Distillery in St. Petersburg, Florida, in 2017. The men were some of the first Green Berets to fight in Afghanistan after the September 11, 2001, attacks. In retirement, they opened the distillery and now produce Horse Soldier Bourbon, inspired by distillery co-owners Bob Pennington and Mark Nutsch, who commanded a small element of Fifth Special Forces Group soldiers, known as the Horse Soldiers, in Afghanistan in 2001.

Without a doubt, there are other whiskey-focused craft distilleries owned or operated by veterans. More will open after the publication of this book. Bourbons, ryes, wheat whiskeys, single-malts, and experimental whiskeys will come and go. Selfless service to the nation, however, and the tradition of veteran-made American whiskey, will endure forever.

Acknowledgments

I have so many people to thank. Mary Dudley, Robbie, and Mary Grace Tramazzo are the loves of my life and supported me unconditionally. Robert and Lynn Bertram believed in the project from the beginning and provided me with all of the books and bourbon I needed to turn an interesting idea into a manuscript. Charlie, Sharon, and Susan Tramazzo, Will, Lauren, Sarah, and Charles Bertram, and Jeff and Whitney Thweatt provided constant support.

I am grateful beyond words for the time and assistance provided by Janet Patton, Steve Mayeux, Kim Handy, Amy Preske, Stephanie Schmidt, Julian Van Winkle III, Sissy Van Winkle, Sally Van Winkle Campbell, Joe Magliocco, Freddie Johnson, John Trowbridge, Richard Wolf, Al Young, Ken Mannshardt, Fred Minnick, and many others.

I am perhaps most grateful for the editors and staff at the University of Nebraska Press, who recognized the value in this multiyear project. Tom Swanson, Natalie O'Neal, Abby Stryker, Ann Baker, and Rosemary Sekora are true professionals. Finally, I owe copyeditor Jesse Arost an entire barrel of bourbon for his expert editing work. Cheers!

Appendix

HAPPY HOUR

In April 1914 Mexican soldiers arrested nine American sailors for entering off-limits areas in the port city of Tampico. The sailors were released, but Rear Admiral Henry T. Mayo demanded an apology and a twenty-one-gun salute. Gen. Morelos Zaragoza offered a sincere apology to an American emissary, but Admiral Mayo wanted more. He again demanded that the American flag be hoisted "in a prominent position on shore" and saluted by twenty-one guns.[1]

The Mexican general, backed by controversial President Victoriano Huerta, refused the salute, infuriating the U.S. Navy and President Woodrow Wilson, who believed Huerta to be a ruthless dictator. Later in the week, when U.S. forces discovered a German vessel delivering machine guns and ammunition to Huerta, President Wilson ordered the U.S. Navy's Atlantic Fleet to occupy the port of Veracruz and block the shipment.

On April 21, 1914, several hundred U.S. Marines from the Second Advanced Base Regiment commanded by Col. John A. Lejeune and 285 armed sailors from the U.S. ships *Florida* and *Utah* occupied Veracruz by force. The Atlantic Fleet's flagship, USS *Arkansas*, also contributed

17 officers and 313 enlisted men, who fought through and secured the city. Two of the *Arkansas*'s crewmen were killed in the fighting, and another two, John Grady and Jonas H. Ingram, received Medals of Honor for their actions.

The violence quickly leveled off, and by April 30, 1914, the *Arkansas*'s detachment was back on the vessel, where it remained until September. Daily life in the port became tedious for the sailors and war correspondents traveling with the Atlantic Fleet. The *Arkansas* crew passed time by holding "happy hours," semiweekly smokers that included "moving pictures, boxing bouts, chorus singing of popular songs, and dramatics."[2] At the time, sailors could still lawfully drink alcohol onboard their ships. After several popular reports of "happy hours" emerged in the pages of *Our Navy*, other vessels in the fleet began holding weekly "happy hours," a navy tradition that continued well into the 1950s.

Happy hour went mainstream in 1959 when the *Saturday Evening Post* published an article entitled "The Men Who Chase Missiles," a profile of U.S. airmen stationed on remote island bases to track intercontinental ballistic missiles launched from Florida's Cape Canaveral.[3] The author noted how the airmen had nowhere to spend their money, "except during happy hour" at the bars on their distant outposts. The phrase, like the custom of drinking before dinner, took off in the United States.

Like happy hour, many American cocktails trace their roots to wartime experiences, necessity, relationships, and ingenuity. The Aviation, Cuba Libre (aka rum and coke), daiquiri, French 75, gin and tonic, Gunfire, Irish Coffee, Kamikaze, Sidecar, and Singapore Sling all originated in the military. Even Angostura bitters were invented as a tonic for soldiers and sailors suffering from stomach ailments. So enjoy your next happy hour, and toast your next cocktail to the service members who brought the tradition home!

LIGHT INFANTRY

Light infantry is a designation reserved for foot soldiers. Light infantrymen rely on speed and mobility to skirmish with their enemies in advance of main battles. The Light Infantry cocktail features American rye whiskey and French Lillet, a blend of Bordeaux wine and citrus liqueur. I recommend rye whiskey from Colorado's 10th Mountain Whiskey & Spirit Company, named in honor of the U.S. Army's light infantry division currently based at Fort Drum, New York.

> *2 ounces 10th Mountain Whiskey & Spirit Company rye whiskey*
> *1 ounce Lillet blanc*
> *½ ounce Cocchi Vermouth de Torino*
> *4 dashes orange bitters*
> *1 large, thick orange peel, for garnish*
> *1 maraschino cherry, for garnish*

Place rye, Lillet, vermouth, and bitters in a shaker with ice and stir. Rub orange peel around rim of a chilled martini glass. Strain drink into glass. Twist orange peel over drink to release its oils and add to glass. Garnish with a cherry.

CHATHAM ARTILLERY PUNCH

One legend holds that when George Washington visited Savannah, Georgia, in 1791, he gifted the Chatham Artillery with two cannons his troops had captured during the Battle of Yorktown. In return, they celebrated with dinners and toasts and a strong whiskey punch.

An alternative history traces the punch's roots to the 1850s and a unit called the Republican Blues. After returning to Savannah from drill in Macon, Georgia, the men were welcomed back by Sgt. A. B. Luce and the Chatham Artillery. Luce concocted a punch using a horse bucket filled with finely crushed ice to which a quart of brandy, whiskey, and rum were poured and lemon and sugar added. The bucket was filled with champagne and stirred to "delirious deliciousness."

> *8 lemons*
> *1 pound of superfine sugar*
> *1 bottle of bourbon or rye whiskey*
> *1 bottle of cognac*
> *1 bottle of dark Jamaican rum*
> *3 bottles champagne or other sparkling wine*
> *Nutmeg*

Squeeze and strain the lemons to make sixteen ounces of juice. Peel the lemons and muddle the peels with the sugar. Let the peels and sugar sit for an hour, then muddle again. Add the lemon juice and stir until sugar has dissolved. Strain out the peels. Fill a two- to three-gallon bucket or bowl with crushed ice or ice cubes. Add the lemon-sugar mixture and the bourbon, Cognac, and rum. Stir and add the champagne. Taste and adjust for sweetness. Grate nutmeg over the top and serve.

THE FIGHTING SIXTY-NINTH

Gen. Thomas Francis Meagher, commander of the Irish Brigade in the Civil War (a contingent of Massachusetts, Pennsylvania, and New York soldiers, including the Sixth-Ninth New York Infantry Regiment) liked to drink his whiskey with Vichy water. On one occasion, his aide was unable to find Vichy water, so he returned with champagne. Meagher liked the new mixture, and the drink stuck. (Be careful, General Meagher drunkenly fell from his horse during the Battle of Antietam.)

Others say the cocktail was created during the unit's service in the Champagne region of France during World War I. One of the first books on mixing drinks, Jerry Thomas's *The Bon Vivant's Companion* (1862), describes the 69th Regiment Punch as consisting of one ounce of Irish whiskey, one ounce of Scotch whisky, a teaspoon of sugar, and four ounces of hot water.

2 parts champagne
1 part Irish whiskey

PATTON'S ARMORED DIESEL

In the early 1940s, Gen. George S. Patton created a drink he called the Armored Diesel to create camaraderie amongst his newly formed armored division. The division carried its mobile bar across France and into Germany. The general was known to serve libations from oil cans that had been transformed into cocktail goblets by sawing off the bottoms and soldering the can tips onto them.[4] (Be careful, General Patton had no sense of taste or smell to speak of.)

1 ounce Old Crow bourbon whiskey
1 ounce Johnny Walker Red Label Scotch whisky
1 ounce Southern Comfort
California white wine to taste
Splash of lemon juice
Sugar to taste
Mix well with ice

MACARTHUR PUNCH

A World War II–era cocktail named for the general of the army, who appreciated stiff whiskey.

1½ ounces rye whiskey
1 ounce dry red wine
1 ounce cherry heering
1 ounce dry orange curacao
2 ounces orange juice
1 ounce lime juice
1 ounce sparkling water

Combine all ingredients except sparkling water in a cocktail shaker. Shake. Strain into a glass filled with crushed ice. Top with sparkling water.

THE OMAR BRADLEY

Gen. Omar Bradley was a highly distinguished senior officer in the U.S. Army during and after World War II. He was the last man to wear five stars and the rank of general of the army. He served as the commander of the Eighty-Second Airborne Division, the commander of American ground forces for the 1944 D-Day invasion at Normandy, as army chief of staff, chairman of the joint chiefs of staff, and, later, as the U.S. secretary of veterans affairs. General Bradley, a Missourian with family roots in Kentucky, liked bourbon. His wartime driver was a former bartender. He was known for giving bottles of liquor to his aides and subordinates. His staff threw plenty of cocktail parties during the war, and he attended more than a few. On one occasion during the war,

General Bradley sought an orange to muddle for an Old Fashioned. With no oranges available, the General improvised with a dollop of orange marmalade and a new drink was born.

2 ounces bourbon whiskey
1 tsp. orange marmalade
1 squeeze fresh lemon juice
1 dash Angostura bitters

Shake well with ice and strain into an Old Fashioned glass with fresh ice. Garnish with a cherry.

NOTES

INTRODUCTION

1. Ross, *The General's Wife*, 38–43.
2. White, *American Ulysses*, 103.
3. White, *American Ulysses*, 74, 85.
4. White, *American Ulysses*, 103.
5. Keegan, *A History of Warfare*, 6.

1. BOURBON AND BULLETS

1. Theobold, "When Whiskey Was the King of Drink," *Colonial Williamsburg Journal*, Summer 2008, http://www.history.org/foundation/journal/summer08/whiskey.cfm.
2. Parker, *The Sugar Barons*, 322.
3. Smith, *The World of the American Revolution*, 369.
4. Carson, *The Social History of Bourbon*, 10, 30.
5. Cheever, *Drinking in America*, 163, 176.
6. Ratliff, *How to Be a Revolutionary War Soldier*, 18.
7. Letter from General George Washington to the president of the Continental Congress, August 16, 1777, George Washington Papers, series 4, General Correspondence, Library of Congress, https://www.loc.gov/resource/mgw4.043_0699_0702; General George Washington, General Orders, August 7, 1756, in Fitzpatrick, *Writings of George Washington*, 1:441.

8. U.S. Naval Institute Staff, "A Hundred Years Dry: The U.S. Navy's End of Alcohol at Sea," *U.S. Naval Institute News*, July 1, 2014, https://news.usni.org/2014/07 /01/hundred-years-dry-u-s-navys-end-alcohol-sea.

9. Minnick, *Bourbon Curious*, 41.

10. Hogeland, *The Whiskey Rebellion*, 114.

11. Hogeland, *The Whiskey Rebellion*, 99.

12. Hogeland, *The Whiskey Rebellion*, 217.

13. See generally Pogue, *George Washington and the Beginnings of the American Whiskey Industry*; see also Natasha Gelling, "Long Before Jack Daniels, George Washington Was a Whiskey Tycoon," *Smithsonian Magazine*, May 12, 2014.

14. Joyce, *Moonshine*, 40.

15. Julia Edwards, "Making Whiskey at George Washington's Distillery," *Washington Post*, March 27, 2013, https://www.washingtonpost.com/lifestyle/style/making -whiskey-at-george-washingtons-distillery/2013/03/27/3f6dc1b0–9189–11e2–9cfd -36d6c9b5d7ad_story.html?utm_term=.1bf09289fc14.

16. Quisenberry, *Kentucky Troops in the War of 1812*, 50.

17. Stone Jr., *Kentucky Fighting Men*, ix.

18. Crowgey, *Kentucky Bourbon*, 67.

19. "Anecdotes about Grant, Col. Stewart's Recollections of the Great Soldier," *The World*, August 7, 1885.

20. Sometime in the 1790s, pioneers Wattie Boone and Aaron Atherton established a small distillery on the banks of Knob Creek, where the water was "as nearly perfect as could be found for the manufacture of fine beverage whiskey." Thomas Lincoln briefly worked at the distillery on Knob Creek, where he fashioned whiskey barrels for the distillers. Tom's son Abe apparently assisted his father. As the legend goes, Wattie Boone predicted that young Abe Lincoln was "bound to make a great man, no matter what trade he follows," adding, "if he goes into the whiskey business, he'll be the best distiller in the land."

21. Carson, *The Social History of Bourbon*, 75.

22. Fisher, *Food in the American Military*, 36–37.

23. Belanger, *Deep Freeze*, 328.

24. Detzer, *Allegiance*, 208; see also Letter from Maj. Robert Anderson to Col. S. Cooper, Fort Sumter, South Carolina, March 6, 1861, *Miscellaneous Documents of the House of Representatives for the Second Session of the Fifty-Second Congress, 1892–93* (Washington DC: Government Printing Office, 1893), ch. 1, p. 191.

25. Carson, *The Social History of Bourbon*, 79.

26. Other Civil War whiskey nicknames included "bust-head," "pop-skull," "old red eye," "spill skull," "knock-knee," "tanglefoot," "oh, be joyful," and "nockum stiff."

27. See generally Lucas, *Sherman and the Burning of Columbia*.

28. Lankford, *Richmond Burning*, 164, 200.

29. Coffey, *The Civil War Months*, 398.

30. Wheelan, *Their Last Full Measure*, 291.

31. See generally Schultz, *Quantrill's War*.

32. Bill Samuels Jr. interview, November 18, 2013, Louie B. Nunn Center for Oral History, University of Kentucky Libraries.

33. Samuels Jr., *Maker's Mark*, 30–31.

34. See generally Hartigan, *Bill W.*

35. Veach, *Kentucky Bourbon Whiskey*, 101.

36. Letter from General Brehon Somervell to Mr. Lewis Rosenstiel, June 7, 1945, in Schenley Distillers Corp., *Remarks of Merit*, October 1945, Sazerac Company Archives, Buffalo Trace Distillery, Frankfort KY.

37. McCullough, *Truman*, 1,023.

38. Letter from President Harry S. Truman to Tom L. Evans, June 21, 1958, box 5, folder 2, Papers of Tom L. Evans, Harry S. Truman Presidential Library, Independence MO.

39. Distilled Spirits Council 2017 Economic Briefing, New York City, February 1, 2018, 43, https://www.distilledspirits.org/wp-content/uploads/2018/03/Distilled _Spirits_Council_Annual_Economic_Briefing_Feb_1_2018_Final.pdf; see also Minnick, *Bourbon*, 195.

40. Mitenbuler, *Bourbon Empire*, 241.

41. Mitenbuler, *Bourbon Empire*, 244.

42. Steve Ury, "The Complete List of American Whiskey Distilleries & Brands," *Sku's Recent Eats*, http://recenteats.blogspot.com/p/the-complete-list-of-american -whiskey.html.

43. Heaven Hill Distilleries Inc. executive Harry J. Shapira (1947–2013) designed the Evan Williams Bourbon Experience in downtown Louisville and the Bourbon Heritage Center in Bardstown. Shapira served in the U.S. Army for two years during the Vietnam War.

44. Thomas Sherman interview by author, October 19, 2016.

45. Corey Barnes interview, March 3, 2016.

46. "U.S. Army Is Generous with Equipment but Is Inexorable about Accounting," *Indianapolis Star*, May 25, 1941.

47. Amanda Macias, "One Group Buys More Barrels of Jack Daniel's Whiskey Than Anyone Else on the Planet," *Business Insider*, November 1, 2016, http://www .businessinsider.com/us-military-loves-jack-daniels.

48. Mitenbuler, *Bourbon Empire*, 132.

49. Julian Van Winkle III interview, April 20, 2010, Louie B. Nunn Center for Oral History, University of Kentucky Libraries.

50. Van Winkle Campbell, *But Always Fine Bourbon*, 87.

2. RED LIKKER

1. 27 Code of Federal Regulations § 5.22(b) (1969).

2. Minnick, *Whiskey Women*, 16.

3. Veach, *Kentucky Bourbon Whiskey*, 13.

4. Minnick, *Bourbon*, 21, citing the *Western Citizen* (Bourbon County KY), June 26, 1821.

5. 27 Code of Federal Regulations § 5.22(b)(iii) (1969).

6. Wiley, *An Autobiography*, 67.

7. Wiley, *An Autobiography*, 70–71.

8. Michael Veach, "President Taft Inducted to the Kentucky Bourbon Hall of Fame," *Filson Historical Society Blog*, December 22, 2009, http://filsonhistorical .org/president-taft-inducted-to-the-kentucky-bourbon-hall-of-fame.

9. While serving as a judge in 1869, Alphonso Taft presided over a lawsuit filed by the government of Japan against Ohio-based whiskey merchants. The basis of the lawsuit was an objection to rectifiers exporting rectified whiskey labeled as straight whiskey. Taft ruled that products containing neutral spirits could not be called whiskey, a precedent that likely influenced his son's ruling four decades later.

10. William Howard Taft, "The Proposal for a League to Enforce Peace: Affirmative," *Faculty Scholarship Series*, 1916, Paper 3939, http://digitalcommons.law.yale.edu /fss_papers/3939.

11. Mangan, *On This Day in Connecticut History*, 77.

12. 27 Code of Federal Regulations § 5.22(b)(1)(i) (1969).

13. Kleber et al., *The Kentucky Encyclopedia*, 480–81.

14. Bober, *Thomas Jefferson*, 134.

15. Jouett's grandson James Edward served with Admiral David Farragut in the Civil War and was mentioned in Farragut's famous command: "Damn the torpedoes! Four bells! Captain Drayton go ahead! Jouett full speed!"

16. The Bucks breached the agreement by failing to provide Jouett with the whiskey, which compelled a lawsuit. Records from the litigation led modern archaeologists to the site of his distillery on Craig's Creek Road, southwest of Versailles, Kentucky.

17. Staples, *The History of Pioneer Lexington*, 18.

18. Crowgey, *Kentucky Bourbon*, 62.

19. Purvis, *The Ethnic Descent of Kentucky's Early Population*, 261.

20. Alvey, *Kentucky Bluegrass Country*, 110.

21. Dieterle, *Economics*, 445.

22. Chernow, *Alexander Hamilton*, 468.

23. Swett, *Who Was the Commander at Bunker Hill?*, 18.

24. Syrett and Cooke, *The Papers of Alexander Hamilton*, 99.

25. Slaughter, *The Whiskey Rebellion*, 188.

26. C. M. Ewing, "The Causes of That So-Called Whiskey Insurrection of 1794," Washington and Jefferson College, 1930.

27. Syrett and Cooke, *The Papers of Alexander Hamilton*, 306.

28. Slaughter, *The Whiskey Rebellion*, 177–78.

29. Diane E. S. Widmer and Annabelle Caldwell, "Whiskey Rebellion 1791–1794," *Monongahela Area Historical Society*, 1990.

30. Slaughter, *The Whiskey Rebellion*, 183.

31. Proclamation, George Washington, August 7, 1794, Founders Online website, National Archives, last modified February 1, 2018, http://founders.archives.gov/documents/Washington/05-16-02-0365.

32. Cheever, *Drinking in America*, 70.

33. Hogeland, *The Whiskey Rebellion*, 238.

34. Slaughter, *The Whiskey Rebellion*, 177.

35. Onuf, *Establishing the New Regime*, 255–56.

36. 27 Code of Federal Regulations § 5.22(b)(1)(i) (1969).

37. Work, *Wood, Whiskey, and Wine*, 49.

38. Work, *Wood, Whiskey, and Wine*, 47–49.

39. Veach, *Kentucky Bourbon Whiskey*, 19.

40. Minnick, *Bourbon*, 133.

41. Sondhaus, *Naval Warfare*, 2.

42. Laplander, *Finding the Lost Battalion*, 679.

43. Bryson, *Tasting Whiskey*, 144.

44. Macdonald, *Whisky*, 57.

45. Coulombe, *Rum*, 45.

46. The Whisky Professor, "Why Is Scotch Whisky Bottled at 40% ABV?" *Scotch Whisky*, January 4, 2017, https://scotchwhisky.com/magazine/ask-the-professor/12295/why-is-scotch-whisky-bottled-at-40-abv/.

47. S. Con. Res. 19, 88th Cong., 78 Stat. 1208 (1964); see also Mark Wayne Podvia, "Bourbon and the Law: A Brief Overview," *Newsletter of the Legal History and Rare Books SIS of the American Association of Law Libraries* 21, no. 2 (June 19, 2015). Congress's two spellings of the word *whisk(e)y* was likely a mistake.

48. The Kentucky representatives in the 88th Congress were Thruston Ballard Morton, John Sherman Cooper, Frank Stubblefield, William Huston Natcher, Gene Snyder, Frank Chelf, Eugene Siler, John C. Watts, and Carl Perkins. Neither Snyder, who was thirteen at the outbreak of WWII, nor Watts, a farmer and lawyer from Lexington, served in the armed forces.

49. Richard Harwood, "John Sherman Cooper Obituary," *Washington Post*, February 23, 1991.

50. Morton was a descendant of Revolutionary War hero and whiskey distiller George Rogers Clark. His brother Rogers Clark Ballard Morton married Anne Prather Jones, the great-granddaughter of Col. Warner Paul Roland Jones, whose brother, Paul L. Jones Jr., founded Four Roses after serving in the Civil War.

51. Dorothy J. Gaiter, "Thruston B. Morton Is Dead at 74; Served as Senator from Kentucky," *New York Times*, August 15, 1982.

52. Mitenbuler, *Bourbon Empire*, 225.

53. Mitenbuler, *Bourbon Empire*, 3.

54. "Extension of Bonding Period on Liquor: Hearings before the Committee on Finance," Senate, 83rd Cong. 2 (1954), 4.

55. Mitenbuler, *Bourbon Empire*, 228.

56. Aime J. Forand Papers (1918–1972), Providence College, Phillips Memorial Library, Special and Archival Collections.

57. "Biography of Aime Joseph Forand (1895–1972)," U.S. House of Representatives, History, Art & Archive website, http://history.house.gov/People/Detail/13294.

58. Mitenbuler, *Bourbon Empire*, 228.

59. Mitenbuler, *Bourbon Empire*, 234.

60. "1964 Congressional Resolution Declaring Bourbon 'America's Native Spirit' Comes to Kentucky," *Kentucky Distillers' Association*, May 9, 2014, http://kybourbontrail.com/1964-congressional-resolution-declaring-bourbon-americas-native-spirit-comes-kentucky/.

61. See generally Seward, *The Bourbon Kings of France.*

62. Newton, *Angry Mobs and Founding Fathers*, 66.

63. Clary, *Adopted Son,* 479.

64. Crowgey, *Kentucky Bourbon*, 124.

65. McGirr, *Tarascon of Shippingport at the Falls of the Ohio*, 89–100.

66. Veach, *Kentucky Bourbon Whiskey*, 28; Reigler, *Kentucky Bourbon Country*, 13.

67. Din and Harkins, *New Orleans Cabildo*, 7.

68. Killikelly, *The History of Pittsburgh*, 123.

69. Veach, *Kentucky Bourbon Whiskey*, 25.

70. Minnick, *Bourbon*, 29.

71. Minnick, *Bourbon*, 29.

72. Minnick, *Bourbon*, 19–29.

73. Minnick, *Bourbon*, 26.

74. "Proceedings of the Mississippi Valley Historical Association, Volume IX for the Years 1915–1918," *Mississippi Valley Historical Association*, 141, 144.

75. Spears, *The Spears Saga*, 37.

76. Spears, *The Spears Saga*, 37.

77. *Advocate-Messenger* (Danville KY), February 27, 1977, 34.

78. General Clark, the son of Virginia farmer distiller John Clark, founded Louisville in 1780. Clark was pressured to retire after abusing whiskey on duty and left the service in significant debt, as he personally funded his unit's campaign during the revolution. In 1809, following what was likely a drunken fall into a burning fireplace, Clark moved into his brother's Locust Grove estate in Louisville, where farmhands operated a gristmill and small whiskey distillery. He died there in 1818.

79. Illinois State Historical Society, *Transactions of the Illinois State Historical Society for the Year 1903*, 177. Col. Abraham Bowman's great-grandson Abram Smith Bowman opened a whiskey distillery near Reston, Virginia, in 1934. His products included Fairfax County and Virginia Gentleman. Today the Sazerac Company owns the A. Smith Bowman Distillery, which relocated to Fredericksburg, Virginia, in 1988.

80. Minnick, *Bourbon*, 23.

81. Minnick, *Bourbon*, 21, citing the *Western Citizen* (Bourbon County KY), June 26, 1821.

82. Crowgey, *Kentucky Bourbon*, 122–23.

83. Crowgey, *Kentucky Bourbon*, 123.

84. Veach, *Kentucky Bourbon Whiskey*, 25.

3. WAR AND WHISKEY PERSIST

1. Carson, *The Social History of Bourbon*, 62.

2. Fisher, *Food in the American Military*, 36–37.

3. "An Act to Increase the Present Military Establishment of the United States," 25th Cong. 2, sec. 17 (1838).

4. Homans, *The Army and Navy Chronicle*, 331.

5. Petition of Andrew Jackson, February 12, 1803, HR 7A-F1.1, U.S. House of Representatives (NAID 306666).

6. Bell, *Circling Windrock Mountain*, 33.

7. Prucha, *Army Life on the Western Frontier*, 126.

8. Mahan, *Old Fort Crawford and the Frontier*, 263.

9. Selcer, *Civil War America*, 419.

10. Miller and Munoz, *Controlling Your Drinking*, 37.

11. Bowers, *Stonewall Jackson*, 140.

12. Wiley, *Life of Johnny Reb*, 40.

13. Wiley, *Life of Johnny Reb*, 223.

14. Letter from General Robert E. Lee to Fitzhugh Lee, May 30, 1858, George Bolling Lee Papers, Virginia Historical Society, 18411868, microfilm reels C27 and C278.

15. Bowers, *Stonewall Jackson*, 140.

16. Johnson, *In the Footsteps of Stonewall Jackson*, 190.

17. Bowers, *Stonewall Jackson*, 342.

18. Gienapp, *The Civil War Diary of Gideon Welles*, 262.

19. Gienapp, *The Civil War Diary of Gideon Welles*, 207.

20. Barton and Logue, *The Civil War Soldier*, 134.

21. Burton, *Melting Pot Soldiers*, 123.

22. Tim Omarzu, "Whiskey and the War: Alcohol Played a Role in the Civil War," *Times Free Press* (Chattanooga TN), October 21, 2012, http://www.timesfreepress .com/news/life/entertainment/story/2012/oct/21/whiskey-and-the-war-civil -war/90673/.

23. Losson, *Tennessee's Forgotten Warriors*, 325; see also McDonough, *Nashville*, 76.

24. Davis, *Crucible of Command*, 575; see also Rick Beard, "General Grant Takes a Spill," *New York Times*, September 4, 2013, https://opinionator.blogs.nytimes .com/2013/09/04/general-grant-takes-a-spill/.

25. Carson, *The Social History of Bourbon*, 75.

26. See generally Cadwallader, *Three Years with Grant*.

27. Carson, *The Social History of Bourbon*, 72.

28. Mingus, *The Louisiana Tigers in the Gettysburg Campaign*, 67.

29. Mingus, *The Louisiana Tigers in the Gettysburg Campaign*, 77.

30. Mingus, *The Louisiana Tigers in the Gettysburg Campaign*, 148.

31. Roy Morris Jr., ed., "America's Civil War: January 1998 from the Editor," *Weider History Group*, September 23, 1998, http://www.historynet.com/americas-civil-war-january-1998-from-the-editor.htm.

32. Rowland, *Strange and Obscure Stories of the Civil War*, 160.

33. Carson, *The Social History of Bourbon*, 72.

34. Carson, *The Social History of Bourbon*, 72.

35. Carson, *The Social History of Bourbon*, 72.

36. Carson, *The Social History of Bourbon*, 73.

37. Carson, *The Social History of Bourbon*, 77.

38. Bruce E. Stewart, "Distillers and Prohibitionists: Social Conflict and the Rise of Anti-Alcohol Reform in Appalachian North Carolina, 1790–1908" (dissertation, University of Georgia, 2007), 101–2.

39. Christ, *Civil War Arkansas*, 139.

40. Mitenbuler, *Bourbon Empire*, 100.

41. Perrin, *Kentucky*, 725.

42. Perrin, *Kentucky*, 711.

43. Federal Publishing Company, *The Union Army*, 338.

44. Jack Sullivan, "Wiley Searcy: Kentucky Distiller in War and Peace," *Those Pre-Pro Whiskey Men!*, June 22, 2013, http://pre-prowhiskeymen.blogspot.com/2013/06/wiley-searcy-kentucky-distiller-in-war.html.

45. Zoeller, *Bourbon in Kentucky*, 237–38.

46. Another "Morgan's Brigade" trooper was John Lewis Mock (1841–1915), the son of prominent Kentucky distiller John J. Mock, whose Old Mock bourbon brand was acquired by Pappy Van Winkle's Stitzel-Weller Distillery after the repeal of Prohibition. John Mock was taken prisoner in 1863 but escaped to Canada and participated in the St. Alban's Raid with the Confederate Secret Service in Vermont.

47. "Ripy Brothers Distilling Company," *Anderson News*, Souvenir Supplement, June 1906, 38; see also "Distillery Now Bottling Plant," *Anderson News*, Centennial Edition, August 1, 1977, 19.

48. Cecil, *The Evolution of the Bourbon Whiskey Industry in Kentucky*, 16.

49. Charles F. Conlon, "Taxation in the Alcoholic Beverage Field," *Law and Contemporary Problems* 7 (Fall 1940): 743.

50. McDonald, *Secrets of the Great Whiskey Ring*, 20.

51. Lucius E. Guese, "St. Louis and the Great Whiskey Ring," *Missouri Historical Review* 36, no. 2, State Historical Society of Missouri, January 1942, 172.

52. McDonald, *Secrets of the Great Whiskey Ring*, 256–59, 281.

53. McDonald, *Secrets of the Great Whiskey Ring*, 228.

54. McDonald, *Secrets of the Great Whiskey Ring*, 56.

55. Coffey, *The Reconstruction Years*, 269.

56. David McCullough, *Historical Encyclopedia of Illinois and History of Peoria County*, vol. 2. (Chicago: Brookhaven Press, 1902), 510–11.

57. Spoelman and Haskell, *Dead Distillers*, 137.

58. Pfanz, *Gettysburg*, 140–41.

59. Gurock, *American Jewish History*, vol. 1, 32–33.

60. Spoelman and Haskell, *Dead Distillers*, 137.

61. Bernie Drake, "When Peoria Tried to Monopolize Whiskey," *Peoria Magazines*, February 2016, http://www.peoriamagazines.com/ibi/2016/feb/when-peoria -tried-monopolize-whiskey.

62. Drake, "When Peoria Tried to Monopolize Whiskey."

63. Drake, "When Peoria Tried to Monopolize Whiskey."

64. Downard, *Dictionary of the History of the American Brewing and Distilling Industries*, 213–14.

65. *Congressional Record*, vol. 34, pt. 1, 56th Cong. 2, Senate, January 4, 1901, 118.

66. C. E. Littlefield, "Anti-Canteen Legislation and the Army," *North American Review* 178, no. 568 (March 1904): 398.

67. Wiley, *Beverages and the Adulteration, Origin, Composition, Manufacture, Natural, Artificial, Fermented, Distilled, Alkaloidal, and Fruit Juices*, 275.

68. Lyle W. Dorsett, "The Problem of Ulysses S. Grant's Drinking during the Civil War," *Hayes Historical Journal* 4, no. 2 (Fall 1983).

69. *Congressional Record, Volume LV, Appendix and Index to Parts 1–8*, 65th Cong. 1, October 2–6, 1917, 472.

70. Keene, *The United States and the First World War*, 41.

71. Morone, *Hellfire Nation*, 313.

72. "Yale Alumni Work for Dry Reunions," *New York Times*, May 8, 1917.

73. Josephus Daniels, General Order No. 99, *Navy Department*, Washington DC, June 1, 1914.

74. Zion, *The Republican Challenge*, 114.

75. Veach, *Kentucky Bourbon Whiskey*, 80.

76. Ross, *World War I and the American Constitution*, 189.

77. Keene, *The United States and the First World War*, 40; see also Veach, *Kentucky Bourbon Whiskey*, 80–81.

78. Buxton and Hughes, *The Science and Commerce of Whisky*, 74–75.

79. Duncan, *Pubs and Patriots*, 136.

80. Duncan, *Pubs and Patriots*, 104.

81. Duncan, *Pubs and Patriots*, 106.

82. Frederick Arthur McKenzie, "Soldiers' Unanimous Vote for Rum," 1914. https:// www.greatwarforum.org/

83. Gately, *Drink*, 361.

84. Tim Cook, "Rum in the Trenches," *Legion*, September 1, 2002, https:// legionmagazine.com/en/2002/09/rum-in-the-trenches/.

85. Mansergh, *Whitehaven in the Great War*, 8.

86. Graves, *Good Bye to All That*, 163.

87. Duncan, *Pubs and Patriots*, 68.

88. Minnick, *Bourbon*, 83.

89. "Thompson, Ex-president of Glenmore, Dies at Age 94," *Louisville Courier-Journal*, February 28, 1990.

90. Carol V. Dowden, "Col. Frank B. Thompson Is Just As He Appears in Those Whisky Ads," *Louisville Courier-Journal*, August 21, 1960.

91. Veach, *Kentucky Bourbon Whiskey*, 80.

92. Cecil, *The Evolution of the Bourbon Whiskey Industry in Kentucky*, 17.

93. Maynard, *Woodrow Wilson*, 179.

94. Kentucky Army National Guard Archives, February 21, 1922.

95. Pacult, *American Still Life*, 183.

96. Veach, *Kentucky Bourbon Whiskey*, 81–82.

97. "Our Story Begins in Henderson Co. Kentucky," Kentucky Peerless Distilling website, https://kentuckypeerless.com/our-story/the-peerless-timeline/.

98. Zoeller, *Bourbon in Kentucky*, 69; see also Minnick, *Bourbon Curious*, 42.

99. Dowden, "Col. Frank B. Thompson Is Just As He Appears."

100. Reeves, *Ol' Rum River*, 356–57.

101. Burk, *The Corporate State and the Broker State*, 80.

102. "War Veterans Raise Voices against Prohibition, Say It Flies Directly in the Face of God's Teachings," *Marin Journal* 12 (March 20, 1919): 3.

103. Franklin D. Roosevelt, "Address to the American Legion Convention," Chicago, Illinois, October 2, 1933, http://www.presidency.ucsb.edu/ws/?pid=14521.

104. Connor, *Watering Hole*, 72.

105. Reeves, *Ol' Rum River*, 350.

106. Stelze, *Why Prohibition!*, 56–70.

107. Pacult, *American Still Life*, 184.

108. Presidential Proclamation, December 5, 1933, identifier 299967, National Archives and Record Administration website, https://catalog.archives.gov/id/299967.

109. Veach, *Kentucky Bourbon Whiskey*, 92.

110. See generally Hartigan, *Bill W.*

111. "Soldier Invented 'Rhino Tank' to Smash Hedgerows after They Slowed Drive near St. Lo," *St. Louis Post-Dispatch*, July 2, 1945.

112. Borch, *Medals for Soldiers and Airmen*, 128.

113. Carafano, *GI Ingenuity*, 137.

114. Dwight D. Eisenhower, "Remarks upon Receiving the Hoover Medal Award," January 10, 1961.

115. "Fort Knox Building Named for Ingenious Jersey Guardsman," *Armor Magazine*, November–December 1989, 51.

116. Schenley Distillers Corp., *Remarks of Merit*, March 1944, , Sazerac Company Archives, Buffalo Trace Distillery, Frankfort KY.

117. Minnick, *Bourbon Curious*, 229.

118. "Deaths: McCarthy, Thomas Raynolds," *New York Times*, May 3, 1997.

119. Astor, *Semper Fi in the Sky*, 145.

120. Waymack and Harris, *The Book of Classic American Whiskeys*, 160–61.

121. "Eighth Infantry Division, a Combat History by Regiments and Special Units [U.S. Army, Thirteenth Infantry Regiment]," 1946, *World War Regimental Histories*, 84.

122. Scott Owens, "Soldier's Stories: Lt. Everett C. Owens; Forward Observer," Forty-Fifth Field Artillery Battalion, http://www.fatherswar.com/8thinfdiv/ww2/soldier%20stories/ww2_individual%20stories%20%20everett%20owens.html.

123. "Distiller Ernest Ripy, Jr. Dies at 89," *Lexington Herald-Leader*, March 27, 2002.

124. "Thompson, Ex-president of Glenmore, Dies at Age 94."

125. Colonel Thompson was succeeded at Glenmore by his son Frank Jr., who served in the U.S. Air Force from 1956 to 1958. The elder Thompson died in the winter of 1990 at the age of ninety-four and was inducted into the Kentucky Bourbon Hall of Fame in 2002, along with George T. Stagg, George Garvin Brown, and Julian "Pappy" Van Winkle, a fitting salute to the bourbon baron and war hero.

126. Lambert Willett et al. v. Commissioner, 16 T.C.M. 840, 845 (1957).

127. "Obituary: Robert E. Willett, Sr. Bardstown," *Nelson County Gazette*, April 7, 2017.

128. Two of Charlie's sons, Gerard Jude "Jerry" Willett and Charles D. "Sam" Willett Jr., followed in their father's footsteps by serving in the navy after graduating from the U.S. Naval Academy in 1976 and 1979, respectively.

129. Louis Forman Business Papers, accession 2290, Hagley Museum and Library, Wilmington DE.

130. Veach, *Kentucky Bourbon Whiskey*, 101.

131. Pacult, *American Still Life*, 112.

132. Reigler, *Kentucky Bourbon Country*, 91–92.

133. Minnick, *Whiskey Women*, 121–24.

134. Galatin, *Take Her Deep!*, 49.

135. Sulzberger, *World War II*, 193.

136. Winters and Kingseed, *Beyond Band of Brothers*, 46.

137. Ambrose, *Band of Brothers*, 279.

138. Tate, *Walkin' with the Ghost Whisperers*, 248.

139. Wilson, *Scotch*, 92.

140. Williams, *SS Leibstandarte*, 147.

141. Hall, Jake, "A Farewell to Sobriety, Part Two: Drinking during World War II," *War on the Rocks*, June 5, 2015, https://warontherocks.com/2015/06/a-farewell-to-sobriety-part-two-drinking-during-world-war-ii/.

142. Luther Huston, "Bourbon on the Potomac," *New York Times Sunday Magazine*, December 15, 1946.

143. Miscamble, *The Most Controversial Decision*, 69.

144. The family that ran Haig & Haig distillery included Field Marshal Douglas Haig, commander of the British Expeditionary Force during World War I. After leaving military service, he devoted his life to the welfare of veterans.

145. McCullough, *Truman*, 453.

146. Oe, *Hiroshima Notes*, 123.

147. Holdstock and Barnaby, *Hiroshima and Nagasaki*, 2.

148. Shannon, *Finding Japan*, 197.

149. Clay Risen, "The Billion-Dollar Bourbon Boom," *Fortune*, February 6, 2014, http://fortune.com/2014/02/06/the-billion-dollar-bourbon-boom/.

150. Veach, *Kentucky Bourbon Whiskey*, 106.

151. Veach, *Kentucky Bourbon Whiskey*, 106–7; see also Pacult, *American Still Life*, 193.

152. Mitenbuler, *Bourbon Empire*, 229.

153. Timothy Dunn, "The Passing of Lt. O'Connor," *Vietnam Veterans Memorial Fund*, March 7, 2000, http://www.vvmf.org/Wall-of-Faces/38332/brian-R-O'connor ?page=3#remembrances.

154. "Hall of Valor Silver Star Citation, Second Lieutenant Brian Richard O'Connor," *Military Times*, http://valor.militarytimes.com/recipient.php?recipientid=40897.

155. Dunn, "The Passing of Lt. O'Connor."

156. Ed St. Clair, "Ramled's Vietnam Journal," serial 40, March 31, 2008, http://www .archivum.info/vwar@lists.opn.org/2008-04/00016/(Vwar)-Ramled's-Vietnam -Journal-Serial-Nr-40.html.

157. Joe Galloway, "Remarks to Vietnam Helicopter Pilot Association Reunion," Washington DC, 2006.

158. Austin Wilcox, "Guest Book Comments," First Battalion, Twentieth Infantry Regiment website, December 31, 2007, http://www.1–20infantry.org/guestresultsy.htm.

159. John O'Meara, "A Present for Miss Tu," *Veterans Writing Project*, June 12, 2015, https://o-dark-thirty.org/2015/06/12/a-present-for-miss-tu/.

160. Richard Boyd, reply to "Vietnam Trivia," Leatherneck.com forums, May 16, 2004, http://www.leatherneck.com/forums/showthread.php?14608-Vietnam -Trivia&p=74510&viewfull=1#post74510.

161. Nick Marrapode, James Mulvaney interview, May 17, 2012, https://www .pritzkermilitary.org/files/1813/8445/9485/MulvaneyTranscript.pdf, 28.

162. Pacult, *American Still Life*, 134.

163. Pacult, *American Still Life*, 135.

164. Minnick, *Bourbon*, 191.

165. Paul Vitello, "Elmer T. Lee, 93, Kentucky's Bourbon Sage," *New York Times*, July 24, 2013.

166. Minnick, *Bourbon*, 193.

167. Vitello, "Elmer T. Lee, 93, Kentucky's Bourbon Sage."

168. Janet Kelly, Barry Kornstein, and Ryan Marshall, "The Economic and Fiscal Impacts of the Distilling Industry in Kentucky," *Urban Studies Institute*, University of Louisville, January 2017.

4. GEORGE WASHINGTON

1. Clary, *George Washington's First War*, 169.
2. Hening, *The Statutes at Large*, vol. 10, 19.
3. Fitzpatrick, *The Writings of George Washington*, 441.
4. Ford, *The True George Washington*, 296.
5. Ford, *The True George Washington*, 295.
6. Randall, *George Washington*, 102.
7. Gardner and Charles, *Election Law in the American Political System*, 2nd ed., 2.
8. Burns, *The Spirits of America*, 21.
9. Lisa Bramen, "Swilling the Planters with Bumbo: When Booze Bought Elections," *Smithsonian.com*, October 20, 2010, https://www.smithsonianmag.com/arts-culture/swilling-the-planters-with-bumbo-when-booze-bought-elections-102758236; see also Abbot, *The Papers of George Washington*, vol. 5, 349.
10. McCardell, *Ill-Starred General*, 188.
11. "The Indians, seeing them in this apparently desperate condition, thought they were an easy prey, and drawing their scalping knives and raising the war-whoop dashed toward them. The line never wavered; but, waiting until the Indians were but a few paces off, Captain Bullitt gave the order to fire, when instantly every gun was brought up, steadily aimed, and fired. Almost every shot is supposed to have taken effect, and the execution was such that the attacking force fell back and Bullitt retreated, covering also the retreat of the entire force, which otherwise would have been lost" (Bullitt, *My Life at Oxmoor*).
12. Bullitt, *My Life at Oxmoor*, 2.
13. Abbot, *The Papers of George Washington*, vol. 6, 120–23.
14. Upham, *The Life of General Washington*, 80.
15. Michael Beschloss, "George Washington, the Whiskey Baron," *New York Times*, February 14, 2016.
16. Frank J. Prial, "One Family's Story: From Apples to Applejack," *New York Times*, May 4, 2005.
17. Kaminski, *George Washington*, 20.
18. Crowgey, *Kentucky Bourbon*, 18.
19. Kosar, *Whiskey*, 92.
20. Phillips, *Alcohol*, 183.
21. Lender and Martin, *Drinking in America*, 32.
22. Minnick, *Whiskey Women*, 45.
23. Lender and Martin, *Drinking in America*, 32.
24. "An Act to Ascertain and Fix the Military Establishment of the United States," 4th Cong, 1, chap. 39 (1796).
25. Prial, "One Family's Story."
26. Fitzpatrick, *The Writings of George Washington from the Original Manuscript Sources 1745–1799*, vol. 24, 261.

27. Fitzpatrick, *The Writings of George Washington from the Original Manuscript Sources 1745–1799*, vol. 23, 106.

28. Fitzpatrick, *The Writings of George Washington from the Original Manuscript Sources 1745–1799*, vol. 33, 358.

29. Lengel, *First Entrepreneur*, 239.

30. Letter from George Washington to James Anderson, January 8, 1797, Founders Online website, National Archives, last modified February 1, 2018, http://founders.archives.gov/documents/Washington/99-01-02-00159.

31. Ford, *The True George Washington*, 123.

32. Joyce, *Moonshine*, 40.

33. See generally Pogue and White, *George Washington's Gristmill at Mount Vernon*.

5. EVAN AND ISAAC SHELBY

1. Draper, *King's Mountain and Its Heroes*, 411.

2. Hanna, *The Wilderness Trail*, 60.

3. Hinton, *The North Carolina Booklet*, 113.

4. Crowgey, *Kentucky Bourbon*, 23.

5. Crowgey, *Kentucky Bourbon*, 23–24.

6. Crowgey, *Kentucky Bourbon*, 30–31.

7. Crowgey, *Kentucky Bourbon*, 32.

8. Hinton, *The North Carolina Booklet*, 115.

9. Hinton, *The North Carolina Booklet*, 115.

10. Hinton, *The North Carolina Booklet*, 113.

11. Russell, *The American Revolution in the Southern Colonies*, 196.

12. Crowgey, *Kentucky Bourbon*, 140.

13. Harrison built a commercial farm and grew "very superior corn," some of which he converted into whiskey, "an article more portable and profitable." In the years preceding his presidency, however, Harrison closed his distillery, ceased drinking alcohol, and decried whiskey as "poison to the body and the soul"; see Burr, *The Life and Times of William Henry Harrison*, 257, 258, 295.

14. The toast was first delivered in 1938 by then-governor Albert "Happy" Chandler. Chandler signed up for Reserve Officers' Training Corps training in 1918 while a student at Transylvania College, but World War I ended before he graduated. During World War II, he served on the U.S. Senate's Committee on Military Affairs and traveled the world inspecting U.S. military bases.

6. THE WELLER FAMILY

1. A. W. Cissel, "Jacob Weller: America's First Manufacturer of Stick Matches," *Thurmont Scrapbook*, Greater Emmitsburg Area Historical Society, http://emmitsburg.net/history_t/archives/people/weller.htm.

2. Tracey and Dern, *Pioneers of Old Monocacy*, 210.

3. Nead, *The Pennsylvania-German in the Settlement of Maryland*, 232.

4. Smith, *The History of Kentucky*, 882.

5. Brumbaugh and Hodges, *Revolutionary Records of Maryland*, 24.

6. John Miller, "The Unit History of the Tom's Creek Hundred's Game Cock Company," *Greater Emmitsburg Area Historical Society*, http://www.emmitsburg .net/archive_list/articles/history/rev_war/game_cock_unit_history.htm.

7. "The People of the Mountain: Archaeological Overview, Assessment, Identification, and Evaluation Study of Catoctin Mountain Park, Maryland, Volume I," *Louis Berger Group*, June 2011, 18.

8. Weller Family Papers, tab 6, "John Weller, Patriot," Filson Historical Society, Louisville KY.

9. Daniel Weller of Lancaster, Pennsylvania (1754–1824), and Daniel Weller of Sharon, Connecticut (1760–1829), both served as privates in the Revolutionary War. There are thirteen Wellers listed in the Daughters of the American Revolution rolls as veterans of the war, an indication of the larger Weller family's proliferation and impact.

10. Frederick County, Maryland, Wills, Liber G.M. #2, folio 434, Maryland State Archives, Annapolis.

11. Smith, *The History of Kentucky*, 882.

12. Veach, *Kentucky Bourbon Whiskey*, 17.

13. Will of Daniel Weller, Nelson County, Kentucky, Will Book C, 462–63.

14. Sugden, *Tecumseh*, 189.

15. Eckert, *A Sorrow in Our Heart*, 214.

16. Sugden, *Tecumseh*, 198–201.

17. Sugden, *Tecumseh*, 201.

18. "American Military History," *Army Historical Series* 30, no. 21 (2005): 132.

19. "American Military History," 132.

20. Wilder, *Kentucky Soldiers of the War of 1812*, 12.

21. Wilder, *Kentucky Soldiers of the War of 1812*, 290.

22. Letter from David Weller to Samuel Weller, January 6, 1815, Mss.A.W4482, Miscellaneous Papers, Filson Historical Society, Louisville KY.

23. Kanon, *Tennesseans at War*, 167.

24. Quisenberry, *Kentucky Troops in the War of 1812*, 50.

25. See generally Dillin, *The Kentucky Rifle*.

26. Tenkotte and Claypool, *The Encyclopedia of Northern Kentucky*, 617.

27. "W. L. Weller Dead," *Courier-Journal* (Louisville KY), March 24, 1899.

28. Tim Talbott, "Louisville Legion," *Kentucky Historical Society*, http://explorekyhistory .ky.gov/items/show/208.

29. Register of Kentucky State Historical Society, vol. 16, no. 46, January 1918, 13, Kentucky State Historical Society, Frankfort.

30. Martin, *General Braxton Bragg*, 59.

31. Bradford, *A Companion to American Military History*, 81.

32. "W. L. Weller Dead."

33. Van Winkle Campbell, *But Always Fine Bourbon*, 22–23

34. Jack Sullivan, "William L. and the Distilling Wellers of Kentucky," *Those Pre-Pro Whiskey Men!*, October 24, 2013, http://pre-prowhiskeymen.blogspot.com/2013/10/william-l-and-distilling-wellers-of.html.

35. Zoeller, *Bourbon in Kentucky*, 109.

36. U.S. Food and Drug Administration, "Notices of Judgment under the Food and Drugs Act, Issue 5501, Part 6000," August 9, 1915, 161.

37. Kleber et al., *The Kentucky Encyclopedia*, 583.

38. Van Winkle Campbell, *But Always Fine Bourbon*, 22.

39. Consolidated Illustrating, *Louisville of To-Day*, 100.

7. THOMAS HUGHES HANDY

1. Handy, *Annals and Memorials of the Handys and Their Kindred*, 216.

2. Winkler, *Journal of the Secession Convention of Texas*, 120–23.

3. "1861 New Orleans City Directory," Louisiana Division, Main Branch, New Orleans Public Library, http://files.usgwarchives.net/la/orleans/history/directory/1861hi.txt.

4. Bergeron, *Guide to Louisiana Confederate Military Units*, 28.

5. Hearn, *The Capture of New Orleans*, 252.

6. Scriber and Scriber, *The Fourth Louisiana Battalion in the Civil War*, 287.

7. U.S. War Department, *The War of the Rebellion*, series 2, vol. 4, 446.

8. Booth, *Records of Louisiana Confederate Soldiers and Louisiana Confederate Commands*, vol. 3, pt. 1, 174.

9. Mayeux, *Earthen Walls, Iron Men*, 46.

10. La Bree, *The Confederate Soldier in the Civil War*, 419.

11. Mayeux, *Earthen Walls, Iron Men*, 68.

12. Mayeux, *Earthen Walls, Iron Men*, 70, 266.

13. Jones, *Southern Historical Society Papers*, vol. 1, 97.

14. Jones, *Southern Historical Society Papers*, vol. 1, 94–96.

15. Mayeux, *Earthen Walls, Iron Men*, 92.

16. Mayeux, *Earthen Walls, Iron Men*, 92.

17. "Compiled Service Records of Confederate Soldiers Who Served in Volunteer Units from Louisiana," microcopy 320, roll 52 (Washington DC: National Archives Microfilm Publication, 1961).

18. Mayeux, *Earthen Walls, Iron Men*, 267.

19. Mayeux, *Earthen Walls, Iron Men*, 175.

20. Mayeux, *Earthen Walls, Iron Men*, 195.

21. McPherson, *War on the Waters*, 196.

22. Moss, *Southern Spirits*, 184.

23. Moss, *Southern Spirits*, 184.

24. Moss, *Southern Spirits*, 184.

25. Moss, *Southern Spirits*, 185.

26. Moss, Robert F. "The Unexpurgated History of the Sazerac Cocktail," June 7, 2013, http://www.robertfmoss.com/p/i-will-warn-you-in-advance-that-this.html.
27. Personal journal of Steven M. Mayeux.

8. PAUL L. JONES JR.

Epigraph. McKittrick, a soldier with the Sixteenth South Carolina, was killed several weeks later near Atlanta.

1. Pankey, *John Pankey of Manakin Town, Virginia, and His Descendants*, 141.
2. Paul L. Jones Jr.'s middle name was most likely Lavalle.
3. The 1860 federal census for Obion County, Tennessee, reflects twenty-year-old Paul and thirty-year-old Warner living next door to one another.
4. Tennessee Historical Commission, *Tennesseans in the Civil War, Part I*, 244.
5. See generally Campbell, "Thirty-Third Tennessee Infantry."
6. Kleber et al., *The Kentucky Encyclopedia*, 216.
7. Tennessee Historical Commission, *Tennesseans in the Civil War, Part I*, 245.
8. Tennessee Historical Commission, *Tennesseans in the Civil War, Part I*, 245.
9. Lindsley, *Military Annals of Tennessee*, 485.
10. Lindsley, *Military Annals of Tennessee*, 486.
11. Lindsley, *Military Annals of Tennessee*, 486.
12. Tennessee Historical Commission, *Tennesseans in the Civil War, Part I*, 245.
13. Young, *Four Roses*, 20.
14. McDonough, *Stones River*, 58.
15. McDonough, *Stones River*, 58.
16. McDonough, *Stones River*, 96.
17. Elliot, *Soldier of Tennessee*, 69.
18. Elliot, *Soldier of Tennessee*, 70.
19. McDonough, *Stones River*, 104.
20. McDonough, *Stones River*, 104.
21. McWhiney, *Braxton Bragg*, 354.
22. McDonough, *Stones River*, 105.
23. Lindsley, *Military Annals of Tennessee*, 705.
24. Martin, *General Braxton Bragg*, 11.
25. McDonough, *Stones River*, 152.
26. McDonough, *Stones River*, 105.
27. Bergeron, *Paths of the Past*, 60.
28. U.S. Government Printing Office, "Index to the Miscellaneous Documents of the House of Representatives," for the First Session of the Fiftieth Congress," 726–27.
29. Lindsley, *Military Annals of Tennessee*, 484.
30. Jones and Sword, *Gateway to the Confederacy*, 208.
31. Martin, *General Braxton Bragg*, 369.
32. Jones, *Generals in Blue and Gray*, 256.

33. Worsham, *The Old Nineteenth Tennessee Regiment*, 121.

34. Worsham, *The Old Nineteenth Tennessee Regiment*, 122.

35. Cope, *The Fifteenth Ohio Volunteers and Its Campaigns*, 456.

36. "From the Front," *Daily Conservative* (Raleigh NC), July 5, 1864.

37. Allardice, *Confederate Colonels*, 222.

38. Marszalek, *Sherman*, 273.

39. Cobb, *Irvin S. Cobb's Own Recipe Book*, 35.

40. Cobb, *Irvin S. Cobb's Own Recipe Book*, 35; Kleber et al., *Kentucky Encyclopedia*, 453.

41. John Lipman and Linda Lipman, "American Whiskey: A Visit to the Four Roses Distillery in Lawrenceburg, Kentucky," November 15, 2005, http://www.ellenjaye .com/4roses.htm.

42. "Dr. R. M. Rose Dies Suddenly," *Atlanta Constitution*, July 22, 1910.

43. Lipman and Lipman, "American Whiskey."

44. "Rufus M. Rose House," City of Atlanta, Georgia, website, https://www.atlanta .gov/government/departments/city-planning/office-of-design/urban-design -commission/rufus-m-rose-house.

45. Zoeller, *Bourbon in Kentucky*, 105.

9. GEORGE THOMAS STAGG

1. Dyer, *A Compendium of the War of the Rebellion*, 1206.

2. After the war, Samuel Woodson Price enjoyed a prominent career as a portrait artist. In 1868, he painted an oil portrait of General Rosecrans, which hangs in the Smithsonian National Portrait Gallery today.

3. Speed, *The Union Regiments of Kentucky*, 488.

4. Speed, *The Union Cause in Kentucky*, 286.

5. Jack Sullivan, "The Trials and Ascent of George T. Stagg," *Those Pre-Pro Whiskey Men!*, April 30, 2016, http://pre-prowhiskeymen.blogspot.com/2016/04/the -trials-and-ascent-of-george-t-stagg.html.

6. Harding, *History of Decatur County, Indiana*, 549.

7. Dwyer, *The Day Is Ours!*, 19.

8. Demarest, *The Demarest Family*, 508. Upon his death, James Stagg was buried near Col. John Bowman, whose grandnephew Abram Smith Bowman became a successful Virginia landowner and whiskey distiller.

9. Dyer, *A Compendium of the War of the Rebellion*, 1206.

10. Speed, *The Union Cause in Kentucky*, 491.

11. U.S. War Department, *The War of the Rebellion*, ch. 32, series 1, vol. 20, pt. 1, Reports, serial no. 29, 613.

12. Sauers, *Civil War Battlegrounds*, 102.

13. U.S. War Department, *The War of the Rebellion*, ch. 43, series 1, vol. 31, pt. 2, Reports, serial no. 55, 499.

14. U.S. War Department, *The War of the Rebellion*, ch. 43, series 1, vol. 31, pt. 2, Reports, serial no. 55, 499.

15. U.S. War Department, *The War of the Rebellion*, ch. 52, series 1, vol. 45, pt. 1, Reports, Correspondence, Etc., serial no. 93, 204.

16. Speed, *The Union Regiments of Kentucky*, 493.

17. "Index to the Miscellaneous Documents of the House of Representatives for the First Session of the Forty-Fifth Congress" (Government Printing Office, 1876), 398.

18. See generally Geo. T. Stagg Co. v. Taylor, 16 Ky.L.Rptr. 213, 95 Ky. 651, 27 S.W. 247 (1894); Taylor v. Geo. T. Stagg Co., 18 Ky.L.Rptr. 680, 37 S.W. 954 (1896); and Geo. T. Stagg Co. v. E. H. Taylor & Sons, 24 Ky.L.Rptr. 495, 113 Ky. 709, 68 S.W. 862 (1902).

19. Cazentre, *Spirits and Cocktails of Upstate New York*, 96.

20. Minnick, *Bourbon*, 66.

21. "Reports of Committees of the Senate of the United States for the First Session of the Forty-Seventh Congress" (*Government Printing Office*, 1882), 85.

10. JULIAN PROCTOR VAN WINKLE JR.

1. Van Winkle Campbell, *But Always Fine Bourbon*, 39.

2. "World War II Army Enlistment Records," National Archives and Records Administration, record group 64, box 0177.

3. Letter from Julian Van Winkle Jr. to Julian "Pappy" Van Winkle, December 29, 1944, in the possession of the Van Winkle family, Louisville KY.

4. Knox, *The Muted Trumpet's Call*, 226.

5. Knox, *The Muted Trumpet's Call*, 227.

6. Knox, *The Muted Trumpet's Call*, 235.

7. Letter from Julian Van Winkle Jr. to Julian "Pappy" Van Winkle, July 6, 1944, in the possession of the Van Winkle family, Louisville KY.

8. Letter from Julian Van Winkle Jr. to Julian "Pappy" Van Winkle, July 6, 1944, in the possession of the Van Winkle family, Louisville KY.

9. Letter from Julian Van Winkle Jr. to Julian "Pappy" Van Winkle, July 6, 1944, in the possession of the Van Winkle family, Louisville KY.

10. Imperato, *General MacArthur Speeches and Reports*, 124.

11. Knox, *The Muted Trumpet's Call*, 240.

12. Peterson, *An Analytical History of World War II*, vol. 2, 702.

13. Prefer, *Leyte, 1944*, 124.

14. Mark G. Hunter interview, 12th Armored Reunion, October 31, 1998, uploaded by 12th Armored Museum, previously on YouTube at https://web.archive.org/web/20160408092954/https://www.youtube.com/watch?v=juh-xsgixs4.

15. Verbeck, *A Regiment in Action*, 28.

16. Knox, *The Muted Trumpet's Call*, 247.

17. Personal journal of Julian Van Winkle Jr., January 15, 1945, in the possession of the Van Winkle family, Louisville KY.

18. Bradstreet, *Hellcats*, vol. 2, 36.

19. Letter from Julian Van Winkle Jr. to Julian "Pappy" Van Winkle, January 1, 1945, in the possession of the Van Winkle family, Louisville KY.

20. Knox, *The Muted Trumpet's Call*, 268.

21. Personal journal of Julian Van Winkle Jr., January 10, 1945.

22. Prefer, *Leyte, 1944*, 146.

23. Astor, *Crisis in the Pacific*, 512.

24. "Japs Deliberately Tried to Starve Prisoners, Van Winkle Says, Telling of Manila Liberation," *Louisville Courier-Journal*, March 18, 1945.

25. "Japs Deliberately Tried to Starve Prisoners."

26. "Japs Deliberately Tried to Starve Prisoners."

27. "Japs Deliberately Tried to Starve Prisoners."

28. Stone Jr., *Kentucky Fighting Men*, 110.

29. Letter from Julian Van Winkle Jr. to Julian "Pappy" Van Winkle, December 29, 1944, in the possession of the Van Winkle family, Louisville KY.

30. Totani, *Justice in Asia and the Pacific Region*, 21.

31. "Taro Leaf," *24th Infantry Division Association* 19, no. 4 (1965–1966): 3.

32. Van Winkle Campbell, *But Always Fine Bourbon*, 95.

33. *Louisville Courier-Journal*, June 12, 1990.

34. Van Winkle Campbell, *But Always Fine Bourbon*, 95.

35. Van Winkle Campbell, *But Always Fine Bourbon*, 107.

36. Van Winkle Campbell, *But Always Fine Bourbon*, 187.

37. Van Winkle Campbell, *But Always Fine Bourbon*, 176.

38. Van Winkle Campbell, *But Always Fine Bourbon*, 185.

39. Bill Cowern, "Bourbon Stories," *Sku's Recent Eats*, December 31, 2015, http://recenteats.blogspot.com/2015/12/bourbon-stories.html.

40. Jim Thompson, *Louisville Courier-Journal*, June 29, 1972.

41. The last master distiller at the Van Winkles' Stitzel-Weller / Old Fitzgerald Distillery before it closed in 1992 was Edwin "Ed" Foote. After graduating from high school, Foote enlisted in the U.S. Army as the conflict in Korea raged. After basic training at Fort Knox, he spent a brief army career at Fort Devens, Massachusetts, and left the military after two years. Foote attended Western Kentucky University on the GI Bill and went to work as a teacher for a short time after earning his degree. In 1961, Foote answered a classified advertisement for a position at Seagram's and was hired to work in its quality control lab in Louisville. He was eventually promoted to beer chemist, and began working as a full-time distiller in the mid-1960s. Foote was hired at Old Fitzgerald after working for Seagram's from 1961 to 1982. While at Old Fitzgerald, he produced "wheated" bourbons made famous by Pappy Van Winkle and Julian Van Winkle Jr. (e.g., Cabin Still, Rebel Yell, and the Old Fitzgerald and W. L. Weller lines). When the distillery was acquired by United Distillers and closed, Ed Foote was transferred to Bernheim Distillery, where he served as the master distiller until his retirement in 1997. While he did not personally know Julian Van Winkle Jr.,

he became acquainted with Julian Van Winkle III in the 1980s. Van Winkle III purchased whiskey produced by Foote at Old Fitzgerald to launch the Pappy Van Winkle line in 1997. According to Van Winkle, "Ed Foote made our label [Pappy Van Winkle] famous as most of our popularity came while we were bottling whiskey he made. It was arguably the best on the planet according to some. I sure enjoyed it."

11. ELMER TANDY LEE AND JAMES B. JOHNSON JR.

1. See generally Dorr, *B-29 Superfortress Units of World War 2*.
2. Elmer T. Lee interview, October 30, 2008, Louie B. Nunn Center for Oral History, University of Kentucky Libraries.
3. "Annual Report," Jarman Shoe Company, October 1940.
4. Presidential Proclamation no. 7259, 3 C.F.R. 1999 Comp., 147 (December 7, 1999).
5. Elmer T. Lee interview, October 30, 2008.
6. Ralph Swann, "A Unit History of the 315th Bomb Wing, 1944–1946," Air Command and Staff Research Report 86-2460, March 1986, http://www.dtic.mil /dtic/tr/fulltext/u2/a168128.pdf, 12.
7. Swann, "A Unit History of the 315th Bomb Wing, 1944–1946."
8. Preston Crans, "History of the 16th Bombardment Group (VH)," September 14, 2005, http://www.315bw.org/16bg_hb.html.
9. Elmer T. Lee interview, October 30, 2008.
10. "Memoirs of Herbert C. Bach, June 6th to October 4th 1945," January 5, 2005, 315th Bomb Wing Association website, http://www.315bw.org/Herb_Bach.htm.
11. Dorr, *B-29 Superfortress Units of World War 2*, 1.
12. Elmer T. Lee interview, October 30, 2008.
13. Elmer T. Lee interview, October 30, 2008.
14. Jimmy and Freddie Johnson interview, October 16, 2008, Louie B. Nunn Center for Oral History, University of Kentucky Libraries.
15. Veach, *Kentucky Bourbon Whiskey*, 102.
16. Jimmy and Freddie Johnson interview, October 16, 2008.
17. "Enlisted Record and Report of Separation, Honorable Discharge, James B. Johnson II," November 1944, photocopy in possession of author.
18. See generally Pearson, *Engineer Aviation Units*.
19. Jimmy and Freddie Johnson interview, October 16, 2008.
20. Scott and Scott, *Images of America*, 68.
21. National Historic Landmark Nomination, "George T. Stagg Distillery," February 27, 2013, https://www.nps.gov/nhl/find/statelists/ky/StaggDistillery.pdf, 69.
22. Mitenbuler, *Bourbon Empire*, 243–44; Minnick, *Bourbon*, 180–87.
23. Moss, *Southern Spirits*, 282.
24. Teaford, *Cities of the Heartland*, 221; see also *Maryland Historical Magazine* 85, no. 4 (Winter 1990): 346.
25. Elmer T. Lee interview, October 30, 2008.

26. Elmer T. Lee interview, October 30, 2008.

27. Clay Risen, "The Billion-Dollar Bourbon Boom."

28. Richard Wolf interview by author, January 24, 2017.

12. RICHARD J. NEWMAN

1. See generally Sandler, *The Korean War*.

2. Hess, *Presidential Decisions for War*, 9.

3. Truman's Democratic party lost several key elections in the winter of 1950. According to author Larry Blomstedt in *Truman, Congress, and Korea*, "an aide recalled that election night in 1950 was the only time he saw the chief executive using liquor to drown his sorrows."

4. See generally Smith, *U.S. Marines in the Korean War*.

5. Berry, *Hey, Mac, Where Ya Been?*, 234.

6. Berry, *Hey, Mac, Where Ya Been?*, 233.

7. Berry, *Hey, Mac, Where Ya Been?*, 234.

8. Berry, *Hey, Mac, Where Ya Been?*, 235.

9. Berry, *Hey, Mac, Where Ya Been?*, 235.

10. Smith, *U.S. Marines in the Korean War*, 238.

11. Berry, *Hey, Mac, Where Ya Been?*, 237.

12. Berry, *Hey, Mac, Where Ya Been?*, 237.

13. Berry, *Hey, Mac, Where Ya Been?*, 237.

14. Berry, *Hey, Mac, Where Ya Been?*, 238.

15. Berry, *Hey, Mac, Where Ya Been?*, 238.

16. Berry, *Hey, Mac, Where Ya Been?*, 239.

17. "1st Marine Division Command Diary," January 1953, Korean War Project Digital Initiative website, http://www.koreanwar2.org/kwp2/usmc/001_2/M001_CD16 _1953_01_1211.pdf.

18. Berry, *Hey, Mac, Where Ya Been?*, 239.

19. Berry, *Hey, Mac, Where Ya Been?*, 239.

20. Newman and Wild Turkey master distiller Jimmy Russell briefly considered purchasing Lou Forman's Michter's Distillery in Schaefferstown, Pennsylvania, as both men had an affinity for Michter's quaint history and well-made rye whiskey, but they ultimately passed on the opportunity.

21. Jura Koncius, "Today's Feather Report," *Washington Post*, April 25, 1980.

22. Koncius, "Today's Feather Report."

23. Jeremy Main and Robert Steyer, "Companies That Float from Owner to Owner," *Fortune Magazine*, April 28, 1986.

24. Main and Steyer, "Companies That Float From Owner to Owner."

25. Joseph Magliocco interview by author, October 2015.

26. Joseph Magliocco interview.

27. Joseph Magliocco interview.

13. THOMAS E. BULLEIT JR.

1. "Defense Casualty Analysis System," U.S. National Archives website, Vietnam Conflict Extract File, https://www.archives.gov/research/military/vietnam-war/casualty-statistics.html.
2. DeYoung, *Soldier*, 82, 87.
3. Dougan and Weiss, *Nineteen Sixty-Eight*, 68.
4. Fred Minnick, "Bulleit Proof," *The American Legion*, October 28, 2011, https://www.legion.org/magazine/92238/bulleit-proof.
5. Janet Patton, "Ky. Bourbon Industry Gets Boon with $115 million Bulleit Distillery," *Lexington Herald-Leader*, August 21, 2014, http://www.kentucky.com/news/business/bourbon-industry/article44504460.html.

14. DAVID STEVEN PICKERELL

1. Jim Michaels, "In the 1970s, the U.S. Military Struggled with Morale," *USA Today*, July 3, 2013, https://www.usatoday.com/story/nation/2013/07/03/afghanistan-advisers-george-lepre-haynes-vietnam-conrad-crane/2484665/.
2. Scales, *Certain Victory*, 6.
3. David Pickerell interview by author, November 11, 2015.
4. David Pickerell interview, November 11, 2015.
5. David Pickerell interview, November 11, 2015.
6. David Pickerell interview, November 11, 2015.
7. David Pickerell interview, November 11, 2015.
8. David Pickerell interview, November 11, 2015.
9. David Pickerell interview, November 11, 2015.
10. Nino Marchetti, "Master Whiskey Wizard Dave Pickerell Interview: Part 1," *The Whiskey Wash*, September 17, 2015, https://thewhiskeywash.com/whiskey-styles/american-whiskey/master-whiskey-wizard-dave-pickerell-interview-part-1/.
11. Clay Risen, "Meeting Mr. Whiskey," *Garden & Gun*, February/March 2014, http://gardenandgun.com/articles/gg-interview-mr-whiskey/.
12. Marchetti, "Master Whiskey Wizard Dave Pickerell Interview: Part 1."
13. Risen, "Meeting Mr. Whiskey."
14. Nino Marchetti, "Master Whiskey Wizard Dave Pickerell Interview: Part 3," *The Whiskey Wash*, September 23, 2015, https://thewhiskeywash.com/whiskey-styles/american-whiskey/master-whiskey-wizard-dave-pickerell-interview-part-3/.
15. "About Us: A New Tradition," Union Horse Distilling Company website, last modified 2018, http://www.unionhorse.com/about-us/.
16. Solera is a process for aging whiskey, wine, beer, vinegar, and brandy by fractional blending in such a way that the finished product is a mixture of ages. A solera system is composed of several rows of barrels stacked on top of each other. Liquid moves from the top row to the bottom row before being bottled over the period of several years.

15. VETERANS IN CRAFT WHISKEY

1. Rorabaugh, *The Alcoholic Republic*, 87.
2. Pacult, *American Still Life*, 56; Carson, *The Social History of Bourbon*, 86.
3. Michael Kinstlick, "The U.S. Craft Distilling Market: 2011 and Beyond," April 2012, https://coppersea.com/wp-content/uploads/2012/04/Craft_Distilling_2011_White_Paper_Final.pdf.
4. Moss, *Southern Spirits*, 112; Pacult, *American Still Life*, 56.
5. Zoeller, *Bourbon in Kentucky*, 29.
6. Elmer T. Lee interview, October 30, 2008.
7. Risen, "Meeting Mr. Whiskey."
8. Kline, Slocum, and Cavaliere, *Craft Beverages and Tourism*, 27.
9. Jorg Rupf interview by Shanna Farrell, November 19, 2014, West Coast Cocktail Oral History Project, University of California, Berkeley.
10. Hearn, *Carriers in Combat*, 217.
11. Ken Mannshardt interview by author, November 20, 2017.
12. Not far from where Dietrich and his team craft their extremely popular Diamond Peak and Snowflake whiskeys, the 10th Mountain Whiskey & Spirit Co. in Gypsum, Colorado (owned by the grandson of an World War II Tenth Mountain Division veteran), produces bourbon and rye whiskey from Rocky Mountain grain and snowmelt.
13. "Speaking with Rob Dietrich, Head Distiller of Stranahan's Whiskey and Combat Veteran," *Mutineer Magazine*, November 7, 2014.
14. Michael Kinstlick, "The U.S. Craft Distilling Market: 2011 and Beyond," April 2012, http://www.parkstreet.com/wp-content/uploads/ArtisanSpirit_Issue017_CSDP.pdf.
15. Chris Lozier, The Craft Spirits Data Project, http://www.parkstreet.com/wp-content/uploads/ArtisanSpirit_Issue017_csdp.pdf.
16. "Texas Bourbon News," Garrison Brothers Distillery Blog, October 15, 2012, http://blog.garrisonbros.com/2012/10/15/texas-bourbon-news-fall-2012/.
17. Paul Tomaszewski interview by author, December 10, 2015.
18. Willie Blazer interview by author, September 12, 2016.
19. Jack Landers interview by author, April 3, 2016.
20. Travis Barnes interview by author, October 17, 2016.
21. Travis Barnes interview, October 17, 2016.
22. Travis Barnes interview, October 17, 2016.
23. Susan Laughlin, "All American Spirits at Smoky Quartz Distillery," *New Hampshire Magazine*, November 2015.
24. Pat Levy interview by author, November 14, 2017.
25. Pat Levy interview, November 4, 2017.

APPENDIX

1. Eisenhower, *Intervention!*, 99.
2. Jessica Leigh Hester, "A Brief History of 'Happy Hour,'" *City Lab*, October 16, 2015, https://www.citylab.com/life/2015/10/a-brief-history-of-happy-hour /410989/.
3. Harold H. Martin, "The Men Who Chase Missiles," *Saturday Evening Post*, April 25, 1959.
4. Totten, *The Button Box*, 327.

BIBLIOGRAPHY

Abbott, William W., ed. *The Papers of George Washington, Colonial Series.* 10 vols. Charlottesville: University of Virginia Press, 1983–95.

Acitelli, Tom. *Whiskey Business: How Small-Batch Distillers Are Transforming American Spirits.* Chicago: Chicago Review Press, 2017.

Alden, John R. *The American Revolution, 1775–1783.* New York: Harper & Row, 1954.

Allardice, Bruce S. *Confederate Colonels: A Biographical Register.* Columbia: University of Missouri Press, 2008.

Alvey, R. Gerald. *Kentucky Bluegrass Country.* Jackson: University Press of Mississippi, 1992.

Ambrose, Stephen E. *Band of Brothers: E Company, 506th Regiment, 101st Airborne from Normandy to Hitler's Eagle's Nest.* New York: Touchstone, 1992.

Anderson, Marie C., and Donald O. Anderson. *The Reasoner Family: Traditional, Historical, Genealogical, Pictorial, 1665-1990.* Midvale UT: Seagull Printing, 1990.

Antal, Sandy. *Wampum Denied: Procter's War of 1812.* Ottawa: Carleton University Press, 1998.

Arthur, Anthony. *Bushmasters: America's Jungle Warriors of World War II.* New York: St. Martin's, 1987.

Astor, Gerald. *Crisis in the Pacific: The Battles for the Philippine Islands by the Men Who Fought Them.* New York: Random House, 1996.

———. *Semper Fi in the Sky: The Marine Air Battles of World War II.* New York: Presidio Press, 2005.

Ballenger, Lee. *The Final Crucible: U.S. Marines in Korea.* Vol. 2, *1953.* Washington DC: Potomac Books, 2001.

Bartlett, Napier. *Military Record of Louisiana.* New Orleans: L. Graham, 1875.

Barton, Michael, and Larry M. Logue, eds. *The Civil War Soldier: A Historical Reader.* New York: New York University Press, 2002.

Barton, Robert T. *The First Election of Washington to the House of Burgesses.* Richmond: Virginia Historical Society, 1892.

Bassett, Mary C., and Sarah Hall Johnston. *Lineage Book: National Society of the Daughters of the American Revolution.* Vol. 38. Harrisburg: Telegraph Printing, 1914.

Battle, J. H., W. H. Perrin, and G. C. Kniffin. *Kentucky: A History of the State.* Louisville: F.A. Battey, 1885.

Beirne, Francis F. *The War of 1812.* New York: Dutton, 1949.

Belanger, Dian O. *Deep Freeze: The United States, the International Geophysical Year, and the Origins of Antarctica's Age of Science.* Boulder: University Press of Colorado, 2006.

Bell, Augusta Grove. *Circling Windrock Mountain: Two Hundred Years in Appalachia.* Knoxville: University of Tennessee Press, 1998.

Bergeron, Arthur W. *Guide to Louisiana Confederate Military Units, 1861–1865.* Baton Rouge: Louisiana State University Press, 1996.

Bergeron, Paul H. *Paths of the Past: Tennessee, 1770–1970.* Knoxville: University of Tennessee Press, 1979.

Berkin, Carol. *A Sovereign People: The Crises of the 1790s and the Birth of American Nationalism.* New York: Basic Books, 2017.

Berry, Henry. *Hey, Mac, Where Ya Been? Living Memories of the U.S. Marines in the Korean War.* New York: St. Martin's Press, 1988.

Bilby, Joseph G. *Irish Brigade in the Civil War: The 69th New York and Other Regiments of the Army of the Potomac.* Cambridge MA: Da Capo, 1995.

Black, Rachel. *Alcohol in Popular Culture: An Encyclopedia.* Santa Barbara: ABC-CLIO, 2010.

Blomstedt, Larry. *Truman, Congress, and Korea: The Politics of America's First Undeclared War.* Lexington: University Press of Kentucky, 2016.

Bober, Natalie S. *Thomas Jefferson: Draftsman of a Nation.* Charlottesville: University of Virginia Press, 2007.

Booth, Andrew B. *Records of Louisiana Confederate Soldiers and Louisiana Confederate Commands.* 3 vols. Spartanburg SC: Reprint Company Publishers, 1984. First published 1920.

Borch Fred L., III. *Medals for Soldiers and Airmen: Awards and Decorations of the United States Army and Air Force.* Jefferson NC: McFarland, 2013.

Bowers, John. *Stonewall Jackson: Portrait of a Soldier.* New York: William Morrow, 1989.

Bradford, James C., ed. *A Companion to American Military History.* Vol. 1. Malden MA: Wiley-Blackwell, 2010.

Bradstreet, Ken. *Hellcats, 12th Armored Division Association.* 2 vols. Paducah KY: Turner, 1990.

Brumbaugh, Gaius M., and Margaret R. Hodges. *Revolutionary Records of Maryland.* Baltimore: Clearfield, 1924.

Bryson, Lewis M., III. *Tasting Whiskey: An Insider's Guide to the Unique Pleasures of the World's Finest Spirits.* North Adams MA: Storey, 2014.

Bullitt, Thomas W. *My Life at Oxmoor: Life on a Farm in Kentucky before the War.* Louisville: John P. Morton, 1911.

Burk, Robert F. *The Corporate State and the Broker State: The Du Ponts and American National Politics, 1925–1940.* Cambridge: Harvard University Press, 1990.

Burns, Eric. *The Spirits of America: A Social History of Alcohol.* Philadelphia: Temple University Press, 2004.

Burr, Samuel Jones. *The Life and Times of William Henry Harrison.* New York: L.W. Ransom, 1840.

Burton, William L. *Melting Pot Soldiers: The Union's Ethnic Regiments.* Ames: Iowa State University Press, 1988.

Buxton, Ian, and Paul S. Hughes. *The Science and Commerce of Whisky.* Cambridge: Royal Society of Chemistry Publishing, 2014.

Cadwallader, Sylvanus. *Three Years with Grant.* New York: Knopf, 1955.

Campbell, Alex W. "Thirty-Third Tennessee Infantry." In *The Military Annals of Tennessee. Confederate,* comp. and ed. John Berrien Lindsley. Wilmington NC: Broadfoot, 1995. First published 1886.

Campbell, R. Thomas. *Voices of the Confederate Navy: Articles, Letters, Reports, and Reminiscences.* Jefferson NC: McFarland, 2008.

Carafano, James J. *GI Ingenuity: Improvisation, Technology, and Winning World War II.* Mechanicsburg PA: Stackpole, 2006.

Carson, Gerald. *The Social History of Bourbon.* Lexington: University Press of Kentucky, 1963.

Cazentre, Donald. *Spirits and Cocktails of Upstate New York: A History.* Charleston: American Palate, 2017.

Cecil, Sam K. *The Evolution of the Bourbon Whiskey Industry in Kentucky.* Paducah KY: Turner, 1999.

Cheever, Susan. *Drinking in America: Our Secret History.* New York: Grand Central, 2016.

Chernow, Ron. *Alexander Hamilton.* New York: Penguin, 2004.

Christ, Mark K. *Civil War Arkansas, 1863: The Battle for a State.* Norman: University of Oklahoma Press, 2010.

Clark, Thomas D. *A History of Kentucky.* Lexington: John Bradford, 1954.

Clary, David A. *Adopted Son: Washington, Lafayette, and the Friendship That Saved the Revolution.* New York: Random House, 2007.

———. *George Washington's First War: His Early Military Adventures.* New York: Simon & Schuster, 2011.

Clements, J. Reginald. *History of First Regiment of Infantry: The Louisville Legion and Other Military Organizations.* Whitefish MT: Kessinger, 2011.

Cobb, Irvin S. *Irvin S. Cobb's Own Recipe Book.* Louisville: Frankfort Distilleries, 1934.

Coffey, Walter. *The Civil War Months: A Month-by-Month Compendium of the War between the States.* Bloomington IN: AuthorHouse, 2012.

———. *The Reconstruction Years: The Tragic Aftermath of the War between the States.* Bloomington IN: AuthorHouse, 2014.

Coleman, J. Winston. *Sketches of Kentucky's Past.* Lexington: Winburn, 1979.

Coles, Harry L. *The War of 1812.* Chicago: University of Chicago Press, 1965.

Connelley, William E., and Ellis Merton Coulter. *History of Kentucky.* Vol. 4. Chicago: American Historical Society, 1922.

Connor, Matt. *Watering Hole: The Colorful History of Booze, Sex, and Death at a New Jersey Tavern.* Bloomington IN: AuthorHouse, 2003.

Consolidated Illustrating. *Louisville of To-Day: A Souvenir of the City for Distribution during the G.A.R. Encampment.* Louisville KY: Consolidated Illustrating, 1895.

Cope, Alexis. *The Fifteenth Ohio Volunteers and Its Campaigns, 1861–1865.* Columbus: Alexis Cope, 1916.

Coulombe, Charles A. *Rum: The Epic Story of the Drink That Conquered The World.* New York: Citadel Press, 2004.

Cowdery, Charles K. *Bourbon, Straight: The Uncut and Unfiltered Story of American Whiskey.* Chicago: Made and Bottled in Kentucky, 2004.

Crowgey, Henry G. *Kentucky Bourbon: The Early Years of Whiskeymaking.* Lexington: University Press of Kentucky, 1971.

Davis, William C. *Crucible of Command: Ulysses S. Grant and Robert E. Lee—The War They Fought, the Peace They Forged.* Boston: Da Capo, 2014.

Demarest, Mary A., and William H. S. Demarest. *The Demarest Family: David Des Marest of the French Patent on the Hackensack and His Descendants.* New Brunswick NJ: Thatcher-Anderson, 1938.

Detzer, David. *Allegiance: Fort Sumter, Charleston, and the Beginning of the Civil War.*

DeYoung, Karen. *Soldier: The Life of Colin Powell.* New York: Vintage Books, 2006.

Dieterle, David A., ed. *Economics: The Definitive Encyclopedia from Theory to Practice.* Vol. 1, *Foundations of Economics.* Santa Barbara: Greenwood, 2017.

Dillin, J.G.W. *The Kentucky Rifle.* Washington DC: National Rifle Association, 1924.

Din, Gilbert C., and John E. Harkins. *New Orleans Cabildo: Colonial Louisiana's First City Government, 1769–1803.* Baton Rouge: Louisiana State University Press, 1996.

Dorr, Robert F. *B-29 Superfortress Units of World War 2.* Oxford: Osprey, 2002.

Dougan, Clark, and Stephen Weiss. *Nineteen Sixty-Eight: The Vietnam Experience.* Boston: Boston Publishing, 1983.

Dowdall, Denise M. *From Cincinnati to the Colorado Ranger: The Horsemanship of Ulysses S. Grant.* Dublin: Historyeye, 2012.

Downard, William L. *Dictionary of the History of the American Brewing and Distilling Industries.* Westport CT: Greenwood, 1980.

Draper, Lyman C. *King's Mountain and Its Heroes.* Cincinnati: Thomson, 1881.

Dreazan, Yochi. *On Jim Beam: The Invisible Front; Love and Loss in an Era of Endless War.* New York: Crown, 2014.

Duncan, Robert. *Pubs and Patriots: The Drink Crisis in Britain during World War One.* London: Liverpool University Press, 2013.

Dwyer, William M. *The Day Is Ours! An Inside View of the Battles of Trenton and Princeton, November 1776–January 1777.* New Brunswick NJ: Rutgers University Press, 1983.

Dyer, Frederick H. *A Compendium of the War of the Rebellion.* Des Moines: Dyer, 1908.

Eckert, Allan W. *A Sorrow in Our Heart: The Life of Tecumseh.* New York: Bantam Books, 1992.

Eisenhower, John S. D. *Intervention! The United States and the Mexican Revolution, 1913–1917.* New York: W.W. Norton, 1993.

Elliott, Sam D. *Soldier of Tennessee: General Alexander P. Stewart and the Civil War in the West.* Baton Rouge: Louisiana State University Press, 2004.

Falk, Stanley L. *Decision at Leyte.* New York: W.W. Norton, 1999.

Federal Publishing Company. *The Union Army: A History of Military Affairs in the Loyal States 1861–65—Records of the Regiments in the Union Army—Cyclopedia of Battles—Memoirs of Commanders and Soldiers.* Vol. 4. Madison: Federal Publishing Company, 1908.

Fisher, John C., and Carol Fisher. *Food in the American Military: A History.* Jefferson NC: McFarland, 2011.

Fitzpatrick, John C., ed. *The Writings of George Washington from the Original Manuscript Sources, 1745–1799.* 39 vols. Washington DC: Government Printing Office, 1931–44.

Ford, Paul L. *The True George Washington.* Philadelphia: J.B. Lippincott, 1896.

Foster, Dave. *Franklin: The Stillborn State and the Sevier/Tipton Political Feud.* Johnson City: Overmountain, 2000.

Galatin, Ignatius J. *Take Her Deep! A Submarine against Japan in World War II.* Annapolis: Naval Institute Press, 2007.

Gardner, James A., and Guy-Uriel Charles. *Election Law in the American Political System.* 2nd ed. New York: Wolters Kluwer, 2018.

Gately, Iain. *Drink: A Cultural History of Alcohol.* New York: Gotham, 2008.

Gienapp, William E., and Erica L. Gienapp, eds. *The Civil War Diary of Gideon Welles, Lincoln's Secretary of the Navy.* Urbana: University of Illinois Press, 2014.

Givens, Ron. *Bourbon at Its Best: The Lore and Allure of America's Finest Spirit.* Cincinnati: Clerisy Press, 2008.

Graves, Robert. *Good Bye to All That: An Autobiography.* New York: Doubleday, 1957.

Greene, Heather. *Whisk(e)y Distilled: A Populist Guide to the Water of Life.* New York: Penguin, 2014.

Griffin, G. W. *Memoirs of Colonel Charles S. Todd.* Philadelphia: Claxton, Remsen & Haffelfinger, 1872.

Gurock, Jeffrey S., ed. *American Jewish History.* Vol. 1, *The Colonial and Early National Period 1654–1840.* New York: Routledge, 1998.

Handy, Isaac W. K. *Annals and Memorials of the Handys and Their Kindred.* Ann Arbor: William L. Clements Library, 1992.

Hanna, Charles A. *The Wilderness Trail: or, The Ventures and Adventures of the Pennsylvania Traders on the Allegheny Path with Some New Annals of the Old West, and the Records of Some Strong Men and Some Bad Ones.* New York: The Knickerbocker Press, 1911.

Harding, Lewis Albert, ed. *History of Decatur County, Indiana: Its People, Industries and Institutions.* Indianapolis: B.F. Bowen & Company, 1915.

Hartigan, Francis. *Bill W.: A Biography of Alcoholics Anonymous Cofounder Bill Wilson.* New York: Thomas Dunne Books, 2000.

Hastings, Max. *Overlord: D-Day and the Battle for Normandy.* Reprint, New York: Vintage, 2006.

Hearn, Chester G. *The Capture of New Orleans, 1862.* Baton Rouge: Louisiana State University Press, 1995.

————. *Carriers in Combat: The Air War at Sea.* Mechanicsburg PA: Stackpole, 2005.

Helman, James A. *History of Emmitsburg, Maryland.* Frederick MD: Citizen Press, 1906.

Henderson, Archibald. *Isaac Shelby: Revolutionary Patriot and Border Hero.* Chapel Hill: North Carolina Society, Daughters of the Revolution, 1917.

Hening, William W. *The Statutes at Large: Being a Collection of All the Laws of Virginia.* Vol. 10. Richmond: George Cochran, 1822.

Hess, Gary R. *Presidential Decisions for War: Korea, Vietnam, and the Persian Gulf.* Baltimore: Johns Hopkins University Press, 2001.

Hinton, Mary H. *The North Carolina Booklet: Great Events in North Carolina History, Volume 16, Number 1.* Raleigh: The North Carolina Society Daughters of the Revolution, 1916.

Hogeland, William. *The Whiskey Rebellion.* New York: Simon & Schuster, 2006.

Holdstock, Douglas, and Frank Barnaby, eds. *Hiroshima and Nagasaki: Retrospect and Prospect,* London: Routledge, 1995.

Homans, Benjamin, ed. *The Army and Navy Chronicle, Vol. 6: From January 1 to June 30, 1838.* Washington DC: Benjamin Homans, 1838.

Hopkins, Kate. *99 Drams of Whiskey: The Accidental Hedonist's Quest for the Perfect Shot and the History of the Drink.* New York: St. Martin's Press, 2009.

Huckelbridge, Dane. *Bourbon: A History of the American Spirit.* New York: William Morrow, 2014.

Illinois State Historical Society. *Transactions of the Illinois State Historical Society for the Year 1903, Fourth Annual Meeting of the Society.* Springfield: Illinois State Historical Society, 1904.

Imperato, Ed. *General MacArthur Speeches and Reports 1908–1964.* Nashville: Turner, 2000.

Johnson, Clint. *In the Footsteps of Stonewall Jackson.* Winston-Salem: John F. Blair, 2002.

Jones, Evan C., and Wiley Sword, eds. *Gateway to the Confederacy: New Perspectives on the Chickamauga and Chattanooga Campaigns, 1862–1863.* Baton Rouge: Louisiana State University Press, 2014.

Jones, William, ed. *Southern Historical Society Papers.* Vol. 1. Richmond: Johns & Goolsby, 1876.

Jones, Wilmer L. *Generals in Blue and Gray.* Vol. 2, *Davis's Generals.* Westport CT: Praeger, 2004.

Joyce, Jaime. *Moonshine: A Cultural History of America's Infamous Liquor.* Minneapolis: Zenith, 2014.

Kaminski, John P. *George Washington: The Man of the Age.* Madison WI: Parallel Press, 2004.

Kanon, Tom. *Tennesseans at War, 1812–1815: Andrew Jackson, the Creek War, and the Battle of New Orleans.* Tuscaloosa: University of Alabama Press, 2014.

Keegan, John. *A History of Warfare.* New York: Vintage Books, 1993.

Keene, Jennifer D. *The United States and the First World War.* New York: Routledge, 2014.

Killikelly, Sarah Hutchins. *The History of Pittsburgh: Its Rise and Progress.* Pittsburgh: B.C. Gordon & Montgomery, 1906.

Kitman, Marvin. *George Washington's Expense Account.* New York: Simon & Schuster, 1970.

Kleber, John E. *The Encyclopedia of Louisville.* Lexington: University Press of Kentucky, 2001.

Kleber, John E., Thomas D. Clark, Lowell H. Harrison, and James C. Klotter, eds. *The Kentucky Encyclopedia.* Lexington: University Press of Kentucky, 1992.

Kline, Carol, Susan L. Slocum, and Christina T. Cavaliere, eds. *Craft Beverages and Tourism.* Vol. 1, *The Rise of Breweries and Distilleries in the United States.* Cham, Switzerland: Palgrave Macmillan, 2017.

Knox, Chuck. *The Muted Trumpet's Call: Stories of the Everyday Heroes of World War II.* Bloomington IN: AuthorHouse, 2011.

Kosar, Kevin R. *Whiskey: A Global History.* London: Reaktion Books, 2010.

Kroll, Henry H. *Bluegrass, Belles, and Bourbon: A Pictorial History of Whiskey in Kentucky.* South Brunswick NJ: A.S. Barnes, 1967.

Krueger, Walter. *From Down Under to Nippon: The Story of Sixth Army in World War II.* Washington DC: Combat Forces Press, 1953.

Kyvig, David, and Honorée Fanonne Jeffers. *Repealing National Prohibition.* Kent OH: Kent State University Press, 2010.

La Bree, Benjamin, ed. *The Confederate Soldier in the Civil War, 1861–1865.* Louisville: Prentice Press, 1897.

Lancaster, Roy. *The Story of the Bushmasters.* Detroit: Lancaster, 1945.

Lankford, Nelson. *Richmond Burning: The Last Days of the Confederate Capital.* New York: Penguin Group, 2002.

Laplander, Robert. *Finding the Lost Battalion: Beyond the Rumors, Myths and Legends of America's Famous World War I Epic.* 3rd ed. Waterford WI: Lulu Press, 2017.

Lender, Mark E., and James Kirby Martin. *Drinking in America: A History.* New York: The Free Press, 1982.

Lengel, Edward G. *First Entrepreneur: How George Washington Built His—and the Nation's—Prosperity.* Boston: Da Capo, 2016.

Lindsley, John B. *Military Annals of Tennessee.* Nashville: J.M. Lindsley, 1886.

Losson, Christopher. *Tennessee's Forgotten Warriors: Frank Cheatham and His Confederate Division.* Knoxville: University of Tennessee Press, 1989.

Lott, Major Robert P. *Van Cleve at Chickamauga: The Study of a Division's Performance in Battle.* Cleveland: Pickle Partners, 2014.

Lubbers, Bernie. *Bourbon Whiskey: Our Native Spirit.* 3rd ed. Indianapolis: Blue River Press, 2015.

Lucas, Marion Brunson. *Sherman and the Burning of Columbia.* Columbia: University of South Carolina Press, 2000.

Luce, Robert. *Legislative Principles: The History and Theory of Lawmaking by Representative Government.* Boston: Houghton Mifflin, 1930.

Macdonald, Fiona. *Whisky, a Very Peculiar History.* Brighton: Salariya, 2011.

Mahan, Bruce E. *Old Fort Crawford and the Frontier.* Iowa City: State Historical Society of Iowa, 1926.

Malleck, Dan. *Try to Control Yourself: The Regulation of Public Drinking in Post-Prohibition Ontario, 1927–1944.* Vancouver: University of British Columbia Press, 2012.

Mangan, Gregg. *On This Day in Connecticut History.* Charleston: History Press, 2015.

Mansergh, Ruth. *Whitehaven in the Great War.* Barnsley, England: Pen and Sword Books, 1988.

Marszalek, John F. *Sherman: A Soldier's Passion for Order.* Carbondale: Southern Illinois University Press, 2007.

Martin, Samuel J. *General Braxton Bragg, C.S.A.* Jefferson NC: McFarland, 2011.

Mather, Otis M. *Six Generations of LaRues and Allied Families.* Louisville: C.T. Dearing, 1921.

Mayeux, Steven M. *Earthen Walls, Iron Men: Fort DeRussy, Louisiana, and the Defense of Red River.* Knoxville: University of Tennessee Press, 2007.

Maynard, William B. *Woodrow Wilson: Princeton to the Presidency.* New Haven: Yale University Press, 2008.

McCardell, Lee. *Ill-Starred General: Braddock of the Coldstream Guards.* Pittsburgh: University of Pittsburgh Press, 1958.

McCullouch, David, ed. *Historical Encyclopedia of Illinois and History of Peoria County.* 2 vols. Chicago: Brookhaven Press, 1901–2.

McCullough, David. *Truman.* New York: Simon & Schuster, 1992.

McDonald, John. *Secrets of the Great Whiskey Ring: And Eighteen Months in the Penitentiary.* St. Louis: W.S. Bryan, 1880.

McDonough, James L. *Nashville: The Western Confederacy's Final Gamble.* Knoxville: University of Tennessee Press, 2004.

———. *Stones River—Bloody Winter in Tennessee.* Knoxville: University of Tennessee Press, 1980.

McGirr, Newman F. *Tarascon of Shippingport at the Falls of the Ohio.* Charleston: West Virginia History, 1946.

McPherson, James M. *War on the Waters: The Union and Confederate Navies, 1861–1865.* Chapel Hill: University of North Carolina Press, 2012.

McWhiney, Grady. *Braxton Bragg and Confederate Defeat.* Vol. 1. Tuscaloosa: University of Alabama Press, 1991.

Miller, William R., and Ricardo F. Munoz. *Controlling Your Drinking: Tools to Make Moderation Work for You.* 2nd ed. New York: Guilford Press, 2013.

Mingus, Scott L. *The Louisiana Tigers in the Gettysburg Campaign, June–July 1863.* Baton Rouge: Louisiana State University Press, 2009.

Minnick, Fred. *Bourbon: The Rise, Fall, and Rebirth of an American Whiskey.* Minneapolis: Voyageur, 2016.

———. *Bourbon Curious: A Simple Tasting Guide for the Savvy Drinker.* Minneapolis: Zenith, 2015.

———. *Whiskey Women: The Untold Story of How Women Saved Bourbon, Scotch, and Irish Whiskey.* Lincoln: Potomac Books, 2013.

Miscamble, Wilson D. *The Most Controversial Decision: Truman, the Atomic Bombs, and the Defeat of Japan.* New York: Cambridge University Press, 2011.

Mitchell, Reid. *The American Civil War, 1861–1865.* New York: Routledge, 2001.

Mitenbuler, Reid. *Bourbon Empire: The Past and Future of America's Whiskey.* New York: Viking, 2015.

Morone, James A. *Hellfire Nation: The Politics of Sin in American History.* New Haven: Yale University Press, 2003.

Morrison, Andrew. *The Industries of New Orleans.* New Orleans: J.M. Elstner, 1885.

Moss, Robert F. *Southern Spirits: Four Hundred Years of Drinking in the American South, with Recipes.* Berkeley: Ten Speed Press, 2016.

Murrin, John M. *Liberty, Equality, Power: A History of the American People.* Concise ed., 7th ed. Boston: Cengage, 2016.

Nead, Daniel Wunderlich. *The Pennsylvania-German in the Settlement of Maryland, Part XXV of a Narrative and Critical History Prepared at the Request of the Pennsylvania-German Society.* Lancaster: Pennsylvania-German Society, 1914.

Newton, Michael, E. *Angry Mobs and Founding Fathers: The Fight for Control of the American Revolution.* Phoenix: Eleftheria, 2011.

Oe, Kenzaburo. *Hiroshima Notes.* New York: Grove Press, 1995.

Onuf, Peter S., ed. *Establishing the New Regime: The Washington Administration.* New York: Garland, 1991.

Pacult, F. Paul. *American Still Life: The Jim Beam Story and the Making of the World's #1 Bourbon.* Hoboken: Wiley, 2003.

Palmer, Frederick. *Clark of the Ohio: A Life of George Rogers Clark.* New York: Dodd, Meade, 1929.

Pankey, George Edward. *John Pankey of Manakin Town, Virginia, and His Descendants.* Ruston LA: G.E. Pankey, 1969.

Parker, Matthew. *The Sugar Barons: Family, Corruption, Empire, and War in the West Indies.* New York: Walker, 2011.

Pearson, Natalie M. *Engineer Aviation Units in the Southwest Pacific Theater during World War II.* Fort Leavenworth KS: U.S. Army Command and General Staff College, 2005.

Perrin, William H., J. H. Battle, and G. C. Kniffin. *Kentucky: A History of the State, Embracing a Concise Account of the Origin and Development of the Virginia Colony;*

Its Expansion Westward, and the Settlement of the Frontier beyond the Alleghanies; the Erection of Kentucky as an Independent State, and Its Subsequent Development. Louisville: F.A. Battey, 1887.

Peterson, Edward Norman. *An Analytical History of World War II.* 2 vols. Bern, Switzerland: Peter Lang, 1995.

Pfanz, Harry W. *Gettysburg: Culp's Hill and Cemetery Hill.* Chapel Hill: University of North Carolina Press, 1993.

Phillips, Rod. *Alcohol: A History.* Chapel Hill: University of North Carolina Press, 2014.

Pogue, Dennis J. *George Washington and the Beginnings of the American Whiskey Industry.* Buena Vista VA: Harbour Books, 2011.

Pogue, Dennis, and Esther White. *George Washington's Gristmill at Mount Vernon.* Mount Vernon: Mount Vernon Ladies' Association, 2005.

Prefer, Nathan. *Leyte, 1944: The Soldier's Battle.* Havertown PA: Casemate Publishers, 2012.

Prucha, Francis Paul. *Army Life on the Western Frontier: Selections from the Official Reports Made between 1826 and 1845 by Colonel George Croghan.* Norman: University of Oklahoma Press, 1958.

Purvis, Thomas L. *The Ethnic Descent of Kentucky's Early Population: A Statistical Investigation of European and American Sources of Emigration, 1790–1820.* Frankfort: Kentucky Historical Society, 1982.

Quisenberry, Anderson C. *Kentucky Troops in the War of 1812.* Frankfort: Register of the Kentucky Historical Society, 1912.

Randall, Willard S. *George Washington: A Life.* New York: Henry Holt, 1997.

Ratliff, Thomas. *How to Be a Revolutionary War Soldier.* Washington DC: National Geographic, 2006.

Ravino, Jerry. *Elite: USMC First Reconnaissance Company of the Korean War, 1950–1953.* Sedona: Memory Works, 2009.

Reeves, Ira Louis. *Ol' Rum River: Revelations of a Prohibition Administrator.* Chicago: Thomas S. Rockwell, 1931.

Regan, Gary, and Mardee Haiden Regan. *The Book of Bourbon and Other Fine American Whiskeys.* Shelburne VT: Chapters, 1995.

Reigler, Susan. *Kentucky Bourbon Country: The Essential Travel Guide.* Lexington: University Press of Kentucky, 2016.

Rhodes, Richard. *The Making of the Atomic Bomb.* New York: Simon & Schuster, 1986.

Rice, James M. *Peoria City and County, Illinois: A Record of Settlement, Organization, Progress and Achievement.* Chicago: S.J. Clarke, 1912.

Rorabaugh, W. J. *The Alcoholic Republic: An American Tradition.* Oxford: Oxford University Press, 1973.

Ross, Ishbel. *The General's Wife: The Life of Mrs. Ulysses S. Grant.* New York: Dodd, Meade, 1959.

Ross, William G. *World War I and the American Constitution.* New York: Cambridge, 2017.

Rothbaum, Noah. *The Art of American Whiskey.* Berkeley: Ten Speed Press, 2015.

Rowland, Tim. *Strange and Obscure Stories of the Civil War.* New York: Skyhorse, 2011.

Russell, David L. *The American Revolution in the Southern Colonies.* Jefferson NC: McFarland, 2000.

Samuels, Bill Jr. *Maker's Mark—My Autobiography.* Louisville: Saber, 2000.

Sandler, Stanley. *The Korean War: No Victors, No Vanquished.* Lexington: University Press of Kentucky, 1999.

Sauers, Richard. *Civil War Battlegrounds: The Illustrated History of the War's Pivotal Battles and Campaigns.* Minneapolis: Zenith, 2013.

Scales, Robert H. *Certain Victory: The U.S. Army in the Gulf War.* Washington DC: Potomac Books, 1993.

Schultz, Duane. *Quantrill's War: The Life & Times Of William Clarke Quantrill, 1837–1865.* New York: Thomas Dunne, 1996.

Scott, Berkeley, and Jeanine Scott. *Images of America: The Kentucky Bourbon Trail.* Charleston: Arcadia, 2009.

Scriber, Terry G., and Theresa Arnold-Scriber. *The Fourth Louisiana Battalion in the Civil War: A History and Roster.* Jefferson NC: McFarland, 2008.

Selcer, Richard F. *Civil War America, 1850 to 1875.* New York: Infobase, 2006.

Seward, Desmond. *The Bourbon Kings of France.* London: Thistle, 2013.

Shannon, Anne. *Finding Japan: Early Canadian Encounters with Asia.* Victoria: Heritage House, 2012.

Shulimson, Jack, Leonard A. Blaisol, Charles R. Smith, and David A. Dawson. *U.S. Marines in Vietnam: The Defining Year, 1968.* Washington DC: History and Museums Division, Headquarters, U.S. Marine Corps, 1997.

Slaughter, Thomas P. *The Whiskey Rebellion.* New York: Oxford University Press, 1986.

Smith, Charles R., ed. *U.S. Marines in the Korean War.* Washington DC: History Division, U.S. Marine Corps, 2007.

Smith, James M., ed. *Republic of Letters: The Correspondence between Thomas Jefferson and James Madison 1776–1826.* Vol. 1. New York: W.W. Norton, 1995.

Smith, Justin H. *The War with Mexico: The Classic History of the Mexican-American War.* St. Petersburg: Red & Black, 2011.

Smith, Merril D., ed. *The World of the American Revolution: A Daily Life Encyclopedia.* Vol. 1. Santa Barbara: Greenwood, 2005.

Smith, Ron, and Mary O. Boyle, *Prohibition in Atlanta: Temperance, Tiger Kings & White Lightning.* Charleston SC: American Palate, 2015.

Smith, Zachariah F. *The History of Kentucky: From Its Earliest Discovery and Settlement to the Present Date.* Louisville: Courier-Journal Job Printing, 1892.

Sohn, Anton P. *A Saw, Pocket Instruments, and Two Ounces of Whiskey: Frontier Military Medicine in the Great Basin.* Spokane: Arthur H. Clarke, 1998.

Sondhaus, Lawrence. *Naval Warfare: 1815–1914.* New York: Routledge, 2001.

Spears, Joseph F. *The Spears Saga.* Alexandria: J.F. Spears, 1982.

Speed, Thomas. *The Union Cause in Kentucky.* New York: G.P. Putnam's Sons, 1907.

———. *The Union Regiments of Kentucky.* Louisville: Courier-Journal Job, 1897.

Spoelman, Colin, and David Haskell. *Dead Distillers: A History of the Upstarts and Outlaws Who Made American Spirits*. New York: Abrams, 2016.

Staples, Charles R. *The History of Pioneer Lexington, 1779–1806*. Lexington: University Press of Kentucky, 1939.

Stelze, Charles. *Why Prohibition!* Bedford: Applewood Books, 1918.

Stewart, Richard W. *American Military History: The United States Army and the Forging of a Nation, 1775–1917*. Washington DC: Center of Military History, 2009.

Stone, Richard G., Jr. *Kentucky Fighting Men: 1861–1946*. Lexington: University Press of Kentucky, 1982.

Sugden, John. *Tecumseh: A Life*. New York: Henry Holt, 1997.

Sulzberger, Cyrus L. *World War II*. Boston: Houghton Mifflin, 1969.

Swett, Samuel. *Who Was the Commander at Bunker Hill? With Remarks on Frothingham's History of the Battle*. Boston: Wilson, 1850.

Syrett, Harold C., and Jacob E. Cooke., eds. *The Papers of Alexander Hamilton*. Vol. 1. New York: Columbia University Press, 1962.

Tate, J. R. *Walkin' with the Ghost Whisperers: Lore and Legends of the Appalachian Trail*. Mechanicsburg PA: Stackpole, 2006.

Teaford, Jon C. *Cities of the Heartland: The Rise and Fall of the Industrial Midwest*. Bloomington: Indiana University Press, 1993.

Tenkotte, Paul A., and James C. Claypool, eds. *The Encyclopedia of Northern Kentucky*. Lexington: University Press of Kentucky, 2009.

Tennessee Civil War Centennial Commission. *Tennesseans in the Civil War: A Military History of Confederate and Union Units with Available Rosters of Personnel*. Nashville: Civil War Centennial Commission, 1964.

Thian, Raphael P. *Legislative History of the General Staff of the Army of the United States (Its Organization, Duties, Pay, and Allowances), from 1775 to 1901*. Washington DC: U.S. Adjutant General's Office, 1901.

Totani, Yuma. *Justice in Asia and the Pacific Region, 1945–1952: Allied War Crimes Prosecutions*. New York: Cambridge University Press, 2015.

Totten, Ruth Ellen Patton. *The Button Box: A Daughter's Loving Memoir of Mrs. George S. Patton*. Columbia: University of Missouri Press, 2005.

Tracey, Grace L., and John P. Dern. *Pioneers of Old Monocacy: The Early Settlement of Frederick County, Maryland, 1721–1743*. Baltimore: Genealogical Publishing, 1987.

Tucker, Glenn. *Poltroons and Patriots: A Popular Account of the War of 1812*. Vol. 2. Indianapolis: Bobbs-Merrill, 1954.

Ullrich, Robert C., and Victoria A. Allrich, eds. *Germans in Louisville: A History*. Mount Pleasant SC: Arcadia, 2015.

U.S. Government Printing Office. "Index to the Miscellaneous Documents of the House of Representatives for the First Session of the Fiftieth Congress." In *Congressional Serial Set*, vol. 10, 1877–88. Washington DC: U.S. Government Printing Office, 1889.

U.S. War Department. *The War of the Rebellion: A Compilation of the Official Records of the Union and Confederate Armies.* Washington DC: Government Printing Office, 1899, 446

Upham, C. W., ed. *The Life of General Washington: First President of the United States.* Vol. 1. London: Office of the National Illustrated Library, 1852.

Van West, Carroll. *The Tennessee Encyclopedia of History and Culture.* Nashville: Rutledge Hill, 2002.

Van Winkle Campbell, Sally. *But Always Fine Bourbon: Pappy Van Winkle and the Story of Old Fitzgerald.* Louisville: Limestone Lane, 1999.

Veach, Michael R. *Kentucky Bourbon Whiskey: An American Heritage.* Lexington: University Press of Kentucky, 2013.

Vego, Milan N. *The Battle for Leyte, 1944: Allied and Japanese Plans, Preparations, and Execution.* Annapolis: Naval Institute Press, 2006.

Verbeck, William J. *A Regiment in Action.* [West Point NY?]: World War Regimental Histories, 1946.

Vermilya, Daniel. *The Battle of Kennesaw Mountain.* Mount Pleasant SC: Arcadia, 2014.

Wallis, Frederick A., and Hambleton Tapp. *A Sesqui-Centennial History of Kentucky.* Hopkinsville KY: Historical Record Association, 1945.

Walthall, Melvin C. *We Can't All Be Heroes: A History of the Separate Infantry Regiments in World War II.* Hicksville NY: Exposition, 1975.

Ward, Christopher. *The War of the Revolution.* Vol. 2. Old Saybrook CT: Konecky & Konecky, 2006. First published 1952.

Waymack, Mark H., and James F. Harris. *The Book of Classic American Whiskeys.* Chicago: Open Court, 1995.

Wheelan, Joseph. *Their Last Full Measure: The Final Days of the Civil War.* Cambridge MA: Da Capo, 2015.

White, Ronald C. *American Ulysses: A Life of Ulysses S. Grant.* New York: Random House, 2016.

Wilder, Minnie S., ed. *Kentucky Soldiers of the War of 1812.* Baltimore: Clearfield, 1969.

Wiley, Bell Irvin. *The Life of Johnny Reb, the Common Soldier of the Confederacy.* Indianapolis: Bobbs-Merill, 1943.

Wiley, Harvey W. *An Autobiography.* Indianapolis: Bobbs-Merrill, 1930.

———. *Beverages and the Adulteration, Origin, Composition, Manufacture, Natural, Artificial, Fermented, Distilled, Alkaloidal, and Fruit Juices.* Philadelphia: Blakiston, 1919.

Williams, David G. *SS Leibstandarte, Ace of the Waffen SS, Werner Herman Gustav Pötschke.* Two Moons Rising, 2015.

Will-Weber, Mark. *Muskets and Applejack: Spirits, Soldiers, and the Civil War.* Washington DC: Regnery, 2017.

Wilson, Ross. *Scotch: Its History and Romance,* Melbourne, Australia: Wren, 1973.

Winkler, E. W., ed. *Journal of the Secession Convention of Texas.* Austin: Austin Printing, 1912.

Winters, Dick, and Cole C. Kingseed. *Beyond Band of Brothers: The War Memoirs of Major Dick Winters.* New York: Penguin, 2006.

Wolf, Simon. *The American Jew as Patriot, Soldier and Citizen.* Vol. 3. Philadelphia: Levytype, 1895.

Wondrich, David. *Imbibe!* New York: TarcherPerigee, 2007.

Work, Henry H. *Wood, Whiskey, and Wine: A History of Barrels.* London: Reaktion Books, 2014.

Worsham, W. J. *The Old Nineteenth Tennessee Regiment, C.S.A. June, 1861–April, 1865.* Knoxville: Paragon, 1902.

Wrobel, Sylvia, and George Grider. *Isaac Shelby: Kentucky's First Governor and Hero of Three Wars.* Danville KY: Cumberland, 1974.

Young, Al. *Four Roses: The Return of a Whiskey Legend.* Louisville: Butler Books, 2010.

Zion, Roger H. *The Republican Challenge: Building the Case for Action.* Indianapolis: Guild Press, 1995.

Zoeller, Chester. *Kentucky Bourbon Barons: Legendary Distillers from the Golden Age of Whiskey Making.* Louisville: Butler, 2014.

Zoeller, Chester. *Bourbon in Kentucky: A History of Distilleries in Kentucky.* 3rd ed. Louisville: Butler, 2015.

INDEX